THE SAINT AND THE SULTAN

THE SAINT

AND

THE SULTAN

The Crusades, Islam, and
Francis of Assisi's Mission of Peace

PAUL MOSES

DOUBLEDAY RELIGION
New York   London   Toronto   Sydney   Auckland

ꭰꭰ

DOUBLEDAY

Published in the United States by Doubleday Religion, an
imprint of the Crown Publishing Group, a division of Random
House, Inc., New York.
www.crownpublishing.com

DOUBLEDAY and the DD colophon are registered trademarks of
Random House, Inc.

Library of Congress Cataloging-in-Publication Data
Moses, Paul.
The saint and the sultan: the Crusades, Islam, and Francis of
Assisi's mission of peace / by Paul Moses. —1st ed.
p. cm.
Includes bibliographical references and index (pp. 277, 291).
1. Francis, of Assisi, Saint, 1182–1226. 2. Malik al-Kamil
Muhammad, Sultan of Egypt and Syria, 1180?–1238.
3. Crusades. 4. Missions to Muslims—Egypt. I. Title.
BX4700.F6M675 2009
261.2'709022—dc22   2009005203

ISBN 978-0-385-52370-7

PRINTED IN THE UNITED STATES OF AMERICA

Design by Jennifer Daddio / Bookmark & Media Inc.

1   3   5   7   9   10   8   6   4   2

First Edition

FOR BERNARD AND ANNE MOSES

Pace e bene—e grazie

Contents

CONTENTS

CONTENTS

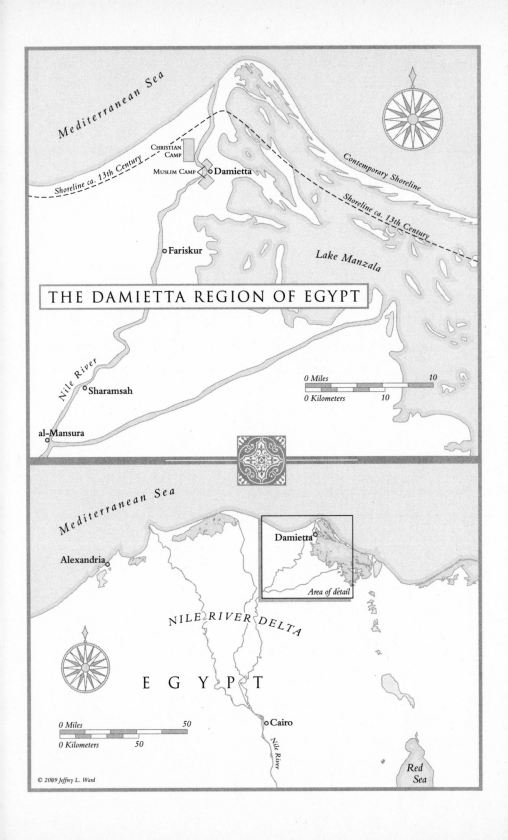

THE DAMIETTA REGION OF EGYPT

Mediterranean Sea

Shoreline ca. 13th Century

Contemporary Shoreline

Shoreline ca. 13th Century

CHRISTIAN CAMP

MUSLIM CAMP

Damietta

Fariskur

Lake Manzala

Nile River

Sharamsah

al-Mansura

0 Miles 10
0 Kilometers 10

Mediterranean Sea

Alexandria

Damietta

Area of detail

NILE RIVER DELTA

EGYPT

Cairo

Nile River

Red Sea

0 Miles 50
0 Kilometers 50

© 2009 Jeffrey L. Ward

THE SAINT AND THE SULTAN

Introduction

Francis stood before the sultan of Egypt.

He had yearned for such an audience with a Muslim leader for at least seven years, embarking on dangerous journeys three times during that period. Now his moment had arrived, in the midst of a Crusade that was killing thousands of people in the sweltering heat on the banks of the Nile late in the summer of 1219. The leader of the Christian army—Cardinal Pelagius himself—had warned the friar from Assisi that it would be folly to traverse the battlefield between the two armies to seek out this Sultan Malik al-Kamil. Francis, no stranger to the cruelty of men at war, knew full well the torture and mutilation that both armies inflicted on suspected spies. He had been told that the sultan was a monster, a cruel tyrant likely to order his death. But Francis had traveled a long way to see the sultan and insisted to the cardinal that he must go.

God willed it.

The sultan looked over the odd duo in his tent, Francis and his traveling companion, Friar Illuminato, barefoot monks dressed in coarse, patched brown tunics. His soldiers had found the two wandering around the outskirts of the Muslim camp and seized them roughly. Francis and

Illuminato had cried out, "Sultan! Sultan!" That these unarmed Christians had survived their initial encounter with the sultan's troops was wonder enough. What could they want? The sultan thought that perhaps the Franks, as Muslims called all Crusaders, had sent them to his tent with a response to his latest peace proposal. The sultan, made weary by war, desperately wanted a deal that would end the Christians' siege of Damietta, a city at the mouth of the Nile where his people were dying of disease and starvation.

"May the Lord give you peace." Francis surprised the sultan with his words. It was the friar's standard greeting—most unusual for Christians in his time, especially during war. It perplexed the sultan. Uncertain about his visitors' intention, the sultan asked if they had come as representatives of the pope's army.

"We are ambassadors of the Lord Jesus Christ," Francis responded.

The sultan, a subtle, philosophical man who was schooled in the ways of Christians, could not have missed the distinction Francis drew in asserting that he was God's ambassador, not the pope's. This daring little man and his companion intrigued him—they even resembled the severely dressed Sufi holy men the sultan revered for their mystical insight into Islam.

"If you wish to believe us," Francis continued, "we will hand over your soul to God."

Sultan Malik al-Kamil gave this man permission to continue. Then he listened closely as Francis began to speak.

This is a story about peace, one that is nearly eight hundred years old but still resonates in an era when Christians and Muslims look at one another with suspicion.

In the midst of war Francis of Assisi and Sultan Malik al-Kamil found common ground in their encounter outside the besieged city of Damietta, Egypt, in 1219. By that time the Crusades had been fought for more than a century. Christians had seized Jerusalem from the Muslims in 1099 but suffered a devastating blow when the great warrior Saladin took it back eighty-eight years later. In the decades that followed, the popes launched one failed military venture after another to win back territory in the Holy Land. The interreligious warfare would continue for centuries as Christians fought Muslim armies in Europe.

This is the story of how one man tried, in his own way, to stop this cycle of violence. I have written it because the example of Francis and the sultan calls out from the past to be recovered as a glimmer of hope in our own time.

Sultan al-Kamil, Saladin's nephew, clearly was taken by this charismatic monk who dared to cross into his encampment. Francis, one of the greatest Christian saints, was changed by the experience and came away deeply impressed with Islamic spirituality. In a revolutionary departure for his time, he urged his brothers to live peacefully among Muslims even as the Fifth Crusade clattered on to its deadly and fruitless conclusion. This encounter endures as a memorable forerunner of peaceful dialogue between Christians and Muslims. I've written this book with the hope that it will encourage others to build on the example of the saint and the sultan.

Spectacular as it was, Francis's journey to Damietta plays little role in the timeworn portrayal of the saint as a pious, miracle-working mystic and a quaintly impoverished friend to animals and nature. As a journalist for some three decades, I'll just say, in the language of the newsroom, that the truth about Francis and his relationship to Islam and the Crusades was covered up. The key early biographies of Francis were written under the influence of powerful medieval popes—the same men who organized the Crusades and used the battering ram of excommunication to force reluctant rulers to take part. With the medieval papacy at the zenith of its theocratic power in the thirteenth century, the early biographers could not say what really happened in Damietta—that Francis, opposed to the Crusade, was on a peace mission and hoped to end the warfare by converting the sultan to Christianity.

Journalistic training tells me to be skeptical about the tendency in our day to re-cast Francis as a medieval flower child, a carefree, peace-loving hippie adopted as the patron saint of the Left. Francis was far too devoted to suffering, penance, obedience, and religious orthodoxy to be cast as an ancestor to the hippies of the 1960s or the New Age movement. Yet a probing look at the early documents concerning Francis reveals that the quest for peace—a peace encompassing both the end of war and the larger spiritual transformation of society—was at the core of Francis's ministry and thus at the heart of his mission to the sultan's court.

The major problem faced in trying to recover the Francis of history is that these medieval documents, however detailed and informative, cannot be taken at face value. Their aim is to portray Francis's saintliness, not to provide a true history of his life. For me, that has meant trying to approach the material on Francis as an investigative reporter would, looking for the agendas and "spin" in the accounts. In deciding which portions of the medieval documents to accept as historical and which to reject, I've kept in mind that the accounts of Francis's life were written to fulfill various needs: to enhance his cult as a saint; to convince the church hierarchy of the Franciscan order's orthodoxy; to appease competing factions within the order. I've relied mainly on accounts from the first half of the thirteenth century because the later ones tend to be much more embellished. I've also given heavy weight to clues in Francis's own writings, which show that he favored a peaceful solution to the conflicts between Christian and Muslim.

The method used in this book to seek the true story of Francis and the sultan is a journalist's version of the detective work Scripture scholars have done to find the historical Jesus in the gospels. In both cases, the accounts in question need to be viewed in the context of their own times: the audiences they were written for, the political pressures at hand, the writers' theological goals in telling the story. By doing that, it's possible to decode the early documents and uncover the story of Francis, the sultan, and what their encounter can mean today.

The *Life of Saint Francis* by the friar Thomas of Celano was the first in a long series of biographies, appearing two to three years after Francis's death in 1226. It was written on commission from Pope Gregory IX, who wanted to memorialize the newly canonized saint's great deeds. Celano wrote in this work that Francis preached to the sultan, who "was deeply moved by his words," listening to him "very willingly." Thomas's second and more complex biography of Francis, *The Remembrance of the Desire of a Soul,* which appeared in 1247, was the work of a more assertive writer. It vividly described Francis's opposition to what turned out to be one of the most disastrous attacks for the Crusaders during the Battle of Damietta. Having become convinced that an attack would end badly for the Christian forces, Francis decided to warn the Crusade's leaders to cancel their plans: "The saint leapt to his feet, and rushed to the Christians crying out warnings to save them, forbidding war and threatening disaster." Historians have long debated whether this ambiguous passage meant that he opposed doing battle only on that particular day, or whether he was "forbidding war" altogether. The answer can be found by piecing together other evidence from the saint's early life: that Francis, an aspiring knight, turned away from the battlefield to adopt a life of peace and reconciliation. It is the contention of this book that Francis, having suffered terribly as a young man during a clash between Assisi and the city's rival Perugia, had come to oppose war, not just a particular battle.

Francis's attempt to intervene during the Fifth Crusade should be viewed in the context of his constant opposition to warfare and the pride and avarice that often caused it. He preferred not to argue. His message to the powers of the day was delivered largely, although not solely, by his countercultural example of a life of poverty, compassion, and nonviolence. His humility challenged the arrogance of the papal court, and his dedication to peace confronted the violent culture of his day. At a time when the wealthy indulged in falconry, he preached to the birds.

The truth about Francis's devotion to peacemaking, which glimmered through a number of the early accounts of the saint's life, was concealed in an influential biography that the great medieval theologian Saint Bonaventure wrote while minister general of the Franciscan order. Bonaventure was named leader of the order's feuding friars at a time of crisis. The pope had forced out the previous minister general when some Franciscans fell into a heresy based on supposed biblical prophecies. These dissidents believed, among other things, that Francis was the harbinger of a new spiritual age in which Christians would unite with nonbelievers and the church hierarchy would no longer be needed. Bonaventure faced a difficult task in writing about Francis, needing to unite the feuding factions within the Franciscan order in a common vision of their founder and to purge dissent in an effort to win back the pope's approval. In the process, the story of Francis as peacemaker was virtually eliminated from the pages of Bonaventure's *The Major Legend of Saint Francis* and a much more confrontational version of the saint's encounter with the sultan was added. Then in 1266 the General Chapter of the Franciscans voted to make *The Major Legend* the authorized history of Francis and to destroy all previous accounts. Bonaventure's version, elevated above all others, would set the tone for centuries to come.

For Bonaventure, and indeed for Thomas of Celano, Francis sought the sultan out of his ardent desire to be martyred—not to seek peace. Too many people over the years have accepted this account as historical. It is not history, however, but hagiography—stories that idealize the lives of the saints. Joseph Ratzinger, the future Pope Benedict XVI, recognized this side to Bonaventure's life of Francis in a doctoral thesis in theology he wrote in 1959 while a young priest in Germany: "It may well be that all the various *Legenda* of St. Francis depict a theologically interpreted 'Francis of faith' instead of the simple 'Francis of history.'" Historians who believe Francis supported the Crusades seem to have set aside the evidence showing how deeply he despised war. Nor have they adequately considered that the early biographies were written at a time when the popes were pushing hard for the increasingly reluctant faithful to continue the faltering drive to recapture the Holy Land. It would not have done much good for Bonaventure, as head of a Franciscan order that had come under close scrutiny from Rome as a source of heresy, to portray the founder as a peacemaker who had found common ground with the enemy. The Inquisition, already in swing during the time of these writings, treated opposition to the Crusade as evidence of heresy.

This book will put the meeting of Sultan al-Kamil and Francis in the larger context of their lives. To that end, I have included a good deal of biographical background and an account of the Fifth Crusade, with the aim of better illuminating what occurred between Francis and the sultan when they met. For Francis, that means starting with the story of how warfare traumatized him, and culminating with a look at how his encounter with the sultan changed and shaped him in the last years of his life.

The story begins with Francis's participation in a vicious battle between his city, or commune, of Assisi and neighboring Perugia and his subsequent imprisonment. Francis's jolting experience as a soldier and prisoner of war led to the wealthy young merchant's famous conversion to a life of poverty—a change that transported him away from the greed underlying the war between Assisi and Perugia. His conversion began when, after being released from jail and convalescing, he rode off on horseback to join a new military campaign fought, most likely, on behalf of the pope. His decision to reject this knightly role marked the beginning of his commitment to a new life of radical poverty that made it impossible to go to war again. It also separated him from the values of a voracious, honor-bound culture in which competition for wealth and glory bred constant violence between classes, cities, and the forces of the pope and emperor. He took the words of Jesus to "turn the other cheek" in the face of violence quite literally. He even barred members of his Third Order—established for lay people who want to live holy lives without becoming friars or sisters—from possessing weapons.

Francis's yearning for peace with Islam is especially apparent in his suggestion that his brothers live quietly among Muslims and "be subject" to them rather than engage in disputes, a provision that appears in an early version of the code of conduct for his order, its *Rule.* He wrote it shortly after returning in 1220 from his trip to Egypt—convincing evidence that the encounter with Sultan al-Kamil affected him deeply. All of this, and much more, needs to be considered to understand that Francis was trying to make peace in his historic encounter with Sultan al-Kamil.

The sultan too was an intriguing personality, a statesman adept at both making war and seeking peace. The Western portrait of him was skewed by Crusader propaganda and the Christian writers' basic lack of knowledge of the Muslim world. Any humanity emerging from what one thirteenth-century bishop called the "cruel beast" was presented as the result of Francis's charismatic intercession. Yet Sultan al-Kamil was far from the Western Christian writers' caricature of him. In Egypt he was known for his tolerance toward the Christian minority. He was a cultured man who loved learned conversation with scholars in his court. While fully capable of the ruthlessness his position required, he preferred to negotiate with enemies rather than engage them in combat. His father, Sultan Malik al-Adil, had similar qualities. Even his father's brother Salah ad-Din Yusuf ibn Ayyub, or Saladin, the conquering hero whose name flows so easily from the lips of radical Islamists today more than eight hundred years after his death, knew how to negotiate with Western powers for commercial and military purposes.

While Francis initiated their encounter, al-Kamil shaped its outcome. This is very much the story of two unique men, the saint and the sultan.

I first became interested in the story of Francis and Sultan al-Kamil shortly after the terrorist attacks of September 11, 2001, occurred in my hometown of New York City and in Washington, D.C. At the time I was just leaving a job as the religion writer for the New York newspaper *Newsday* to become a journalism professor. I had only recently written an article on the religious beliefs of al-Qaeda terrorists convicted in New York of killing hundreds of people by bombing two U.S. embassies in Africa in 1998. One of the defense lawyers at that trial had sought to spare his client the death penalty by arguing that the defendant's Islamic beliefs mitigated his responsibility for the crime. In other words, in his religious zeal, the terrorist didn't really understand he was doing evil. U.S. prosecutors countered by producing an imam to dispute that interpretation of Islam. The government lawyers praised the faith for its devotion to peace.

I spent September 11 writing the main story of the attacks on the World Trade Center and the Pentagon. Late in the afternoon a reporter in the paper's Washington bureau called with a few paragraphs quoting a source as saying that al-Qaeda was the prime suspect in the attack. Given the magnitude of what happened that day, it was noted only briefly in a long story. I wasn't sure at first whether to believe it. Early reports after the bombing of the Alfred P. Murrah Federal Building in Oklahoma City on April 19, 1995, had errantly identified an Arab taxi driver from my native Brooklyn as the suspect. Yet as I made my way home that night across the vacant streets of a spooked city, recalling the courtroom debate over the nature of Islam, the thought that religious belief was in some way responsible for the World Trade Center horror stayed with me. Sometime afterward, in search of some spiritual reading, I picked up *The Little Flowers of Saint Francis,* a still-popular account of Francis's life dating to the century after the saint's death. There I read a version of the story of Francis and the sultan and was struck at the added layer of meaning it took on in the wake of the so-called "clash of civilizations" between the West and radical Islam. My encounter with that book ultimately led to this book, which is both a journalist's investigation into Francis, Malik al-Kamil, and the Crusades and a reflection on what the meeting of saint and sultan can mean today.

Of course, ever since the September 11 attacks, references to the Crusades have emerged time and again in the public square. Al-Qaeda leaders referred to their enemies as "Crusaders and Jews," an odd pairing if ever there was one, since the Crusaders were a plague to the Jews. Osama bin Laden has called his jihadists "descendants of Saladin." Lt. Gen. William Boykin, deputy U.S. undersecretary of defense, sounded as if he were preaching the Crusade when he gave speeches that cast the war on terrorists as a spiritual fight against Satan. "I knew that my God was bigger than his," he said of a Muslim fighter in a widely quoted remark. "I knew that my God was a real God and his was an idol." His comment (which he later said was misunderstood) paralleled the Crusader practice of depicting the monotheistic Muslims as pagans.

Pope John Paul II felt the burden of the history of Christian-Muslim relations in the moments after learning that his emissary had been unable to persuade President George W. Bush against attacking Iraq in March 2003. His former personal secretary, Cardinal Stanislaw Dziwisz, later recalled that the pope feared the world was moving toward a "holy war." In covering John Paul's journey to Jerusalem in 2000, I wrote about another incident in which memories of the Crusades shadowed the pope. Standing before the thirteen-hundred-year-old Dome of the Rock with a group of Muslim clerics, John Paul was confronted by protesters, one of whom shouted to the pope's Palestinian hosts: "Shame on you! Saladin took the keys; now you have handed them over to the pope."

John Paul's many efforts to build a bridge between Christians and Muslims offered no protection to his successor, Pope Benedict XVI, who immersed himself in hot water by quoting the views of the fourteenth-century Byzantine emperor Manuel II on Islam: "Show me just what Mohammed brought that was new, and there you will find things only evil and inhuman, such as his command to spread by the sword the faith he preached." Benedict had always advocated a tougher approach to Catholic-Muslim relations than did John Paul, and although he prefaced his remark in a speech at Regensburg University in his native Bavaria by saying Manuel had spoken "with a startling brusqueness, a brusqueness that we find unacceptable," it did nothing to quell Muslim outrage or avert outbreaks of protest and even violence in many places.

That furor spurred my plans to write this book because I am convinced that Francis and the sultan have something important to say to us today: we can find common ground despite our differences. Of course, there are efforts today to bridge the divide between Christians and Muslims that did not exist in medieval times. In November 2008 the Vatican hosted a meeting with leading Muslims that Benedict said opened the way to improved relations. Such high-minded, high-level encounters are crucial, but they don't in and of themselves change the hearts and minds of the many Christians and Muslims who view one another with distrust. This is where the dramatic example of Francis and the sultan can help us. If the greatest Christian saint since the time of the apostles had opposed the Crusade and peacefully approached Muslims at a time when they were supposed to be mortal enemies, that action can inspire and instruct us today. So should the fact that al-Kamil, a great sultan of Egypt and a nephew of Saladin, was so tolerant of Christians that he allowed one of them to preach to him in the midst of a Crusade. The story of Francis of Assisi and Sultan Malik al-Kamil says there is a better way than resentment, suspicion, and warfare. It opens the door to respect, trust, and peace.

It needs to be told anew.

PART ONE

THE
ROAD
TO
DAMIETTA

1

Outfitted to Kill

The young man who would one day be known as Saint Francis of Assisi was clad in armor and mounted on a warhorse. It is a difficult image to imagine. Artists have long shied away from putting a lance in hands better known for caressing birds. But as the extravagant son of one of his city's wealthiest merchants, Francis would have bedecked himself for battle in the finest style of the day as Assisi prepared to war with Perugia, its hated neighbor to the west. The city's increasingly powerful merchants had risen up against the local noblemen who often stood in their way, driving them to seek refuge in Perugia. It was now up to the merchants and their sons to defend the city against the belligerent Perugians, who were eager to use the dispute as an excuse to go to war with weaker Assisi.

On that day in November 1202 when Pietro di Bernardone's son mounted his steed and bade farewell to the women of Assisi, there could be little trace of the poverty he would later embody. Francis would have worn the coat of chain mail known as a hauberk as well as the chain hood, gauntlets, and leggings. (The plated armor that would later symbolize the era of chivalry was not yet in use at the start of the thirteenth century.) Since Francis dealt in fine fabrics in his father's business and was very fond of fashion and chivalry, it is sure that he was arrayed to be the very image of knighthood, wearing a striking tunic of the best fabric over his armor.

More to the point, he was outfitted to kill.

Shops were closed and bells rang out as the troops paraded through the center of Assisi and out beyond the fortified city walls. The soldiers' procession led past their beloved Cathedral of San Rufino, where Francis and so many others in Assisi's army had been baptized. The beautiful Romanesque facade of the cathedral was adorned with a vision of the Apocalypse in carved stone figures of a crowned God between star and moon; a Madonna on her throne; and assorted writhing dragons and hideous reptilian birds. The doorway was guarded on each side by stone lions: one was mauling a ram, and the other eating a peasant alive, starting with the head. Eight-year-old Chiara Offreduccio, the future Saint Clare, grew up in a house on the piazza in front of San Rufino but was not home that day. Her aristocratic family had fled town to be safe from the likes of Francis and other merchants who had risen up in anger against the noblemen in a civil war.

The cathedral held the remains of a martyr who was drowned in a river in 238 for refusing to sacrifice to pagan gods. The cult of Rufino, the first bishop of Assisi, had long inspired Assisians in their ancient rivalry with Perugia. One story Francis and his compatriots would have known concerned the cathedral's construction during the twelfth century. It was said that the Perugians ambushed some workers and seized a prized oak beam. When the beam proved to be so heavy that even a team of oxen couldn't budge it, the Perugians saw that the hand of God was against them and gave up.

In the war against Perugia, oxen pulled the *carroccio,* a rolling altar that symbolized the wedding of war and religion in the minds of the people. It was decked not in liturgical splendor but in the city colors of red and blue. It carried Assisi's flag and a bell used to alert residents to be ready for battle. The *carroccio* epitomized the "God and commune" faith Francis was raised in, one that merged Christianity with political aims often contradictory to it—such as fighting a war for economic advantage.

The colorful altar followed an army of archers and foot soldiers, troops from the various craft guilds, and finally the cavaliers. Francis rode with the Compagnia dei Cavalieri, noblemen and merchants wealthy enough to afford horse and armor. History records no swoons, but at roughly age twenty-one, the rich, dark-eyed Francis was as eligible and dashing as a bachelor could be, a young man who sang poetic love songs from Provençal in a sonorous voice and who won friends not only with his natural charisma and leadership but also with his free-spending generosity. His parents scolded him, saying he spent so much money that he seemed to be the son of a prince. Francis, however, would not be deterred. He had bought into the enticing image of knighthood—literally—with his father's money.

Francis was a devotee of chivalry; he loved the French troubadours' songs and, from his birth, was steeped in their culture. His unusual name signaled that. He had been baptized Giovanni, after Saint John the Baptist. But his father, Pietro, on a business trip in France when his son was born, insisted on nicknaming the baby boy Francesco, or Francis. It was akin to calling a schoolboy "Frenchy," as the British writer G. K. Chesterton put it. Pietro evidently was attached to the French.

As Papa's little Frenchman grew, he became well acquainted with the *Chanson de Roland,* a gory French epic romance in which the hot-tempered knight Roland and his uncle Charlemagne fought the Muslims in Spain and tried to convert them through warfare. (Although taken as a factual encounter, the story was fiction; Charlemagne's troops probably fought Christian Basques at Roncesvalles, not Muslims.) The French troubadours' songs of King Arthur and his heroic band of knights also appealed to Francis's imagination, to the point that he would later envision his fledgling order of scruffy friars as a new kind of nonviolent band of brothers. "These brothers of mine are my knights of the round table," he once exclaimed, adding that this would be a brotherhood not of swordplay but of prayer. Francis loved the courtesy and chivalry knights aspired to, even in later years when he rejected their violence.

We should not assume, though, that Francis was acting out a child-hood fantasy as he headed out to battle Perugia that autumn. He may simply have been under pressure from the culture in which he lived to satisfy an obligation. As former Assisi mayor Arnaldo Fortini wrote in 1959 in his comprehensive biography of Francis, *La Nova Vita di San Francesco d'Assisi,* every man in the commune was expected to present himself at the city gate on the way to battle. Those who failed to do so were severely punished. Men who were wealthy enough to afford serving in the cavalry were expected to saddle up. For upwardly mobile urban merchants, it provided the exciting, albeit dangerous, opportunity to adopt the regalia and values of chivalry, including the codes of honor and loyalty. So for Francis, going to war may have been something more than a romantic lark. He had to do it to maintain his family's honor.

Since oaths of loyalty were the foundation of feudal society, it was difficult for young men of the day to avoid being dragged into the constant violence. The historian Lauro Martines observed: "Too often, in the thirteenth-century Italian city, doing the restrained or 'peaceful' thing would have required the renunciation of self-identity." The historian was not referring to Francis, but that observation tells the story of his life. Without a radical change—such as a decision to imitate Jesus as closely as possible—it would have been difficult for Francis to avoid the mayhem. But from all indications, the young Francis was sucked in by the seductive fictions of his time: he longed to be a knight.

Larger historical forces also had conspired to put Francis on the road to battle. "Holy Roman" emperors from Germany had fought to seize control of fractious Italy, clashing with powerful medieval popes who wanted to expand or protect their landholdings. In 1174 merchants in Assisi tried to rid themselves of imperial rule. They failed, and Emperor Frederick assigned Conrad, a ruthless military commander, as Duke of Spoleto to clamp down on the unruly Italian cities. Conrad installed himself as the Count of Assisi in the Rocca Maggiore, a castle that loomed above Assisi. It soon served as a constant reminder of the emperor's unwanted authority.

In the fading days of the twelfth century, the chessboard began to change.

On September 28, 1197, Emperor Henry VI, crowned Holy Roman emperor by the elderly Pope Celestine III, died of malaria at the age of thirty-two in the Sicilian port city of Messina, while preparing to go on Crusade. Celestine III died the following January. With the empire suddenly vulnerable, the College of Cardinals saw an opportunity and voted to name a brilliant and shrewd young canon lawyer, Cardinal Lothar of Segni, to the papacy. Pope Innocent III was destined to be the most powerful of the medieval popes.

Educated in Rome, Paris, and Bologna, Innocent grew up in a noble Roman family. His uncle, who reigned as Pope Clement III from 1187 to 1191, had made him a cardinal at the age of twenty-nine. The speedy choice of the talented, energetic thirty-seven-year-old Innocent signaled that the empire was about to be struck.

Innocent moved quickly to assert control, assuming power over Italian cities and in particular Conrad's Duchy of Spoleto, which included Assisi. He ordered the duke to submit forthwith, and Conrad, knowing that he was outpowered, didn't have much choice. As negotiations continued, the duke went to bargain with papal legates in the city of Narni. That's when the seething merchants of Assisi—tired of the years of abuse and angry that they still faced the prospect of having Conrad lord over them, even as he submitted to the pope—got their opportunity to attack.

They stormed Conrad's hilltop fort, spurning papal representatives who tried to calm them, and battered it into a heap of stones. Most likely the teenaged Francis joined the assault.

More castles fell as the angry merchants attacked the noblemen in their bastions. Then a street war broke out all around Francis and his family in the narrow confines of Assisi. We don't know for sure if Francis participated, but as the son of one of the wealthiest merchants, it is likely that he did. Merchants destroyed one fortified house after another, burning them down. The noblemen fled their palaces. Such economic conflict between imperious overlords and a newly assertive merchant class dragged city after city into chaos and, in an era noted for its violence, the tight quarters made this intracity fighting especially dangerous. Rooftop cata-

Angry merchants—and possibly the young Francis—destroyed the Rocca Maggiore, an imperial castle in Assisi. It was rebuilt in the fourteenth century. *Copyright © 2007 by Paul Moses*

pults, crossbows, fire, and chains stretched across streets to down horsemen were among the weapons of choice.

Girardo di Gislerio, an Assisi aristocrat, sought protection from the rampaging merchants in powerful Perugia. This neighboring city, built on a fifteen-hundred-foot hilltop across the Tiber River, had been battling one community after another to expand its influence. With its easily secured site on the heights overlooking a broad valley, Perugia was becoming the regional powerhouse.

The Assisi nobleman presented himself to the Perugians on January 18, 1200. This act betrayed his city, but di Gislerio had little choice but to seek a new protector after his life in Assisi unraveled. He was lord of Sasso Rosso, one of the castles that the merchant-revolutionaries in Assisi had destroyed after dismantling Conrad's fortress. He also happened to hold a key piece of property in an area called Collestrada. From their respective hilltops about thirteen miles apart, the communes of Perugia and Assisi both ruled over vast valleys with farms, orchards, rivers, and strategic roadways leading to Rome. The Tiber River divided their domains, with the exception of Collestrada, a disputed strip of land on Assisi's side that Perugia claimed. Collestrada was a modest hill with a minor fortification at the top and a hospital for lepers below. The hill sloped gently down toward the Tiber, which could be crossed on the Ponte San Giovanni. Small as this hill was, Collestrada loomed like a mountain in the ancient rivalry between Perugia and Assisi.

The combative Perugians were quick to see that by offering protection to the aggrieved noblemen from Assisi, they had the opportunity to justify war against their neighboring city, which their people had hated from one generation to the next. Acting under the honor-bound codes of chivalry, Perugia, a city that symbolized itself as a griffin, a mythical animal part eagle and part lion, took di Gislerio under its wings and demanded that Assisi rebuild the castle that its rabble had trashed and pay damages.

Assisi's honor was challenged, and amid fevered political speeches in the central piazza near the Bernardones' home, its citizens refused to back down. The city walls were quickly built up—some historians have speculated this was when Francis learned the masonry skills he later used to rebuild derelict churches—and an army was organized. Perugian raiders fought skirmishes, chopped down fruit trees, and destroyed crops in the vulnerable hinterlands.

These were the historical forces that armored Francis and put him on horseback late in the fall of 1202. He and his fellow soldiers took their places a half mile from the Perugians, who gathered on the other side of the Tiber River near the Ponte San Giovanni. The Assisians occupied high ground, seizing a small castle at the top of the Collestrada hill. In a triumphalist history of Perugia written nearly a century after the battle, one can still sense the Perugians' sneers at a foe that had driven its most experienced fighting men into the enemy camp. The author of the *Eulistea,* poet Bonifazio da Verona, likened the Assisians to chickens.

Bonifazio portrayed it as a long and intense battle that ended with the

Perugians slaughtering the retreating Assisians. This is confirmed in the writings of Thomas of Celano. "There was a great massacre in a war between the citizens of Perugia and Assisi," he wrote. The Perugians sent the blood-soaked Assisians fleeing for hiding places in the woods and in caves, then hunted them down like animals. The battlefield was covered with severed limbs, entrails, and mutilated heads, Bonifazio wrote.

There is no record of Francis's exploits on the battlefield, but our modern-day knowledge of the psychology of warfare tells us that it had to be a frightening experience. Strip away any inclination to romanticize combat—especially hand-to-hand medieval warfare—and consider this data from *The American Soldier,* the U.S. Defense Department's official review of the troops' performance in World War II. One-quarter of all U.S. soldiers in the war admitted losing control of their bladders, and an eighth acknowledged defecating in their pants, according to a study cited in the survey.

Francis would likely have taken part in the gut-churning cavalry charge to open the battle. The terror that the young combatant felt in his first cavalry charge cannot be underestimated. Hand-to-hand combat is generally more traumatic than warfare fought from a distance, especially during retreats, when most of the killing is done as the pursuers pick off soldiers from behind. "Any way you cut it, it had to be a stunningly traumatic event, to be defeated, to see your friends killed, to see your city defeated," said Lt. Col. David Grossman, a retired Army Ranger who became a professor of psychology and military science at West Point.

If we are going to understand Francis's transition from warrior to peacemaker, we must consider the uncomfortable notion that Francis killed men on the battlefield. No one can say for sure if Francis slew the enemy, but it is likely he did. His eventual decision to begin a life of penance (which will be addressed in a later chapter) hints that he believed he had sinned seriously on the battlefield. There was a tradition in medieval times that demanded repentance from those who killed in combat. Penitential manuals, which advised confessors on the penance to impose for various sins, told priests to require forty days of atonement for knights who had slain an opponent at war—an indication that the conduct was considered sinful. Similarly, bishops issued a directive after the Battle of Hastings in 1066 that soldiers must do a year of penance for each man they killed and seven years for those who killed in a war they fought for economic gain.

This idea of repentance for the sins of war is reflected in the songs and writing of the day. *The Four Sons of Aymon,* an epic romance, told of how Aymon's warrior son Rinaldo, having challenged Charlemagne and then later battled the Muslims in the East, returned home to do penance through an ascetic life. To atone for his sins on the battlefield, he labored on the cathedral of Cologne. Early in the thirteenth century the English chronicler Roger of Wendover created a fabulist scene in his work *Flowers of History,* about a soldier whose wanton killing had led to his eternal torture in hell. Every time the knight spurred his horse, devils rose up to tear him limb from limb. Then his limbs were reassembled to begin the torture anew.

In Francis's era, an influential confessors' guide written by the English theologian Thomas of Chobham generally permitted knights to fight on orders of their lords, but told priests to question soldiers closely about their deeds in battle, particularly in an unjust war. In that case, he allowed knights to follow their lord into battle but wanted them to avoid drawing blood except in self-defense.

Assisi's cause hardly qualified as a just war, which at the time meant fighting to right a wrong. Assisians fought for commercial advantage, starting with their assault on a castle over the objections of papal legates who were trying to reach a peace treaty with a foe already in retreat. The Perugian demand for Assisi to make good on the damage its citizens caused was intended to provoke, but it didn't have to. In short, this was a war fought because of greed, hardly the sort of chivalrous cause sung by the troubadours. This was the use of force to seek short-term economic gain, to humiliate class enemies, and to save face. Furthermore, the rebellious Assisians were on perilous moral ground because they had elected a *podestà,* or mayor, who had been excommunicated. The reason for his excommunication isn't known, but possibly the mayor was a member of the Cathar sect, a heretic religious movement that attacked the church over its wealth and—much as Francis would someday—sought a return to the simplicity of apostolic times.

When the Assisians refused to throw out the mayor, Gerard of Filiberti, Pope Innocent III barred them from receiving the Eucharist and other sacraments. Consider the morality of this war as it appeared in Francis's day: Assisians, deprived of the sacraments and led by an excommunicate, had begun the hostilities by destroying a castle over the objections of a papal envoy. Their enemy, closely aligned with the papacy, had stepped in to protect a respected citizen seeking help against a campaign of local street violence. Furthermore, it would have appeared obvious in that era that God had punished the Assisians by spurning their prayers and allowing their horrific defeat at Collestrada. For the soldier with a conscience, there was no glory in killing for such a cause, only sin.

For the rest of his life, Francis was thoroughly convinced of his own sinfulness, much to the amazement of those who admired his holiness. He had made a decision "to embark upon a life of penance," he wrote in his last days. The reason could well be that he had killed in behalf of an unjust cause, and knew it.

While poorer men were hunted in the woods to be run through with swords and spears, Francis, who was left intact in that field of gore only because he was rich enough to be ransomed, was taken prisoner. He was dragged across the river and up to the commanding Perugian hilltop. His enemies deposited him in a damp dungeon, giving Francis plenty of time to reflect on the horrors he had seen—and on the consequences his own actions would have on his soul.

2

Shattered

F rancis was shackled in a makeshift prison that was located on the
edge of a steep hilltop beneath what is now a graceful Renaissance building, Il Palazzo del Capitano del Popolo. Today it
has rounded archways over the doors and windows, a sword-
wielding figure of Justice above the entrance, and a pair of crowned and
clawed griffins on the thick, dark brown wooden door. The fifteenth-
century building has served as a court.

On the day Francis was imprisoned on that site, no magistrate was
present. Justice meted out during the Middles Ages was far less formal
than it is today. Prisons as we know them were not built in Europe until
the end of the thirteenth century; before that, they were usually crude
improvisations. In this case, it appears that Francis and his fellow Assisians,
after being hauled up the mountain and marched through the city center,
presumably before a taunting mob, were dumped in an underground
vault in the depths of Perugia's Etruscan ruins. The broad square where it
was located had a commanding view of the valley below, but not one
Francis would have seen.

Early biographers give the impression that prison was easy for Francis.
Yet prisoners taken in such vendetta-driven intercity warfare were tor-

tured and humiliated to induce wealthy relatives to pay ransom. Many were chained to walls, languishing in near-darkness, forced to live in the stench of their own filth. Many died from disease. Francis may indeed have put up a false bravado at first in the belief that his father would quickly come up with the ransom money, but he soon learned that he was in for a brutal experience.

Even under these conditions Francis, although nowhere near his conversion, still gave an inkling of the peacemaker he would one day become. One of the knights from Assisi was so mean-tempered that the others quarreled with and then shunned him. Francis was the only one to befriend the embittered knight and urged the others to make peace with him.

Francis spent a year in prison before negotiations between Perugia and Assisi ransomed him and his fellow captives in November 1203. He left captivity a shattered man: he had fallen ill in prison, probably of malaria, and as a result would have suffered from fever, chills, possible blood and liver disorders, and a general weakness. He would suffer with malaria periodically for the rest of his life.

Beyond his physical ailments, Francis was inevitably shadowed by psychological disturbance. No lights brightened the subterranean cell where he was held; little if any sunlight would have reached him. The consequence of that sensory deprivation would have been devastating. Living with little or no light "would be enough to shatter any human being," says Lt. Col. Grossman, who has written extensively on the psychology of warfare. "...Whatever he [Francis] went in there with, he would have left there fundamentally a changed human being." In addition, he said, Francis would inevitably have felt abandoned as time passed and experienced a strong sense of survivor guilt. Francis had seen the enemy cavalry rip apart other men on the ground while he was permitted to survive because of his family's wealth.

As the earliest account of Francis's life attests, Francis returned home a physical and emotional wreck. He huddled in Assisi with his parents, too ill and depressed to do much of anything. After a while he was able to walk around the house with the support of a cane. Eventually he went outside and gazed at Assisi's fields and vineyards, which had always raised his spirits. He took no delight in them now. He felt hollow and depressed. Francis wondered at this sudden change he was experiencing; the very thing that once moved him to poetry and song—his love of nature—no longer held any meaning for him. He was numb. Yet there was something stirring in him, moving him ever so slightly toward a radically new way of life.

So began his process of conversion. He soon started to "despise himself and to hold in contempt the things he had admired and loved before," Thomas of Celano wrote. The notion that Francis laughed his way through a year of confinement is false. He left prison a hollow man. In time he learned to fill the empty space with God. Having been broken in a subterranean hellhole in Perugia, Francis gradually experienced a spiritual awakening.

Francis became generous to the poor. In one story, the young man takes the finely tailored clothes off his back and gives them to a destitute knight—much as Saint Martin of Tours, one of the most popular saints during the Middle Ages, was said to have done. Celano draws a close comparison between the two.

Born in 316, Martin revolted after his father, a pagan soldier, insisted he follow the emperor's order to join the Roman military. Martin's friend and biographer, Sulpicius Severus, wrote that the young man was forced at the age of fifteen to take the oath of military service. Once in the Roman army, he used most of his pay to feed and clothe the poor, giving away much of the fine clothing the emperor had issued to him. A turning point came when he tore his cloak in two and gave half of it to a freezing, scantily dressed beggar at the gates of Amiens on a dangerously cold winter day. The other soldiers laughed at Martin in his shredded cloak. That night, according to the story, Martin dreamed that he saw Jesus wearing the beggar's half of the torn cloak.

Martin was baptized a Christian at age twenty-two, entering the faith at a time when the Roman authorities no longer considered it subversive. That didn't stop Martin from standing up to Emperor Julian as he prepared a campaign in Worms against barbarians who were invading Gaul.

"I am the soldier of Christ: it is not lawful for me to fight," he told the emperor, refusing to accept bonus pay handed out in anticipation of the coming battle. The emperor flew into a rage and accused Martin of cowardice. Martin offered to stand unarmed before the enemy in the next day's battle, predicting that Jesus would protect him. Julian, who had no use for the Christian faith, decided to force Martin to make good on his word. That proved to be unnecessary; the enemy surrendered before battle. Sulpicius Severus saw the Lord's hand in this outcome.

This is a clue to understanding the real story of Francis's role in the Crusades. By drawing such a clear parallel between Martin and Francis (whether or not the incident with the poor knight is factual), Thomas of Celano may have signaled that Francis opposed war, just as Martin did. Likening Francis to one of the era's favorite saints may have been a way Celano eased concerns about Francis's countercultural nonviolence.

Like Saint Martin, Francis began moving away from material wealth, but he had yet to to renounce its close relative, warfare. Despite his prison experience, Francis decided to return to the battlefield. According to Thomas of Celano, a knight from Assisi persuaded Francis to take up arms again: "A certain nobleman of the city of Assisi was preparing himself in no mean way with military arms, and, puffed up by a gust of vainglory, vowed that he would go to Apulia to increase his wealth and fame." This was not the glorious warfare of which the troubadours sang—it was a mercenary venture aimed at inflating wealth and ego. Francis was taken in.

To understand this event, it's necessary to fill in historical background that Celano, writing under the pressure of a papal commission, could not. The battle being fought in Apulia early in 1205 was the latest in the ongoing war between imperial and papal forces. Pope Innocent III had dispatched an army headed by Count Walter of Brienne, an aristocrat from Champagne, to oust German forces from lands the papacy claimed in southern Italy. The medieval accounts do not say which army Francis hoped to fight for, but most historians believe Francis planned to join the papal force.

Innocent pulled out all the stops, granting those who fought the imperial force the Crusade privilege, which meant they could wear the holy cross and receive the same indulgence as soldiers who took the arduous journey to the East. Since the Crusade was a holy war fought with papal sanction, Innocent elevated the fight for his own landholdings to a sacred cause by granting the privilege. To justify this misuse of the Crusade privilege for his own political purposes, Innocent charged that Markward, the enemy leader, had aided the Muslim foe by delaying papal forces from joining the Crusade. The pope cleverly labeled Markward "another Saladin." He even threatened to divert the Crusade army to Sicily.

Francis, still drawn by dreams of fame, threw himself once more into preparing for war. As Celano wrote, he was "ignoring God's plan" by returning to his warrior ways. What he couldn't say outright is that it was against God's will for Francis to go to war in behalf of Pope Innocent's quasi-Crusade.

The wealthy knight from Assisi introduced Francis to a count from Apulia who was evidently outfitting Count Walter's army and hiring mercenaries. Francis, eagerly hoping to be knighted and to join Walter of Brienne, the flower of French chivalry, once again arrayed himself in the best armor and weaponry his father's money could buy. Then he set out on horseback on the road south from Assisi, heading toward Spoleto on the way to Apulia. A squire probably accompanied him.

Then came the dream—or as it was considered in Francis's time, his visitation from the Lord.

When Francis slept that night, a man appeared and called him by name. "He led him into a palace of unspeakable beauty, filled with military arms, its walls covered everywhere with shining shields emblazoned with crosses," according to *The Anonymous of Perugia,* an account of Francis's life written about 1240. It was actually Francis's house, transformed with a shining display of saddles, spears, and gleaming armor. The image of the cross put the finishing touch on this dream of Crusader glory. In his dream, Francis initially experienced a sense of joy but wondered who the shining weaponry belonged to. He was told that all of it, the glittering palace included, was for him and his knights.

When he awoke, Francis recalled the dream and at first exulted in it as validation of his plan to be knighted. Beaming, he boasted to others, "I know that I shall become a great prince." So Francis set out for Apulia, a long journey away in Italy's southeastern corner. As he rode south to Spoleto, however, he had second thoughts about the meaning of his dream. He began to feel at best "lukewarm" about his military plans and had to force himself to push ahead.

In Spoleto, Francis felt anxious about his trip and a bit ill. Likely his day of galloping south with his squire toward the battle zone, once again clad in chain mail and bearing a shield and deadly weapons, had reawakened in him horrors of the Battle of Collestrada. As he fell asleep, Francis heard a voice ask where he was going—a question as much about the direction of his life as about his immediate plans. Francis took it literally in his dream, explaining that he was to meet up with a count who would knight him.

"Who do you think can best reward you, the Master or the servant?" the voice asked.

"The Master," Francis answered.

"Then why do you leave the Master for the servant, the rich Lord for the poor man?" the voice asked.

Francis's response would mark his next step toward conversion: "Lord, what do you wish me to do?"

Like Moses, like Samuel, like Elijah, like Saul of Tarsus, Francis had been called by God. The divine voice had told him that by going to battle in Apulia, where he sought his own glory, he would be defying God.

"Return to your own place, and you will be told what to do," the voice told him, echoing words in the Acts of the Apostles about Saint Paul's conversion on the road to Damascus.

Dreams were a commanding force, a sort of psychological cinema for the medieval mind. They would have had more power in Francis's time than in our own, with our ready supply of motion picture fantasies on screens of all sizes. Francis awoke from this troubling dream and couldn't fall back to sleep. He pondered its meaning through the night. His hint of uneasiness over the previous night's dream began to increase.

Basilica of St. Francis in Assisi. The statue, a rare image of Francis on horseback, depicts his return from Spoleto. *Copyright © 2007 by Paul Moses*

The beautifully wrought shields he had imagined were now a source of anxiety. The gleaming weaponry he had imagined in his sleep could have been set out in the *Chanson de Roland,* which similarly glamorized the tools of war. Now Francis's psyche had exposed it as a bright, shining lie.

In the dark of night Francis came to a momentous decision: he would not go to Apulia. Despite his lack of sleep, he felt uplifted as morning broke.

According to *Anonymous of Perugia,* Francis couldn't wait to get back home to abandon his armor, weapons, and horse. He stopped off in Foligno, about ten miles south of Assisi, and sold his horse, his clothes, and the equipment he had acquired to fight in Apulia. He put on cheaper clothes and trudged back to Assisi.

Yet even without his warhorse, lance, and armor, he still had money—even more now that he had sold his extravagant weaponry, his steed, and his clothing. As he approached Assisi, Francis stopped at the rundown little Church of San Damiano, which was down the hill from the walled city of Assisi, about fifteen minutes on foot. He approached a poor priest named Peter who lived there, urging that he take all of his money. Father Peter, shocked to see such a treasure and probably afraid of what Francis's father would do to him, refused. Francis left it on a deep windowsill (which can be seen today). From that day on, Francis distanced himself as much as possible from his old life.

For many, Francis's actions seemed irrational, but he was not the first or last war veteran to experience a change after confronting the demons of the battlefield or prison. While many soldiers throughout history have suffered a certain degree of "shell shock" or battle fatigue, it wasn't until the 1970s that psychologists coined the name post-traumatic stress disorder, or PTSD, to define it. Nearly a third of the men and a quarter of the women who fought for the United States in Vietnam at some point developed PTSD. In the Persian Gulf War, fought more quickly and often at greater distance, 10 percent of the soldiers were diagnosed with the syndrome. A study of 2,863 U.S. soldiers who fought in the second war in Iraq found that 16.6 percent of them met the criteria for PTSD one year after their return from combat. "The high prevalence of PTSD and its strong association with physical health problems among Iraq war veterans have important implications for delivery of medical services," psychiatrists at Walter Reed Army Institute of Research concluded. A Pentagon study found an even more severe problem among National Guard soldiers who fought in Iraq, with more than half reporting mental health problems.

The early accounts of Francis's life don't provide enough detail for us to judge whether he would today meet the diagnostic criteria for PTSD. It is clear, however, that he was psychologically changed, and the early documents describe his gradual recovery.

In one story set in the period after Francis returned to Assisi, he went walking in the woods with his closest friend, an unidentified man his age who had a gift for listening. The suffering Francis talked through his deepest fears and aspirations. Then he entered a cave to pray while his companion waited outside. He fought his inner demons there, asking God for forgiveness of his sins. For the rest of his life, he would seek solitude in caves and woods to pray intensely. Prayer helped him to overcome the deep distress, if not mental illness, that stole away his inherent joie de vivre. He would carry this revulsion for combat with him for the rest of his life, shaping him into the unique man he would become.

Francis took another big step toward conversion when he reached out to a leper. The sickly man had stretched out his hand toward Francis for a donation but got something more than the coin. Francis kissed the leper on the hand and the mouth and was overwhelmed with a sense of peace as he turned away from his own inner struggles and focused more on the needs of others. He became devoted to serving lepers, visting a hospice to care for them. At the start of his *Testament,* which Francis wrote shortly before his death in 1226, he looked back on his decision to overcome his revulsion and embrace lepers as an act of penance that became the turning point in his life. "What had seemed bitter to me was turned into sweetness of body and soul," he wrote. When Francis kissed the leper, he risked his own well-being to embrace someone his society despised—much as he would years later risk his life to preach to the sultan.

The gradual change of heart over the months after his return to Assisi paved the road to what has become the best-known moment in his conversion, when he prayed on his knees before a painted crucifix late in 1205 in the broken-down, century-old Church of San Damiano. According to the early accounts, Jesus spoke from his image on the cross: "Francis, go, repair my house, which, as you see, is falling completely to ruin." This is seen as a request not just to repair the Church of San Damiano but to restore the entire Christian church.

It would take a while longer for Francis to define his mission, but at this point the broad outline for a ministry of peace and reconciliation was established. His conversion was rooted in a rejection of all the values that had led him into the disastrous Battle of Collestrada, the prison in Perugia, and the path to war in Apulia. Francis adopted a life of penance for his sins, expiating his guilt and finding himself through radical compassion, defined in the moment when he kissed the leper.

His friends mocked him and whispered rumors about his sanity. Soon accusations were shouted at him in the streets. But Francis's choice to distance himself from the very things that had traumatized him can hardly be considered irrational. The lover of chivalry and the privileged son of a wealthy merchant had been reborn as a peacemaker.

3

His New Way

To escape the warrior life that had led to his physical and psychological debilitation, Francis turned against the values of his father and friends: wealth and honor. Rather than be party to the honor-driven vendettas of his day, Francis adopted what society viewed as a life of shame—one that freed him from all patrons, including his own family patriarch. He knew this would expose him to ridicule and violence. Not yet ready for that, he hid in a pit, weeping and praying that God would free him from the coming persecution. Finally he found the inner strength to emerge from the hole and challenge the status quo. Then the violence began: people he knew all his life threw mud and rocks at him.

From the first Francis accepted violence and abuse without striking back. His father, Pietro, roused to anger by the gossip, landed on Francis "like a wolf on a lamb" and dragged him home. He beat the unresisting young man and imprisoned him, bound once again in an unlit dungeon. Francis's mother, Pica, freed him while Pietro was on a business trip. With Francis living in rags, even his younger brother Angelo taunted him in the streets. When Pietro returned home to find Francis freed from his chains, he beat Pica. Meanwhile their son survived by begging for food while he worked at restoring the Church of San Damiano.

A crazed Pietro, worried more about recovering his honor than about mending his relationship with his son, brought charges against Francis before the Assisi authorities early in 1206. Since Francis had adopted a religious life, he was able to bring the case before Guido, the bishop of Assisi. There, in a famous scene, Francis handed back to his father not only all of his money but also his clothing. He stood naked before bishop, father, and gaping townspeople. The bishop then wrapped Francis in his cloak.

Not even this gesture of protection erased the violence Francis faced. Robbers assaulted the unresisting vagabond as he ventured outside Assisi's protective walls and walked happily through the wintry woods in his rags, singing praise to God in French. He blithely told assailants that he was "the herald of the great King," possibly a reference to his baptismal saint, John the Baptist, who had also wandered the wilderness dressed in eccentric clothing. Francis was hurled into a snowy ditch; he arose singing.

A few young men joined him in his life of poverty—these brothers too wanted to free themselves from the violent culture that surrounded them. Clods of mud were thrown at their heads. "In a word, people considered them most despicable; that is why they nonchalantly and brazenly persecuted them as if they were criminals," according to *The Anonymous of Perugia*. But the brothers "suffered all these things with constancy and patience, as blessed Francis had counseled them." Although they were often taunted, insulted, stripped, beaten, and jailed, they never sought a protective patron. "Amid all these things they strove for peace and gentleness with all," Celano wrote.

From the start Francis adopted the signature greeting "May the Lord give you peace." He wrote in his *Testament* that Jesus had "revealed" this greeting to him for all the brothers to use. Francis did not use the word "revealed" casually—only when he believed he had specific instruction from God.

Though it doesn't seem so now, Francis's greeting of peace was highly unusual for the time. Amid the violence of the Middle Ages, the principle of peace—announced in the gospels and practiced in the early Christian communities—had become an ideal reserved for the monastic life. Those who sought it were on the margins; the heretical Cathars embraced the pacificism of early Christianity and opposed the Crusades. Francis's greeting announced a new path: peace was for everyone. That notion struck people who encountered him and his followers as amazing, even subversive.

One brother told Francis that people hailed in this manner would ask indignantly what "this greeting of yours" meant. The embarrassed brother asked Francis to let him use a different greeting.

"Let them chatter, for they do not understand the ways of God," Francis responded. "Don't feel ashamed because of this, for one day the nobles and princes of this world will respect you and the other friars for this greeting."

This story ended with a remark from Francis that the "little people" were close to God. In a distinctly egalitarian tone, he immediately saw that his greeting of peace challenged the "nobles and princes of this world"—that is, the lords of war. But the greeting encompasses much more than a prayer for an end to warfare: it was a Scripture-based call for a peaceable kingdom—a new world of salvation in which wealthy warmongers will learn the godly wisdom of the meek. It is the transforming peace that Jesus spoke of when he declared that the kingdom of God was at hand—and Francis delivered it with the aim of both transforming the present and bringing on a new age in which all people would be governed by the Sermon on the Mount.

As soon as there were eight brothers in his fledgling group, Francis sent them out in pairs, telling them to go forth announcing "peace and repentance." They were instructed to bless their persecutors. Francis saw nonviolence as the first step toward conversion—not just for himself and his fellow friars but for all. He later wrote in his *Letter to All the Faithful,* "Love our neighbors as ourselves. Anyone who will not or cannot love his neighbor as himself should at least do him good and not do him any harm."

Francis's devotion to Lady Poverty has always received more attention than his peacemaking efforts. The two, however, are closely linked since, as Francis knew, wars are so often fought for economic gain. Even to sympathetic outsiders, the poverty in which he exulted seemed extreme. "It seems to me that it is very hard and difficult to possess nothing in the world," Bishop Guido once told him.

But it made perfect sense to Francis. Keenly aware that voluntary poverty distanced him from the military life that nearly destroyed him, he responded, "My Lord, if we had any possessions we should also be forced to have arms to protect them, since possessions are a cause of disputes and strife, and in many ways we should be hindered from loving God and our neighbor. Therefore in this life we wish to have no temporal possessions." To Francis, poverty meant liberation.

Much as Francis's life of poverty flowed from his thirst for peace, so too did his celebrated compassion for animals. The early Franciscan accounts chronicled how he extended his compassion to hooked fish, caged rabbits, lambs bound for the slaughter, worms on the path, and birds. Francis taught the principles of nonviolence through his astonishing compassion for every creature. "The wild beasts harmed by others used to flee to him," Thomas of Celano wrote. ". . . What love do you think he bore towards the salvation of human beings, since he was so compassionate towards even the lower creatures?"

In addition, Francis's military experience taught him that the violent often met with violence. He demonstrated this point to his followers through his observations of the animal kingdom. According to Thomas of Celano, two robins, male and female, began accepting crumbs from Francis's table for their chicks. Soon the parent robins moved on, and the chicks, becoming tame, came to the brothers for their crumbs. Then one of the larger chicks muscled in on food meant for the smaller ones. Francis predicted that "this greedy one" would "come to a bad end." Soon afterward the bird fell into a pitcher of water and drowned. For Francis, it was yet another demonstration that greed and violence lead to self-destruction.

Francis did not always teach purely by example. On some occasions he was willing to speak truth to power. Early in his ministry, he and his brothers were living in an abandoned stone hut near the Rivo Torto, in the wooded valley below Assisi. On October 4, 1209, Pope Innocent III crowned Emperor Otto IV. On his way home from Rome, Otto with his entourage paraded by the Rivo Torto. Francis had a chance to make a statement: he refused to leave the hovel to see the historic spectacle. He also forbade his followers to do so. But he did send out one brother who, "without wavering, proclaimed to the emperor that his glory would be short-lived."

Celano's punch line is intriguing: "Apostolic authority resided in him; so he altogether refused to flatter kings and princes." Celano did not spell it out, but his readers would have understood that Francis showed better judgment than Pope Innocent III, since Otto later betrayed the pope.

Francis, a fool for God, was no fool when it came to reading the political climate. He disliked the machinations of the powerful but knew he needed help to protect his brothers from the persecution they experienced even from priests and bishops. His solution, risky as it may seem, was to go over the heads of the jealous clergymen to seek papal approval for his new way of life, distinguishing his men from the members of other penitential movements popular at the time. So began a nuanced relationship between Francis and the Roman Curia, a tie that needs to be examined to understand Francis's view of the Crusades and the meaning of his eventual encounter in Egypt with Sultan Malik al-Kamil. Was it possible for Francis to obey the popes and to oppose the popes' wars? Or did Francis, despite his thirst to be a peacemaker, support the Crusades?

Innocent III, the man occupying the chair of Peter, was arguably the most powerful pope ever. It would be hard to imagine a churchman who differed more from Francis, who viewed earthly power as an evil and wanted members of his order to avoid becoming bishops to save them from pride. Innocent took an exalted view of his authority: he began the custom of calling the pope—himself, in this case—the "vicar of Christ" rather than the "vicar of Peter." In the same vein, he liked to use the phrase "We who have been made princes over the whole land"—a reference to Psalm 45:16, the royal wedding song that declares, "You shall make them princes throughout the land."

Despite Innocent's exalted sense of his own power, the energetic young pontiff quickly became known for his drive to reform an increasingly corrupt institution. According to *The Deeds of Pope Innocent III*, written by an anonymous and well-connected chronicler within the papal court, he threw the money changers out of the papal palace and cut down on the fees that curial officials charged for documents. He revived a practice of holding a public consistory three times a week to hear complaints both minor and major. And he built the Hospital of the Holy Spirit for Rome's poor.

So the pontiff whom Francis hoped to see in 1209 or 1210 was aware that the church needed to return to the simple virtues of apostolic times, even as he reigned like a Roman emperor. For a young man from the hinterland to approach the regal Pope Innocent would have been most daunting, but Francis had little choice if his radical way of life was to survive. Various edicts had forbidden unauthorized preaching, and as a layman untrained in theology, Francis could easily have been targeted as a heretic. So Francis and a ragged band of his followers set out for Rome to seek an audience with the pope.

The stories about what happened next differ. According to one, Francis managed to talk his way into the Lateran Palace, where he found the pope meditating in the Hall of the Mirrors. Innocent, a short man with a round face, big eyes, a small mouth, and a resonant voice, abruptly dismissed him.

In a more pointed version, the English Benedictine monk Roger of Wendover wrote that when the unkempt Francis presented his proposed *Rule* during one of the pope's public sessions, Innocent lambasted him: "Go, brother, go to the pigs, to whom you are more fit to be compared than to men, and roll with them, and to them preach the rules you have so ably set forth." The vagabond bowed and left right away. Then he returned to the court, filthy, and said, "My lord, I have done as you ordered me; grant me now, I beseech you, my petition." According to this account, Innocent regretted treating Francis with such contempt. He ordered him to wash up and return. Then, "much moved," Innocent granted Francis permission to preach.

Hovering over the exchange between Innocent and Francis was the church's drive against the Cathar heretics, which Innocent was at the time whipping to full gallop. On January 14, 1208, a Cistercian inquisitor who represented the pope was murdered in southern France. Shortly thereafter Innocent, incensed, ordered a war against the Cathars and the noblemen who tolerated them, known to history as the Albigensian Crusade.

Francis was aware that his life of poverty could be called into question during this war against the Cathars, who argued that the material world was evil. The hard-liners who wanted to crack down on the burgeoning penitential movements held the upper hand in the Curia, but the influential cardinal John of St. Paul urged his colleagues to step back and consider what it meant if the church leadership refused to permit faithful people such as Francis to live the gospel as closely as possible.

This sentiment seems to have struck a chord with Innocent, who was shrewd enough to know that the roving penitents of that time could help him change the church's image—so long as they were truly obedient. Innocent then had a famous dream in which he saw a man resembling Francis supporting the Basilica of St. John Lateran, preventing it from falling over. The institutional church was indeed in danger because of its corrupt clergy, and Innocent knew it. He told Francis to pray for guidance, and when the friar returned, he gave verbal approval to his *Rule*.

Francis's relationship with church authority was complicated. On one hand, he took his promises to respect the clergy seriously because he thought obedience was rooted in powerlessness and humility, which he prized. He did not, however, advocate blind obedience. "A friar is not bound to obey if a minister commands anything that is contrary to our life or his own conscience, because there can be no obligation to obey if it means committing sin," he wrote in the *Earlier Rule*. In his society many men, bound by feudal oaths of loyalty, went to war because they were *only following orders*. He sought to extricate his followers from the system of patronage and loyalty by prohibiting them from seeking favors from church leaders. He used unusually strong language in his *Testament:* "I strictly forbid the friars, wherever they may be, to petition the Roman Curia, either personally or through an intermediary."

Francis's writings demonstrate that he placed a very high value on obeying the pope and other church authorities. But the ultimate authority was Jesus, whose edict to love God and love your neighbor as yourself was foremost in Francis's heart. These competing values—obeying the hierarchy and following Jesus' teaching of love for enemies—created a tension in Francis that would come into play as he discerned how he should relate to the Muslim world in general and to the sultan of Egypt in particular. Francis was convinced that God wanted him to bring the world a message of peace.

4

The Peacemaker

Throughout his ministry Francis turned his yearning for peace into concrete actions aimed at stopping warfare and other violence, even when it meant intervening in affairs of state. His repeated attempts to make peace shed light on what he was trying to accomplish when he visited Sultan Malik al-Kamil.

In one effort, Francis dared to face his old demons by preaching against war in Perugia, where he had been held prisoner. After spending time deep in prayer in a cliff-top dwelling in Greccio, he came to believe that the Perugians were on the brink of the same sort of warfare between noblemen and merchants that Assisi had experienced. With "his soul on fire," he set out to bring harmony to the very people he had battled in his youth.

A crowd gathered in Perugia's main piazza to hear Francis, by then well known for his holiness. But he was quickly met with jeers and harassment from knights who raced their horses around the square, jousting in a show of force. The sounds of clashing weapons and thundering hooves drowned Francis's voice as he spoke. The noblemen storming through the square on horseback viewed him not as a holy man preaching peace but as a runt from Assisi whose merchant father had ransomed him from their jail.

"Listen and understand what the Lord is telling you through me, His servant, and don't say, 'This one is from Assisi,' " he shouted to the knights. "…Your heart is puffed up by arrogance in your pride and might. You attack your neighbors and kill many of them." God had granted great power to Perugia and allowed it to dominate neighboring cities, he declared, adding that such might required its leaders to be humble and merciful.

Francis believed that war was rooted in the sin of pride; dreams of fame, glory, and knighthood had accompanied him to the battlefield years before. Inflamed by the knights' arrogance, Francis warned that their pride had put them on a road to self-destruction. They would be ripped apart in a civil war, he declared, and end up suffering far more than they would in battles with rival cities.

His warning was on target. Within a few days the commoners attacked the knights. Their battles were fought with such cruelty that even the citizens of neighboring towns—who hated powerful Perugia—were moved to pity. The common people drove the knights from the city, but they retaliated by destroying crops—the same tactics of total war that the Perugians had used against Assisi in Francis's youth.

According to *The Assisi Compilation,* anecdotes that the Franciscan order compiled from Francis's friends starting in 1244: "The knights, supported by the Church, destroyed many of their fields, vineyards and trees, doing as much harm as they could." The church was held responsible in this account for helping the rich to destroy the livelihoods of the lower classes.

The early biographers who recounted Francis's preaching in Perugia were interested in demonstrating his miraculous power of prophecy. Leaving aside the question of whether supernatural power was at work, the story shows Francis to be a shrewd observer of the treacherous politics of his day. With insights honed by extended periods of contemplation, he drew on personal experience as a soldier and son of a well-connected merchant to read the signs of the times and foresee the violence in Perugia.

According to another story, Francis saw warfare as quite literally the devil's work. From a hospice outside the walls of the warring Tuscan city of Arezzo, he could hear battle cries and watch fires burn at night in the strife-ripped commune. "He saw devils rejoicing over that place and stirring up the citizens to each other's destruction," Celano wrote. The factions fought with the same viciousness Francis had experienced during the war in Assisi. Deeply moved, he wanted to help but "was not able" to intervene. The account does not say what forces rendered him unable to step in—but he may well have been unable to move forward because of the crippling memories of his own war experiences. Unable to intervene personally, he told Brother Sylvester, an elderly priest traveling with him, to go to the city gate and in a loud voice command the devils to leave. The priest did so, and peace returned to Arezzo shortly afterward. Francis later returned to the city when warfare threatened again, according to *The Assisi Compilation,* and bluntly warned the people against renewed

Benozzo Gozzoli, *The Expulsion of the Devils from Arezzo,* 1452, Church of St. Francis, Montefalco. *Copyright © Scala / Art Resource, NY*

violence. "I speak to you as those in demons' chains," he said, likening them to animals being led to slaughter.

Celano used the story of Francis and Sylvester in Arezzo to give a lesson on Franciscan peacemaking. In Celano's later biography he describes the old priest as an Assisi clergyman who profited from selling stones to one of Francis's friars for repairing a church. When Sylvester complained angrily to Francis that he hadn't been paid in full, Francis smiled but thought to himself that the man was sick with greed. Rather than lecture the priest on his responsibility to the church, Francis filled Sylvester's hands with money without counting it. This pleased the priest for a while, but later he realized his sin and had a vision—a dream of a golden cross coming from Francis's mouth—and experienced a conversion. Celano illustrated the connection between Franciscan poverty and nonviolence: Sylvester was ready to do God's work as a peacemaker only after he was freed from his greed.

Other stories say that Francis's preaching stopped outbreaks of violence in Siena and Bologna. Despite such dramatic interventions, however, he taught primarily through example, not words. He instructed his followers to do the same. In one story told in *The Assisi Compilation,* Francis charged his brothers to shower kindness upon robbers who were hiding in a forest near their hermitage, lying in wait to attack travelers. His instructions: serve them bread and wine. After the meal the brothers were to speak to them of God's love and then to ask the desperados to promise not to strike anyone. That was it; there was no lecture on stealing. Asking for everything at once would not work, Francis taught. The robbers gradually were converted, as the story goes. Some even joined Francis's order.

Beyond the words and example he used to influence the society around him, Francis also took concrete steps within his own order to promote peace and protect life. When he created his Third Order around 1221 for lay people devoted to living simple, holy lives, its *Rule* specified that members "are to be reconciled with their neighbors and to restore what belongs to others . . . They are not to take up lethal weapons, or bear them about, against anybody." This rule made it impossible for men to enter military service. Francis's bar on making oaths also kept members of the Third Order from fighting wars: lords, vassals, and their underlings all swore oaths to go to war when called, perpetuating the violence that dominated Europe in the thirteenth century. Military leaders quickly recognized that this refusal to bear arms or swear oaths was a serious threat to their ability to make war.

Miracle stories that circulated after Francis's death celebrated him as a saint whose intercession undermined powerful men and their violent designs. One such story involved a guard whose dream of Francis protected him from a Roman nobleman who wanted to slay him as he slept. Others stories credited Francis with helping people escape prison, foiling powerful aristocrats and even the pope. For example, a simple-minded innocent named Pietro was arrested in Rome during Pope Gregory IX's crackdown on heresy. The then-deceased Francis freed the man, whose broken chains were later sent to Gregory. In story after story, Francis protects the oppressed.

Francis's yearning for peace is best summed up by a story in which he negotiated a treaty between the people of Gubbio, a town about thirty miles north of Assisi, and a wolf that terrorized them. It did not appear until the fourteenth century in *The Deeds of Blessed Francis and His Companions*. Popularized in an Italian-language version of that work, *The Little Flowers of Saint Francis,* it remains a favorite.

According to the story, the residents of Gubbio were gripped by fear of a huge wolf that had devoured animals and people. So terrifying was the creature that the citizens ventured outside the town walls only if they were armed "as if they were going to war." But their weaponry was useless: "Even with their weapons they were not able to escape the sharp teeth and raging hunger of the wolf."

The townspeople warned Francis that the wolf could kill him if he went out unarmed to meet it. But he went forward "protected not by a shield or a helmet but arming himself with the Sign of the Cross." As people watched from the parapets, the wolf rushed Francis, jaws gaping, then stopped short as Francis made the sign of the cross. On Francis's command, "Brother Wolf" closed its jaws, bowed, and lay at his feet. Then Francis lectured: "Brother Wolf, you have done great harm in this region, and you have committed horrible crimes by destroying God's creatures without any mercy. . . . You therefore deserve to be put to death just like the worst robber and murderer. Consequently everyone is right in crying out against you and complaining, and this whole town is your enemy. But, Brother Wolf, I want to make peace between you and them, so that they will not be harmed by you anymore, and after they have forgiven you all your past crimes, neither men nor dogs will pursue you anymore."

A deal was on the table, and Francis sweetened it by seeing through the wolf's intimidating appearance to the suffering beneath. "I promise you that I will have the people of this town give you food every day as long as you live, so that you will never again suffer from hunger, for I know that whatever evil you have been doing was done because of the urge of hunger," he said. "But, my Brother Wolf, since I am obtaining such a favor for you, I want you to promise me that you will never hurt any animal or man. Will you promise me that?"

Francis took steps to alleviate the animal's pain, carrying out the gospel message to love the enemy. In return, the wolf would avoid acts of violence. For Francis, this was a first step toward conversion. The wolf responded by lifting its paw to Francis in supplication.

The telling of this tale often ends with this image of Francis with the tamed wolf, but there is more to the story. After the wolf's change of heart, it meekly follows the saint inside the city gates. There Francis preaches a sermon in which he calls on the people of Gubbio to repent: "Dear people, come back to the Lord, and do fitting penance, and God will free you from the wolf in this world and from the devouring fire of hell in the next world." Had this occurred today, Francis's remarks might provoke consternation, for were not the people of Gubbio victims of a campaign of terror? One can easily imagine commentators saying today that Francis was wrong to call on the good citizens of Gubbio to repent because they had done nothing wrong.

But the townspeople had indeed sinned by failing to love their enemy.

They knew that the wolf was ferocious because of its hunger, yet they did nothing to slake it, to their own detriment. Instead, they resorted to the weapons of war—which had led only to more deaths.

The wolf lived out its days going door to door in Gubbio for food. "It hurt no one, and no one hurt it," according to *The Little Flowers*. "The people fed it courteously. It is a striking fact that not even a single dog ever barked at it." When the wolf died of old age, the people were saddened; they had grown to love their former enemy.

By writing allegorically about a wolf instead of the hated and feared Muslims, the author of this fable was able to tell the story of Francis's desire for peace, free from the eyes of the inquisitors. It applied deliberately political language—Francis negotiated a "pact" between Gubbio and the wolf—to a fable. Francis, "protected not by a shield or a helmet," shunned the tools of the Crusader—with one exception: the sign of the cross. Francis, a knight of nonviolence, chose to free the world from its self-destructive behavior by calling for repentance and conversion.

His was a radically different approach to dealing with the "wolf" at Christendom's door.

5

Journeys

Years before his dangerous mission to Egypt in 1219, Francis made two failed attempts to preach to Muslims. The first, a journey to the Holy Land in the summer of 1211, collapsed when the ship he boarded picked up a contrary wind that blew the craft northeast across the Adriatic Sea to Dalmatia, then known as Slavonia. Weathering a terrible storm along the way, he returned to his starting point, at the port of Ancona on the Italian peninsula's eastern shore.

In 1213 or 1214 Francis made a second attempt to reach out to the Muslim world, this time through a journey to the court of a powerful sultan in Morocco. Sultan Muhammad an-Nasir, known in the Christian world as the Miramamolin, or "Commander of the Believers," was a member of the Almohad dynasty, which gained power around 1130. The Almohads, who ruled much of North Africa and Spain, built a society renowned for philosophy and sophisticated Islamic architecture. By the thirteenth century, however, the Almohads' power had begun to wane.

On July 16, 1212, Christian forces won their most important victory in the long reconquest of Moorish Spain, triumphing in the Battle of Las Navas de Tolosa. Sultan Muhammad an-Nasir barely escaped with his life. But an estimated one hundred thousand of the sultan's men were killed.

As elation swept through Christendom after the Battle of Las Navas, Francis came to believe that he might be able to convert the weary commander. Although he supported Pope Innocent's goal of converting Muslim leaders, he avoided the pope's aggressive methods. Francis wanted to approach the sultan unarmed.

Francis's early biographers insisted that his interest in Muslim leaders reflected a holy death wish—a "burning desire for martyrdom," as Thomas of Celano wrote in recounting the planned trip to Morocco—and not a plan for evangelization or for peace. The church celebrated martyrdom, the ultimate sacrifice; death for Christ led directly to sainthood. Francis's early biographers used his supposed desire for martyrdom to explain why such a great saint had never endorsed the Crusade and had dealt peacefully with an enemy. These chroniclers did not accept that one of the greatest Christian saints wanted to have civil discourse with Islam, the wolf outside the gate. This is not to say Francis opposed martyrdom; his *Earlier Rule* required that brothers who wanted to preach the Christian faith to Muslims be prepared to die.

Francis began his risky mission to the court of Muhammad an-Nasir by traveling to Spain, most likely walking across southern France and crossing the Pyrenees (although it is possible he sailed the Mediterranean instead). He set off on a pilgrimage to the shrine of Saint James in Galicia, in the northwestern corner of Spain. A tradition had sprung up as far back as the sixth century that the apostle James, brother of John and friend of fellow fisherman Peter, had brought Christianity to Spain. James was said to be buried in a place the Romans considered to be the end of the world, but this notion is difficult to reconcile with the account of his death in the Acts of the Apostles, which says that King Herod Agrippa had James beheaded around the year 44 in Jerusalem. Location posed no obstacle to the medieval imagination. According to legend, James's friends put his body on a boat that miraculously transported him to Spain. Several miracles later it was buried with the permission of the pagan Queen

Lupa, who soon converted to Christianity. The body remained there in obscurity until the shepherd Pelayo discovered it about 813 after being guided by the stars. At this point the local bishop was quick to recognize the value of such an important shrine, and the cult of Saint James blossomed. Its popularity grew enormously in the eleventh century, and the magnificent Romanesque cathedral of Santiago was built in the city of Santiago de Compostela, starting in 1078. The saint's supposed burial place there became one of the most important Christian pilgrimage sites in the medieval world, third only to Jerusalem and Rome.

Devotion to James deepened because of a tale that the saint miraculously appeared during the legendary Battle of Clavijo between Christians and Moors around 844. Riding a white horse, James supposedly led the Christian forces to victory over the Muslims. The image of James on his charger, waving a sword and decapitating enemy soldiers, doesn't resemble the James who died at the swoop of a sword because he had preached the word of a man who also was executed by the authorities. Nonetheless the legend of Santiago Matamoros, or Saint James the Moorslayer, transformed James from beheaded to beheader.

Francis would have encountered other images of the saint, most notably James the Pilgrim, on his journey to Spain. This representation depicted James as a traveling preacher with a floppy hat to ward off the sun, a sturdy walking stick, and a hollow gourd to carry water. He wears a scallop shell, the symbol of Saint James, later worn by thousands of *peregrinos* who have walked the road to Santiago every year.

Francis eagerly followed what was thought to be the path of the pilgrim and evangelizer James across northern Spain. Thomas of Celano wrote that he hurried ahead of his traveling companions. The Camino de Santiago today passes through dozens of tiny villages that date to medieval times, and if today's *peregrinos* have the advantage of Gore-Tex hiking boots and adjustable synthetic walking sticks, they still tread on roads and bridges that go back to Francis's day and earlier, trekking along rushing rivers, up forested hillsides, and through mountain passes dusted with flowers in shades of gold and purple. Reaching the Monte do Gozo, the Mount of Joy, which offers the first glimpse of Santiago de Compostela, remains an emotional experience for exhausted travelers. They can see a modern monument there that memorializes Francis's arrival.

According to fourteenth-century accounts, Francis prayed in the immense Cathedral of Santiago, which had taken a century to build and was completed around the time he was born. It was an important event for Francis because, as *The Little Flowers of Saint Francis* states, "God revealed to St. Francis in that church that he should found many places throughout the world, because his Order was destined to spread and grow to a large number of friars." Thereupon, "as a result of this divine command," Francis began to establish communities of his friars "in various lands." It

Cathedral of Santiago, Santiago de Compostela, Spain. *Copyright © 2007 by Paul Moses*

Statue of St. Francis, Monte do Gozo, outside Santiago de Compostela, Spain.
Copyright © 2007 by Paul Moses

was a watershed moment for Francis: he decided that God wanted him to bring the gospel message to the world—as the apostle James had done.

Although Celano portrayed Francis's trip to Spain as a failed attempt at martyrdom, the revelation that Francis received at one of Christendom's holiest places seems to signify that God had called on Francis not to die but to create a great religious movement that would attract members from all over the world. In the months that followed Francis expanded his small band of brothers by opening houses in Spain where more people could live the humble, nonviolent life of the apostles.

————

Though Francis's objective was to preach to the sultan of Morocco, he never made it to North Africa. Celano tells conflicting stories about his return. In his first biography, he wrote that Francis turned back from seeking martyrdom in Morocco only because he became ill. Two decades later he contradicted this version in his *Treatise on the Miracles of Saint Francis*. There he wrote that Francis sickened "while returning from Spain *after* failing to reach Morocco as he had wished." This later account indicates that Francis had already dropped his plan to preach to the sultan before he became ill. This second account has the ring of truth because it is more vividly detailed, describing how a seriously ill Francis lost his voice for three days after a rude host ejected him and Brother Bernard of Quintavalle from their lodging.

While Celano often provides useful insights into Francis, he seems to have exaggerated the saint's desire for martyrdom. Francis returned home from Spain making excited plans for the future—not the thoughts of a man intent on martyrdom. He was filled with new hope that the movement he had started would grow dramatically. He knew from the start of his ministry, when he refused to resist beatings, that nonviolence required great courage. As Mahatma Gandhi wrote: "Nonviolence cannot be taught to a person who fears to die."

This, however, is not the same as *wanting* to die.

6

A New Crusade

Once again in poor health, Francis left Spain and made his way back to Italy in 1214 or 1215, arriving in Rome in time for the Fourth Lateran Council. Pope Innocent III, now at the peak of his power, gathered four hundred bishops and archbishops along with twice as many abbots and other church officials. His chief order of business was to launch what is now called the Fifth Crusade, the war that would lead Francis to the sultan's court. Although his presence is not documented, Francis was probably somewhere in the crowd in the Lateran Palace.

Whether or not he was present, the Fourth Lateran Council would influence Francis for the rest of his life and shape the church for centuries to come. An impressive array of reforms was enacted at Innocent's request, including measures aimed at cracking down on corruption, philandering, and incompetence among priests and bishops. But the meeting served primarily as a war council devoted to stirring up enthusiasm for a Crusade that, more than any other, was directed from the Vatican palaces. Innocent believed that if he was going to defeat the Cathar heretics in Europe and recapture the Holy Land from the Muslims, clergy and laity alike needed to be holier and more pleasing to God. This keen interest in reforming the church dovetailed—one is tempted to say "hawktailed"—with his plan for a war that he believed could be won only with God's approval.

For several years Innocent had labored to create the sense of urgency needed to justify another war with the Muslim world. His bull *Quia maior,* issued in April 1213, argued for what would today be called a preemptive war. The Muslims had built a new base, Innocent warned, to launch attacks to seize the narrow band of land that the Crusaders continued to hold along the Mediterranean coast. "At this time there is a more compelling urgency than there has ever been before to help the Holy Land in her great need," he wrote. He stressed that the Muslims' new fort on Mount Tabor, traditional site of Jesus' transfiguration, threatened Acre, the capital of the Crusaders' Latin Kingdom. This city, Innocent argued, absolutely had to be defended.

As sometimes happens during campaigns for preemptive wars, the attacker's justification was exaggerated. The sultan, Malik al-Adil, was busy trying to consolidate his power within the Muslim world and was not interested in fighting the Christians. The sultan already had entered into a five-year truce with the Latin Kingdom—with Innocent's approval—in 1212. Furthermore, Innocent secretly withheld information that showed a war might not be necessary. The patriarch of Jerusalem had written a letter to the pope noting that it *would be possible to negotiate* with the sultan and his sons for possession of Jerusalem:

> They are quite willing to return the Holy Land which they [now] hold into the hands of the lord pope for the use of the Christians, provided that they might be sure that their other land was safe from [the attacks of] the Christian people. They would be prepared every year to pay an agreed tribute to the Patriarch of Jerusalem, and they would thus provide a pledge that they would not inflict any further harm upon the Holy Land, where the feet of Our Lord Jesus Christ walked . . . He [Sultan al-Adil] has also fortified all his land and that of his sons, and musters vast armies, but he and his sons wish above all to make peace with the Roman Church as described above.

In his opening sermon at the Lateran on November 11, 1215, Innocent ignored this letter as he scorned the Muslims, saying they had befouled the holy places in Jerusalem. He preached about a frightening vision that the prophet Ezekiel had had before the Babylonians' destruction of the Temple in Jerusalem. In Ezekiel's vision, God dispatched six sword-wielding executioners and a holy man dressed in linen. The man wearing linen was to mark the last letter of the Hebrew alphabet, the *taw*, on the foreheads of those who opposed the idolatry rampant in Jerusalem at the time. Then the executioners killed those not protected with the *taw*.

Innocent told the churchmen gathered at the council that they were in effect the six men given the task of imposing God's vengeance. Omer Englebert, a Catholic priest who wrote one of the major modern biographies of Francis, has suggested that this speech influenced Francis greatly, noting that Francis afterward began his practice of signing the T-shaped Greek letter *tau*, reminiscent of Jesus' cross, to letters. "He favored the sign of the *tau* over all others," Thomas of Celano said. "With it alone he signed letters he sent, and painted it on the walls of cells everywhere."

If Francis did indeed adopt that sign based on Innocent's sermon, he never echoed the inflammatory language of confrontation that Innocent and his Crusade preachers used. Nor did he cast himself as one of the six sword-toting avengers. Rather, he was the man dressed in linen who saved people from violence with the sign of the *taw*. In adopting this symbol for his own use, Francis appeared to be following the pope's will—but on his own terms, in conformity with his conscience.

Innocent's gripping use of Ezekiel's vision highlighted his intention to use the Fourth Lateran Council to right a slouching church. Under his leadership the council sought to improve the religious observance of all the faithful by creating the Easter duty, which prescribed that all Catholics confess their sins and receive the Eucharist at least once a year. The council decreed that priests must avoid sexual immorality and drunkenness, and that bishops must not take payoffs from priests to overlook misdeeds. Bishops were castigated for partying until dawn, then missing morning mass. Clergymen were ordered not to give their blessing to trial by ordeal—a system of torture in which litigants were immersed in water, boiling or cold, or burned with red-hot irons to determine their truthfulness. Prelates were ordered not to extort money from people seeking their help. Nuns were told not to demand money from those seeking to join their orders.

All of this led up to the final decree on November 30, 1215, for a new Crusade. Never, in more than a century of warring, had church leaders been so involved in directing the troops. But because of the legacy of the Fourth Crusade—Crusaders had sacked Christian-controlled Constantinople in 1204—they had good reason to be more engaged. Innocent determined that the Crusade would set out from the port of Brindisi, near Italy's heel, and from Messina, Sicily, on June 1, 1217. He would launch the army himself, he announced. Those who refused to take part "will have to answer to us on this matter in the presence of the Dreadful Judge on the Last Day of severe Judgment," Innocent declared, putting himself at Jesus' side in the hereafter.

The pressure put on Francis and his followers to support the Crusade was enormous. But as obedient as Francis was to the pope, he would never preach the Crusade. Francis had to find his own way.

Innocent never got to lead the Fifth Crusade: he died on July 16, 1216, while on a diplomatic mission to Perugia. His corpse was bedecked in finery and laid at rest in Perugia, as plans were made for burial. James of Vitry, a leading Crusade preacher and a prolific writer whose accounts give some of the best insights into the era, was in Perugia at the time to be consecrated as bishop of Acre. What he saw disgusted him: thieves stripped the pope's body of its expensive vestments in the night, leaving the corpse naked and decaying in the church. It was a tawdry end for a man who had remolded the church.

Replacing him was a much more cautious Cardinal Cencio Savelli, an aged and devout official in the Curia. The new pontiff, who took the name Honorius III, soon had the difficult task of picking up the many battles Innocent had started, from the war against the Cathars to the struggle with the emperor and the looming Crusade in the Holy Land.

As papal power was changing hands, James of Vitry privately assailed the institutional church he saw in Perugia, writing that the Curia was preoccupied with politics and legal battles. He noted one consolation: Francis's "lesser friars" and the "lesser sisters" headed by Francis's friend, Clare. "They live according to the form of the primitive Church," he wrote, adding that God sent such simple people to shame church authorities.

Francis, looking to realize his movement's potential to help the church, expanded the order's missionary work after the Fourth Lateran Council. He outlined his plans at a chapter meeting, a general meeting of the order, held on May 5, 1217, at the Portiuncula, the small stone Chapel of St. Mary of the Angels that he had restored in the valley below Assisi at the outset of his ministry. He warned the brothers that missionary work would mean enduring shame, hunger, and thirst—and thus, he added, it was only right that he go too. He assigned himself to go to France, but he wanted his order to preach the faith everywhere and to everyone, including the Muslim world. He formalized the order's mission to the East by creating a province there and sending a group of brothers headed by Elias Buonbarone, who would one day head the order. It was an interesting choice, since Elias, hardheaded and authoritarian, lacked the humility of the gentle men who had first joined Francis. He was sent to Acre, the port city and Crusader stronghold where James of Vitry had just been installed as bishop.

Doing missionary work in this outpost north of Jerusalem was a difficult assignment, but Europe was at least as risky, if not more so. The chronicler Jordan of Giano, one of the Franciscan missionaries, reported that brothers who went to France in 1217 were suspected of being Cathars—and were so poorly prepared for the assignment that they didn't know who the Cathars were.

"They themselves were put down for heretics," Jordan wrote, adding that the friars avoided the severe penalties for heresy only after they showed the bishop their *Rule,* which outlined the holy lives they were expected to lead. Similarly, none of the dozens of brothers sent to Germany spoke the local language; no matter what they were asked, they answered, *Ja.* This helped for a while, until they were asked if they were heretics. "Some of them were cast into prison, others were stripped and led naked to a dance and made a ludicrous spectacle before their fellowmen," Jordan wrote.

Still other brothers went to Hungary, and though they were under a local bishop's protection, they were assailed as they walked through the countryside. Shepherds set their dogs on them and struck them with their staffs. Emulating Francis, the brothers gave away their outer tunics. The beatings continued, leading them to give away their inner tunics and then their sole remaining clothing, their breeches.

"One of the brothers told me that he had lost his breeches fifteen times in this way," Jordan wrote. "And since, overcome by shame and modesty, he regretted losing his breeches more than his other clothing, he soiled the breeches with the dung of oxen and other filth, and thus the shepherds themselves were filled with nausea and allowed him to keep his breeches." This organic strategy did not help their evangelizing, though, and the brothers returned to Italy.

For his part, Francis didn't make it to France. He got as far as Florence, where he met the influential Cardinal Ugolino, the late Pope Innocent's nephew. Ugolino, who like his uncle was a canon lawyer trained at the great universities in Paris and Bologna, had been sent out by Pope Honorius to preach the Crusade and to end local wars so that troops would be free to head for the East. As a savvy insider, Ugolino would have known that Francis lacked a well-connected patron in Rome. Previously Cardinal John of St. Paul had supported Francis in the Curia, but he died in 1216. Ugolino rejoiced at seeing the holy vagabond but, according to two early accounts, prohibited him from going to France. Francis was deeply disappointed, responding that if he stayed home while sending the friars out, it would set a poor example.

"Why have you sent your friars to such distant places to die of hunger and undergo other hardships?" the cardinal retorted. Francis responded that the Lord had sent his brothers to preach "for the benefit and salvation of the souls of all men in this world . . . They will be welcomed not only in the countries of the faithful, but in those of unbelievers as well, and they will win many souls."

Francis therefore defended not only his proposed mission to France but all of his order's missionary work among nonbelievers, including Muslims. Though Ugolino admitted that Francis "spoke the truth," he still prohibited the friar from going to France because he was needed closer to home. Francis obediently sent another brother in his place.

The missionary brothers whom Francis sent out with such high hopes came back aching and embittered at the following year's general chapter meeting. They had met resistance not only from pagans but even from jealous bishops and priests, who painted them as heretics. Francis saw plainly that his dream of bringing the Christian faith far and wide would be dashed unless church authorities protected his mission. At the same time he was extremely reluctant to ask any favor from the church hierarchy, since he did not want to become enmeshed in the constant ecclesiastical struggles over power and land. In a dream he saw a small hen unable to gather her wandering chicks under her wings. When he awoke, he recognized himself as the hen and the aimless chicks as his brothers. Francis concluded that his order needed the sheltering wings the institutional church could provide. Sometime in 1218 or early 1219 he went to Rome to renew his acquaintance with Cardinal Ugolino, leading to a long association that would have many consequences for Francis and his order. Ugolino, who would later become the order's official "protector," arranged in 1219 for Pope Honorius to write a letter of endorsement that could be recopied for the missionaries.

Ugolino was evidently uneasy about Francis's desire to reach out to Muslims. We witness this through the work of the poet Henri d'Avranches, whose verses pleased the sensibilities of popes, kings, and the noble class. He wrote *The Versified Life of Saint Francis* for Pope Gregory IX (the former Cardinal Ugolino) in the 1230s, based on Celano's first life of Francis. After addressing the pope—"O greatest of mortals"—Henri presented a Francis who was palatable to those at the pinnacle of power; the flourishes the poet added are a good indication of what the pope and Curia wanted to hear. Interestingly, the pliant poet laureate portrayed Francis as naïve for wanting to preach to Muslims, whom he calls "Syrians." Both Henri and the pope thought Francis was needed to combat heresy in Italy, not to preach to the Muslims:

> With a martyr's death, therefore, longing to crown his labors,
> He sets his mind on making for Parthian regions.
> But with the Church's house in flames within, what is its
> Watchman looking outside it for?

He continued:

> But enough! Certain things may be true but can't always be told.
> Yet the holy simplicity of Francis sustains to the last,
> And has no eyes for sins or for faults.
> Meet he the crafty, he will take them for wise citizens
> Of Italy; nor will he believe they need a schoolmaster.
> And so, he embarks, with his heart set on converting the Syrians.

Henri echoed the position Pope Gregory had taken when he met Francis in Florence—he was needed in Italy but failed to understand that because he had "no eyes for sins or for faults." Although the poem was written after Francis's death, it sheds light on how his plan to convert the sultan was regarded when he was alive. Such attitudes would not keep Francis from setting out in 1219 on his mission of peace to Muslims.

7

The Sultan

Francis did not know much about the powerful sultan he would one day visit on the banks of the Nile River. Christians portrayed Malik al-Kamil and his like in the songs, sermons, and chronicles of the day as sly "beasts" and as pagans who worshiped many gods. Arab chronicles written by both Muslims and Coptic Christians, however, reveal a more nuanced picture that would not have been available to Francis.

Malik al-Kamil Nasir ad-Din Muhammad was born on August 19, 1180, roughly a year and a half before Francis. He was still a boy when the Crusaders surrendered Jerusalem to Muslim forces on October 2, 1187. After getting news of the great defeat, the people of Assisi dressed in sackcloth and spoke constantly of the loss of the holy city. In al-Kamil's world, however, there was joy. Muslims streamed on foot and horseback to visit the Dome of the Rock, the magnificent gold-topped edifice that enshrined the holy black rock from which it was believed Muhammad had ascended to heaven and where Abraham bound his son

Isaac as a sacrifice to God. While the city was under Christian rule, the Muslim holy places had been converted into palaces or churches.

For the seven-year-old future sultan, the jublilation would have been heightened by the knowledge that his family was directly responsible for the victory. His uncle, Salah ad-Din Yusuf ibn Ayyub, known to the Crusaders as Saladin, had led the Muslim army to victory by routing the Christians at the Battle of Hattin three months earlier on July 4, capturing the king of the Latin Kingdom and taking a piece of what was believed to be the cross on which Jesus was crucified.

In addition al-Kamil's father, Malik al-Adil Sayf ad-Din, Saladin's brother and a key adviser, was instrumental in the victory. Troops under his command fought on the broad plain outside the strategic seaside city of Acre and plundered the ancient port city of Jaffa, carrying off the women and imprisoning the men. Outnumbered and on the defensive, the Crusaders in Jerusalem surrendered to Saladin, and the city was taken peacefully.

There is no record of whether the young al-Kamil was in Jerusalem at the time, but an indication in one Arab chronicle suggests that al-Adil's children traveled with him during his campaigns. So quite likely in his later years al-Kamil was able to tell his grandchildren that he had been in the holy city after his uncle Yusuf's glorious victory.

Having taken back Jerusalem eighty-eight years after the Crusaders conquered it, Muslims were outraged to discover that the Franks had chipped away pieces of the sacred rock to sell for their weight in gold. Saladin moved quickly to remove traces of the Christian presence from the Dome of the Rock, eliminating crosses and a portrait of Jesus. Rose water was used to cleanse the sacred rock. Crusader barracks were removed from the nearby al-Aqsa Mosque.

In response to the desecration of Muslim holy places, Saladin turned the Catholics' Church of St. Anne (named for Mary's mother) into a school of Islamic law. The Mount of Olives, where Jesus had gathered with his apostles before his crucifixion, was declared Muslim property. The Tomb of David on Mount Zion, close to the place Christians identified as the Upper Room, where Jesus ate his last supper, was turned into a mosque. Saladin rejected advice to destroy the Church of the Holy Sepulcher, the holiest place in Christendom, where Jesus was believed to have risen from the dead. With or without the edifice, he knew, Christians would still strive to visit the site.

While Saladin retaliated against the Latin church, he allowed the Greek church to continue holding services at the Church of the Holy Sepulcher. He permitted the Georgians to occupy the Monastery of the Cross, said to be built on the site that provided the tree used to make Jesus' cross. Saladin also took an interest in aiding native Arab Christians.

His relations with Arab Christians were not always smooth, however. When he first came to power in Egypt in the 1170s, he had ordered that crosses be taken down from atop churches and that white church buildings be smeared with black mud. Churches were barred from ringing bells, and laws requiring Christians to dress distinctively were enforced, according to *The History of the Patriarchs of the Egyptian Church,* a medieval account of the leaders of Coptic Christianity. Over time Egyptian Christians proved their loyalty and worth and were permitted to take back the key financial jobs they held in the government.

In his early years, while Francis's father was teaching him to be a successful merchant, Malik al-Kamil was schooled in power. One of al-Kamil's great lessons came after the Third Crusade was launched in 1189. This war, the Christians' response to the Muslim triumph in Jerusalem, featured the famed battles between two of history's most dashing leaders, Richard the Lion-Hearted and Saladin. Al-Kamil got a privileged look at the conflict through his father, al-Adil, who was praised for his leadership on the field. Saladin's biographer, a prominent imam at the time, wrote about an instance on July 25, 1190, when the Christians concentrated their forces on the wing al-Adil commanded, penetrating into his camp to loot the tents. Al-Adil "commanded his men to charge, and he himself rushed forward, followed by all the soldiers of the right wing who were on the spot," the chronicler wrote. Saladin, seeing the dust of battle arise from a distance, looked on with "his heart burning with zeal and brotherly love." Al-Adil's soldiers, carrying out Saladin's order to take no prisoners, slaughtered the Christians and left the battlefield covered with their mangled corpses.

The violence of the Third Crusade peaked when Richard, angered that Saladin had failed to pay a ransom supposedly guaranteed when Muslim forces surrendered the city of Acre to the Crusaders, ordered the execution of the 2,700 Muslim prisoners he held, save for a few wealthy enough to fetch a good ransom. According to both Christian and Arab chronicles, the prisoners were led from the city and beheaded within sight of the Muslim army.

As the Third Crusade progressed, Richard won a series of battles, putting Saladin on the defensive. But even though they held the upper hand, the Christians could not take Jerusalem. Saladin, recognizing his own weakness, avoided pitched battles and bided his time. Richard, meanwhile, faced a political plot against him on the home front and also fell ill; he was eager to conclude the Crusade.

Then he came up with a novel peace proposal that thrust al-Kamil's father to center stage. Richard proposed a marriage between his widowed sister Joan, the queen of Sicily, and al-Adil. The deal called for the strange bedfellows to rule Palestine. As outlandish as the idea may sound today, there were actual negotiations between Richard and al-Adil; Richard even sent a message to the pope seeking his approval. Al-Adil notified his brother Saladin, who "consented to the proposals on the spot, for he knew very well that the king of England would not carry them out, and that it was nothing but trickery and mocking on his part," according to an Arab biographer involved in the negotiation. Joan refused to join in her brother's gambit unless al-Adil agreed to convert to Christianity. The offer may have been a clever attempt on Richard's part to divide Saladin from his brother, who would have acquired much power through such a marriage.

All of this opened the door to further peace negotiations between Richard and al-Adil, whom the Christians called "Saphadin," shortening his name. The English king related more easily to the flexible and diplomatic al-Adil than to his brother. That led to another strange turn of events. Richard wasn't able to marry off his sister to al-Adil, but he did have the authority to grant knighthood to the Muslim leader's oldest son. According to one Crusade chronicle, on March 29, 1192, "King Richard at Acre in great state girded with the belt of knighthood Saphadin's son who had been sent there for this purpose." That son was the eleven-year-old Malik al-Kamil.

There is no further documentation of the ceremony, but for a young boy raised in close fidelity to Islamic law to be sent into the Christian king's court to experience a ritual that one historian has described as the "eighth sacrament" must have been staggering. Knighting was not, strictly speaking, a Christian ritual—and it sometimes occurred under less than holy circumstances on the battlefield. But the ceremony was infused with religious symbolism, not to mention Christian prayer and liturgy. Raymond Lull, a philosopher and theologian who was so taken by Francis's ideas that he devoted much of his life (1235–1316) to preaching to Muslims, described the ceremony in *The Book of the Order of Chyvalry.* The service included maintaining an all-night vigil before the altar; attending morning mass; swearing the oath of chivalry before a priest; listening to a sermon; girding on a sword; and participating in a ceremonial kiss and a feast. It's doubtful that al-Kamil experienced the more religious aspects, but that Richard in full pomp vested him with sword and belt is highly significant. The pageantry amounted to diplomacy in action, a symbolic effort by both Richard and al-Adil to show their good faith in peace negotiations.

Christian ways would have been much more familiar to al-Kamil than Muslim customs were to Francis. Another difference between them was that while Francis had rejected his father and adopted a countercultural lifestyle, al-Kamil drew much of his strength from his family tree. The eighty-year Ayyubid dynasty that Saladin founded—relatively brief but nonetheless important to history—is named after Saladin's father, Ayyub, a Kurd who hailed from Duwin in Armenia. Ayyub and his brother Shirkuh migrated from the mountains to modern-day Iraq, where Ayyub was appointed governor of Tikrit, a post his father previously held in the fortified city across the Tigris River from Baghdad. When Ayyub's brother

Shirkuh killed a man, the two brothers fled the caliph. According to Arab chronicles, an infant named Yusuf—later known as Saladin—was born that same night, and the family received shelter from a rival of the caliph. Ayyub and his brother soon found themselves on the right side of history, helping the sultan Nur ad-Din of Aleppo as he conquered Damascus and then Egypt. The powerful sultan appointed Saladin vizier of Egypt in 1169.

Saladin was so adept that Sultan Nur ad-Din grew jealous. Suspecting the younger man's loyalty, the sultan ordered him to march his army north to lay siege to a Crusader castle. After Saladin's officers warned him that it was a trap, he sent a letter telling the sultan that his troops were tied up fighting disorders in Egypt. This angered Nur ad-Din, who sent his army south to confront him. Preparing for battle, Saladin spoke with friends and relatives, gathering assurances of their loyalty. His father, Ayyub, wisely stepped in to make sure his son avoided a battle he was sure to lose.

Ayyub cursed those who pledged their loyalty to his son Saladin, declaring that if Sultan Nur ad-Din were to arrive, he—Ayyub—would dismount from his horse and kiss the ground before him. If the sultan commanded him to put a sword to his son's neck, he would do it, Ayyub said, because the sultan owned both the land and his loyalty.

As Ayyub anticipated, some of those present wrote to Nur ad-Din to describe this startling display of loyalty. Meanwhile Ayyub lectured his son in private, scorning him for telling a large group of supporters that he was planning for battle. Didn't he realize that it would lead Nur ad-Din to attack him? Didn't he understand that all his soldiers would desert him? Ayyub, a wise observer of men, predicted correctly that the sultan would now hear about the loyalty that he had expressed and would not attack. Saladin took his father's advice and sent the sultan gifts—gold, silver, jade, crystal, pearls, rubies, and an elephant. Nur ad-Din continued to eye Saladin with suspicion but delayed his plan to attack him. The sultan died shortly thereafter, as did his plot against Saladin.

It seems Saladin learned his lesson. While he has been praised time and again in both Muslim and Christian accounts as a great warrior, he was also a man of great discretion, inheriting his father's gift for prudent action—a trait that could also be seen in his brother as well as in his nephew, Malik al-Kamil.

Al-Kamil's father, Malik al-Adil, was a capable general whose gift for crafty diplomacy, more than his military acumen, raised him to power. He served his brother with utmost loyalty for some twenty-five years and maintained relationships with Christian leaders that led to key peace treaties. But true power eluded him for years. When Saladin arranged for his empire to be divided among his sons after his death, which occurred in 1193, jealousies among the brothers turned into warfare. Their uncle, al-Adil, was there to intercede. But al-Adil was something more than a disinterested party in those negotiations. Each time he became involved in a bitter family dispute, he wound up with more power. Over time he quietly used his influence to inflame the brothers against each other as he enhanced his own prestige. When one of Saladin's sons died in 1200, he was able to take control in Egypt, and ultimately to win the rest of the empire.

Al-Adil appointed his oldest son, al-Kamil, as viceroy of Egypt at the age of twenty. The second son, Al-Mu'azzam Isa Sharaf ad-Din, became viceroy in Damascus; another son, Al-Ashraf Musa Abu'l-Fath al-Muzaffar ad-Din, was given control of the Jezireh, an area now in northern Iraq.

According to the medieval historian Taqi ad-Din al-Maqrizi, al-Adil took great pleasure in his sons, who took after him in their cunning and instinct for achieving political goals without warfare when possible. Al-Adil taught his sons, al-Maqrizi wrote, that it was better to use finesse against an enemy than to risk a head-on battle.

In a treacherous world of shifting loyalties, al-Adil prospered well into his seventies. He allowed his son al-Kamil to make his own decisions in Egypt. At times al-Kamil even undid some of his father's decisions, especially when it came to dealing with Christians. As a result, he developed a reputation among Christians as the most tolerant of Egypt's sultans. Coptic chroniclers praised him, noting a number of instances in which he was markedly more understanding than his father had been.

The story of a monk from the Monastery of Abba Macarius, an ancient residence some fifty-seven miles north of Cairo, is a good example. The monk, named John, came before al-Kamil to profess Islam. He went off, practiced it for three years, and was frequently seen praying in the mosque. Then, according to *The History of the Patriarchs of the Egyptian Church,* the monk wanted to go back to Christianity. He went before al-Kamil in coarse clothing normally used for burial and asked al-Kamil to either kill him or allow him to return to Christianity.

While the Muslim authorities allowed Christians and Jews to practice their religion, Islamic law seriously penalized Muslims who apostasized. Brother John was ready for the possibility that al-Kamil would order his execution but hoped the Muslim ruler would show mercy. He did. After his meeting with Brother John, al-Kamil signed a document notifying all governors that John was permitted to practice Christianity, allowing the monk to return to the monastery.

All was well until another former Christian who had professed Islam decided to return to Christianity. He picked the wrong day to go to the sultan's court with his petition, for al-Kamil's father was present. The man told Sultan al-Adil that his son, al-Kamil, had been lenient to Brother John and asked for the same consideration. Sultan al-Adil decided to teach a lesson, not only to the former Christian but to his son as well. He decreed that the man be executed unless he renewed his profession of Islam—which he did quickly. Then al-Adil sent a soldier to the Monastery of Abba Macarius to give Brother John the same choice. He also professed.

If al-Adil's actions were intended to make al-Kamil less tolerant of Christians, they didn't work. At one point the young leader was called to intervene in a dispute over ownership of a treasure trove of gold vessels, jewelry, crystal, pearls, and silk veils that were supposedly uncovered during construction of a well at the Monastery of Abba Macarius. When al-Kamil hired experts to evaluate the goods, they discovered Coptic inscriptions and crosses on the gold vessels—evidence that the treasures belonged to the Coptic church. Al-Kamil handed them over to Patriarch John VI. According to *The History of the Patriarchs of the Egyptian Church,* this led to a procession through the streets of Cairo with crosses held aloft.

Another story tells of the time al-Kamil was hunting near a river outside Alexandria when he stopped to converse with a Christian hermit. After al-Kamil told the hermit of a pain in his gut, the hermit prayed over him and gave him some oil, saying that if he anointed the spot that hurt, God would heal him. According to the story, al-Kamil did as the hermit prescribed and felt better immediately. Al-Kamil gave him a gift and took a strong liking to the hermit; Francis, it seems, was not the first Christian holy man to become friendly with al-Kamil.

The sultan's admiration for a Christian hermit may seem strange to some, but the Qur'an speaks affectionately of Christian monks, saying that their eyes brim with tears at the recognition of God's truth. This affectionate recognition is rooted in the earliest days of Islam, when Christian hermits lived with great piety and devotion in the Arabian desert.

"The Prophet of Islam had a great deal of liking for Christian monks," says Seyyed Hossein Nasr, a leading scholar of Islam and professor at George Washington University. ". . . From the beginning of Islam, the Christian monks are always held in respect." This attitude, he said in an interview, would have formed Sultan al-Kamil's view of Francis: "He did not identify the monks with the warriors."

In 1215 and 1216 a huge dispute among Christians raged over choosing a Coptic patriarch to govern the region's churches. Sultan al-Adil favored a priest named David, who traveled often with him as an assistant to the head of the army. The army's leader asked al-Adil to appoint David patriarch, even though David previously had been turned down for a lesser position, in charge of the church in Ethiopia. Al-Adil appointed him without consulting his son al-Kamil. On the evening before David was to be consecrated as patriarch, a crowd of Christians gathered beneath the Citadel, the fortress in Cairo where al-Kamil lived, and asked him to intervene.

According to the Coptic chronicle, al-Kamil sent for the hermit he had met by the river outside Alexandria and ordered that he be brought to Cairo so that *he* could be appointed patriarch. The hermit was taken to the city—weeping as he left his humble home. After he begged to go back, the hermit was returned to the outback. If the story is true, al-Kamil evidently had made a point to the Christians: the next patriarch should be chosen for his virtue, not his political connections. In the end, he prevented David from becoming patriarch, despite the priest's political connections.

Coptic accounts described some of the intense lobbying that occurred, noting that key roles were played by two influential Christians, al-Kamil's personal physician and a scribe who advised al-Adil. In the midst of all this maneuvering, al-Kamil was always portrayed as a conscientious official who tried to heed what the Christian majority wanted. He was shown to be curious about Christians, including the way they chose leaders. He inquired carefully with his personal physician to find out the Coptic Church's proper procedures for choosing a patriarch rather than trying to impose his own solution to the annoying squabble. While al-Adil was not considered harsh in his dealings with Egyptian Christians, his son was unusually sensitive to their concerns.

Al-Kamil's tolerance for Egypt's Christians did not always meet with the approval of his Muslim subjects. H. L. Gottschalk, a German historian who published the leading Western biography of al-Kamil in 1958, wrote that al-Kamil faced the wrath of the crowd after he intervened in a dispute over the proposed construction of a mosque on the site of a church. Muslims insisted there once had been a mosque on the site. When al-Kamil went out to inspect, he announced he had found no sign that there had ever been a mosque. The crowd yelled at him in anger, and with some people throwing stones, he hastened back to the fortress where he lived.

While his willingness to let a Christian hermit pray over him shows his openness to the Christian faith, al-Kamil was, to all evidence, an orthodox Sunni Muslim. He furthered the work that his uncle Yusuf—Saladin—had started in Egypt in the 1170s, stamping out Shiite Islam, which was supported by the Fatimid dynasty that Saladin had displaced.

Al-Kamil imprisoned the remaining members of the Fatimid dynasty in the nether regions of the Citadel, an imposing hilltop fortress that Saladin began and al-Kamil completed. (He was also the first sultan to live there.) He followed Saladin's path in founding schools of Islamic law, another Sunni bulwark against Shiism, and he expanded the Mausoleum of the Imam al-Shafi'i, burial place of a great Sunni theologian who had died in 820. By honoring his memory, al-Kamil further marginalized the Shiites in Egypt; he added to the glory of the site by building an expansive dome over the mausoleum in 1211. When his mother died that year, she was entombed there.

Ruling Egypt, even under his savvy father's watchful eyes, was a difficult task for al-Kamil. When the Nile failed to flood in 1201, not long after he became the viceroy, famine and pestilence followed. Arab chronicles report this was an extraordinarily painful period in Egypt's long history: villages were deserted, parents killed and ate their children, and robbery and murder were rampant. Al-Kamil brought the country through that early crisis and became a first-class administrator who built dams, improved irrigation, created more schools for the study of Islam, and resolved internal disputes before they spun out of control.

He brought the same level of skill to his dealings with Christians from the West, preparing for war but seeking peace through trade. He fortified the walls of the key coastal city of Damietta; his father was so pleased upon inspecting the work that he honored the engineers and builders with robes. At the same time al-Kamil made treaties to build trade between coastal cities in Egypt and Italy.

In 1213 al-Kamil's father got a threatening missive from Pope Innocent warning that the Christians would soon take back Jerusalem. Saladin was able to seize the holy city in 1187 because the Christians' sins had provoked God against them, the pope explained, adding that next time it would be different.

Despite that threat, al-Kamil continued to seek peace by expanding trade relations with the major cities of Italy. He negotiated a trade pact with Venice, and by 1215—the year Pope Innocent proclaimed the next Crusade at the Lateran Council—some three thousand European merchants were living in Egypt. A year later, however, the merchants suddenly migrated from Alexandria to the protection of Acre, a Crusader stronghold.

Malik al-Kamil, viceroy of Egypt and future sultan, was not quite prepared for what came next.

PART TWO

THE
WAR

8

The Siege

I n the spring of 1217 the armies of the Fifth Crusade slowly gathered and headed for the port of Acre. Even in the midst of this mobilization Francis and his brothers didn't preach the Crusade. Others did, however, and their rhetoric stirred the public's fervor. In Friesland (now the northern Netherlands) feelings were so intense in May 1217 that one chronicler said that a crowd, urged to aid the Crusade, saw clouds form an image of Jesus' crucifixion. Another crowd in Friesland was said to have seen a blue cross in the sky, and later a group of thousands saw two clouds form a large white cross and drift to the east.

By September 1217 enough Christian troops had arrived in Acre for military leaders to hold a war council and formulate strategy. They approved a bold plan to attack and conquer Egypt, an idea broached at the Fourth Lateran Council under Pope Innocent's leadership. The Crusade leaders hoped that by conquering Egypt they would deprive Muslim defenders of the wealth of the Nile valley, eliminate the threat of the Egyptian navy, and open a new avenue of attack on Jerusalem from the south.

Since soldiers promised by Emperor Frederick II and the leaders of

Venice, Pisa, Genoa, and the Franks had not yet arrived, the Crusade commanders decided to harass and misdirect the enemy by attacking the new fort on Mount Tabor and other targets in Syria and Jordan. Back in Rome, Pope Honorius was so worried about delays in gathering an army that he called the faithful to the Church of St. John Lateran for a procession through the streets that he led barefoot. It was a sign of penitence and also a way of keeping the public's passion for the war alive.

The campaign began in Acre on November 6, 1217, when Patriarch Ralph of Jerusalem raised aloft what was believed to be a remnant of the True Cross on which Jesus had surrendered his life. "This sweet wood," as Oliver of Paderborn, a German scholastic, called it, was a portion of the cross that remained in Christian hands after Saladin conquered Jerusalem. With the Muslims closing in on the city in 1187, Oliver wrote, the Christians had divided the cross, carrying one piece into battle, where it was lost to Saladin, but retaining another for safekeeping. Rather than serving as a symbol of Jesus' peaceful submission to his enemies, the sacred relic was used for its presumed power to defeat the enemy.

Accompanied by the cross, Christian troops marched east toward the Jordan River and on to the Sea of Galilee before they returned to Acre unscathed. After that show of power, the restless Christians attacked the Muslim fort on Mount Tabor on December 3.

The patriarch of Jerusalem once again went forward with a piece of the True Cross, accompanied in procession by bishops and clergy. They sang psalms as they reached the 1,929-foot mount where, as they believed, the apostles Peter, James, and John had seen Jesus transfigured. The mountain, though not a high one, juts up steeply from a plain, making it difficult for any army to reach the fort at the top. Nonetheless the Christian force led by the French nobleman John of Brienne, the king of Jerusalem, inflicted heavy losses on the Muslims who defended outside the fort's gates. The Christians carried off captives, including children who were later baptized by James of Vitry and sent to live among nuns to receive instruction. A second uphill assault fell short, with knights from two military orders, the Templars and Hospitalers, suffering heavy casualties. Faced with such losses among his best warriors, John of Brienne determined it wasn't worth attacking the new fort again—an ironic decision, given that Pope Innocent had justified the Crusade as a preemptive war to protect the Latin Kingdom from the supposedly great danger that this enemy stronghold posed. Soon afterward Sultan al-Adil dismantled the fortification because it was too difficult to defend.

Late in May 1218 an Egyptian watchman near the mouth of the Nile caught sight of the masts of ships sailing toward him on the Mediterranean. The first Crusader ships had set out from Acre three days earlier, on May 24, the Feast of the Ascension, but other departures were delayed because of squalls at sea. It may have been poorly orchestrated, but from the shore the gradual accumulation of masts gave the impression that a never-ending parade of warships was arriving to unload an immense invading army.

The first soldiers debarked on May 29, and within days most of the ships had landed their men and cargo unopposed about two miles north of the heavily fortified city of Damietta, gatekeeper to the Nile. The soldiers immediately went to work building a trench that would provide their camp with fresh water and, soon after, built a huge siege engine to catapult rocks into the enemy's fortress. The Crusaders were heartened by the sight of a full lunar eclipse. The moon was important to Muslims, who used its phases to calculate feast days. "They attribute great prophetic influence to the increase and decrease of that luminary," the English chronicler Roger of Wendover wrote. The Crusaders took the eclipse as a favorable prophetic sign predicted by Jesus in Scripture: "There will be signs in the sun, the moon and the stars."

So began a trying time for Malik al-Kamil. The Arab historian Ibn al-Athir, a contemporary, noted that the Christian army's arrival in Acre surprised the young leader's father, Sultan al-Adil, who rushed back from Egypt to Syria to protect Damascus. Al-Kamil, in Cairo when he received news by carrier pigeon that the Christians had landed outside Damietta, was left to mobilize troops in Egypt. By this time al-Kamil had ruled in Egypt for some two decades under his father's guidance. But now he was on his own: Sultan al-Adil was in Damascus, trying to prevent another viceroy-son, al-Mu'azzam, from rushing a counterattack against the Crusaders at a point when they were better organized. As a Muslim army gathered, Christians mounted their main attack not against Jerusalem or Damascus, but at the city that guarded the heart of Egypt.

The Crusader feints and attacks to the north had disoriented the Muslims, but the Christians nonetheless faced a difficult road. The Nile protected Damietta on the city's west, and the vast expanse of Lake Manzala, a 660-square-mile saltwater lagoon that sprawled east and south from the mouth of the river, virtually enclosed the city with an immense water barrier, blocking any other approach by land. Swamps surrounding the edge of the lake turned any potential path to the city from the east and south into a quagmire. The threefold walls of Damietta could be approached only from the swirling river. To complicate matters for the invaders, the Egyptians had erected a tower that commanded the river from its island post near the west bank. Heavy iron chains were stretched from the tower to the city walls on the east, blocking the only navigable passage. The channel was further clogged with a bridge of boats lashed one to the other behind the chain. Some of the Crusaders were eager to hurl themselves against the walls of Damietta, but the wiser leaders knew they would only be trapped between the force in the city and the garrison of archers in the tower. The Crusaders had no choice. The chains had to be severed.

Al-Kamil rushed north to Damietta, arriving by June 6 with mostly unseasoned troops who had enlisted hastily for jihad, holy war. They set up a camp on the east bank of the river, several miles south of the city and beside a jutting finger of Lake Manzala. Al-Kamil named the encampment al-Adiliya, after his father.

The Crusaders built a huge mangonel, a powerful catapult capable of hurling rocks on a low arc. Positioning it atop a mound of stones, they used it to heave boulders weighing 200 to 300 pounds more than 150 yards into Damietta. The giant rocks arced over the river from the Crusader camp on the river's west bank, demolishing whatever they hit, including the home of the city's chief official. The Muslims retaliated with medieval artillery of their own and shouted happily when they scored a hit on the enemy siege machine, making its ropes slip. But within days the Christians built an even bigger one, and then four more, and bombarded the stout tower that guarded the river. The battle continued as determined Muslims fired back, shooting arrows and catapulting stones that crashed down into the Crusaders' boats.

It was clear to the Christian leaders that in order to move forward, they had to attack the tower. They launched major assaults on the Muslim stronghold in late June and early July of 1218, using dozens of ships. Many Crusaders drowned when the siege ladders they propped up against the tower tumbled into the turbulent Nile. Javelins hurled from the ramparts killed others. Stones slung from a giant bow pounded the Crusaders' boats. "Greek fire" rained down on their wooden vessels. This weapon of flaming oil, which the Byzantine Greeks invented in the seventh century to destroy their enemies' navies, was especially fearsome because it was difficult to extinguish.

The stone tower, protected by the river's unruly waters, seemed impregnable. But the German scholastic Oliver of Paderborn, a future cardinal who wrote the major Western chronicle of the battle, devised a waterborne attack tower to solve the problem. Two ships were bound together with beams and ropes, and then four masts were built on the deck to serve as the framework for upper and lower levels that were covered on top and the sides with animal skins to ward off Greek fire, arrows, and stones. A ladder extended beyond the ship's prow so that soldiers could assault the upper tower, and a lower bridge was added as a causeway to the base. No one had ever seen such a device—a floating death tower.

Once again the Crusaders turned to their remnant of the True Cross to prepare for battle. Patriarch Ralph of Jerusalem led a barefoot procession with the holy cross on August 18, 1218. A week later three hundred soldiers manned the warship as it was maneuvered with great difficulty down the river against the violently overflowing Nile. The clergy stood barefoot on the shore, praying for the Crusaders' success.

Patriarch Ralph prostrated himself in the dust before the wood of the True Cross and cried out to God as soldiers lashed the attack ship, shifting and heaving in the swirling Nile, to the enemy tower and threw down the anchors. The Muslim troops responded by battering the attack vessel with a torrent of stones cast from a battery of at least a half-dozen machines positioned along the walls of Damietta. Greek fire that "fell on it like lightning" was doused with "vinegar, gravel, and other extinguishing matter," according to Roger of Wendover.

The Crusaders jammed the long wooden ladder on their vessel into the tower. The defenders countered by using their lances to smear the boat with oil, which they lit on fire. Amid the Crusaders' confusion, one of the defenders grabbed the banner of the Duke of Austria, a sign that the Muslims were prevailing. The Christians frantically extinguished the fire and attacked with swords, pikes, and clubs, muscling their way into the upper level of the tower. One young Frisian flailed at the Muslim soldiers with a scythe reinforced with chains—a grim reaper. He cut down the standard-bearer carrying the sultan's saffron pennant and captured the banner. The tower's Muslim defenders abandoned the top level after setting it on fire, forcing the Christians to retreat.

The attack ship's bridge at ground level was used to launch an assault on the base of the tower, despite the rushing depths around it, and soldiers surged forward to surround the stone fortification and pound the door with iron hammers. The attack continued for more than twenty-four hours; some of the Muslims escaped only to drown in the Nile. Eventually the hundred survivors in the garrison agreed to surrender to the Christians if their lives would be spared.

When news of the Christian victory reached Sultan al-Adil at his encampment in Syria, he pounded his chest in grief and took sick, al-

Maqrizi wrote. He was moved to a village near Damascus, where his condition worsened. The sultan died on August 31, 1218.

Al-Kamil, grieving and frightened, received visitors and condolences while trying to discern how to strike back after this major defeat. After his father's death he became the sultan of Egypt, and with this new appointment came a new kind of danger. The transition in power offered jealous emirs opportunity to stage a coup. Even as al-Kamil eyed the Christians before him, he had to watch his back.

With the Nile rising dangerously, the Crusader leader John of Brienne delayed an attack on Damietta, which would have required that the troops cross the swollen river. It must have been an unpopular decision. Oliver of Paderborn wrote that although the Muslims were stricken, the Christian leaders had become lazy. His barb gives an early look at a controversy that would rage among the Christian leaders as the war progressed. The religious leaders insisted on attacking, while the experienced military men looked to wait for the right moment. But whatever Oliver believed, it made sense for John of Brienne to await reinforcements. Pope Honorius had sent a letter promising more troops, and the Crusade force needed them because units that had been there longest were preparing to return home after fulfilling the vow to fight for a year.

John, a dashing and seasoned military man highly respected for his personal bravery and swordsmanship, now had an uneasy grasp on authority. The Christian force was really a loose conglomeration of armies led by men with conflicting agendas. The Crusade's military leaders had chosen John of Brienne to head the army because of his reputation and his role as monarch of the Latin Kingdom of Jerusalem. Yet while he held a grand title, his kingdom did not actually control Jerusalem, which was in Muslim hands. Further, his kingship was under scrutiny because he had not inherited the throne. The youngest of four sons of Count Érard II of Brienne, he had enjoyed a life of profitless adventure. His oldest brother,

Walter, a daring figure in his own right, became the Count of Brienne and inherited the family's lands.

Walter of Brienne was a man Francis would have recognized immediately. He had once planned to find glory by taking part in the quasi-Crusade that the Champagne aristocrat led in the pope's behalf in 1205 against the imperial invader in southern Italy.

John of Brienne, who lived in the shadow of his brothers, was awarded a great opportunity in 1208, when Queen Maria of Jerusalem turned seventeen, old enough to govern without a regent. King Philip asked John, who had a royal bearing and a reputation as a great swordsman, to marry the queen. Strikingly handsome, he "was a huge man, strong and tall, powerful and skilful at war, a veritable second Charlemagne," declared the Franciscan chronicler Salimbene di Adam, who wrote in the 1280s. "And when he went to battle striking here and there with his iron club, the Saracens fled before him as if they were facing the very devil himself or a lion ready to devour them. Indeed, as common report had it, there was no soldier of his time better than he."

But however necessary his military skills were, John was an unusual choice for a kingship, since he had no fortune. There were rumors that Philip had sent him to put an end to a scandal roiling his court involving a love affair between John and the Countess of Champagne. John landed in Acre on September 13, 1210, and married the queen the next day in a political match typical for the nobility of that era. When Maria died in 1212 after giving birth to a daughter, Yolanda (later known as Isabella), John remained in power as regent. He married royalty again two years later, this time to Princess Stephanie of Armenia. But by the time the Battle of Damietta began in 1218, his claim to the throne was fragile. Nonetheless, he had high hopes of expanding his kingdom to Jerusalem and beyond; he knew it could not survive as a sliver of territory pinned against the coastline.

While John delayed attacking Damietta after the Crusaders seized the formidable stone tower in the Nile, dissenters who wanted to hurl the troops at the walls of Damietta soon found an ally in a powerful churchman who arrived from Rome in mid-September 1218. Cardinal Pelagius Galvani, bishop of the see of Albano just south of Rome, had arrived to take charge.

Pope Honorius had sent Pelagius to unite the fractious Christian forces and to preach morality to the troops. He quickly became the most controversial figure of the Fifth Crusade, colliding with nearly everyone—even Francis—as he carried out his mission as papal legate. In *The Chronicle of Ernoul,* a French Crusader chronicle, the writer discusses the fate of two cardinals who arrived in the Crusader camp. While one died, he wrote, "Cardinal Pelagius lived, which was a great shame."

Known for his arrogance, Pelagius, a native of either Spain or Portugal, had served as Pope Innocent's legate in Constantinople after frenzied Western Christians diverted the Fourth Crusade to trash that magnificent city and steal the treasures of the Byzantine Greeks. The Greeks despised him for his high-handed ways and opulence, but Innocent praised Pelagius, who relished authority and the finery of his office.

His assignment as papal legate to the Crusader army in Egypt was no less daunting. The popes—first Innocent, then his successor, Honorius—took charge of the Fifth Crusade in hopes of avoiding the disastrous lack of discipline that had unhitched the Fourth. Pelagius believed that it was essential for the Christian army to strike quickly because, given time, the Muslims would be able to overcome their internal rivalries to mount a far larger force. There was some merit to his argument, which put him on a collision course with John of Brienne, who wanted to wait for reinforcements before attacking the large Muslim army. While John was technically in charge of the army, Pelagius controlled the funding the pope provided, giving him the upper hand.

The cardinal faced an extraordinarily difficult military task, even after the Crusaders' stunning capture of the tower. The treacherous river and the broad lake still blocked an attack. There were also Damietta's fortifications: three sets of walls, all of them heavily fortified, and a deep moat protected the city. Some eighty thousand people lived in close quarters inside those walls, and the Muslim army was determined to beat back the invaders to protect the citizens. The Muslim defenders knew that a defeat at Damietta would open the way for the Crusaders to march into Egypt's heartland and seize Cairo, placing the country under Christian occupation.

The Muslims fortified the east bank of the Nile with high wooden ramparts reinforced with clay. Sunken boats and sharp wooden stakes lurked in eddies beneath the river to gash the Christians' ships. Three ranks of Muslim soldiers stood ominously above the bank—two lines of foot soldiers armed with shields, then a formidable line of horsemen. The Muslims showered the Crusader positions across the river with stones and arrows. Even if the Christians were to succeed in crossing the river, they would have to slog through a muddy riverbank. Arab nomads harassed the Crusader camp with raids at night, trying to deprive the Christians of sleep.

Al-Kamil, aware that boatloads of Christians had gone home, launched an attack on the Crusader camp on October 9, 1218. According to an Egyptian Christian account, fifty to sixty transport ships carried thousands of Muslim soldiers north on the river. The Christian camp was too well protected for a cavalry attack to be launched, but vessels carrying several thousand infantrymen sailed farther and landed men on the west bank of the Nile, just east of the Crusaders. The attackers appeared to be unnoticed—possibly a clever tactic on the Crusaders' part—and penetrated deep into the Christian camp, reaching the tents of a Roman contingent that the pope had sent. The Muslims had blundered too far into the enemy territory; John of Brienne rallied a powerful counterassault that cut them off from the river. The Muslim soldiers were surrounded and slaughtered, many of them beheaded. Beyond those slain in the camp, as many as a thousand more drowned in the Nile as they tried in desperation to swim back to their boats. Many of them, hailing from dry regions such as Syria, didn't know how to swim. So many Muslims were decapitated that the Christians set to hurling their heads into Damietta with their siege engines.

Grieving the loss of some three thousand soldiers, al-Kamil regrouped and dispatched his army to attack the Crusader camp yet again on October 26. According to an anonymous chronicle written by a Christian eye-witness, Pelagius, standing in the forefront with the True Cross, called on God to help the Crusaders, "so that we may be able to convert the perfidious and worthless people, so that they ought duly to believe with us in the Holy Trinity and in Your Nativity and in Your Passion and death and resurrection." For Pelagius, souls were to be won at the point of the sword.

Despite their ability to fend off the sultan's troops, the Crusaders quickly became discouraged. They were able to defend their own camp but foundered in their attacks. Their plight worsened on November 29, when a howling north wind pushed waves of seawater over the Crusaders' camp. During the three-day storm tents and supplies floated away, and fish, Oliver of Paderborn wrote, "piled into our sleeping quarters, and we caught them with our hands, delights nevertheless which we were willing to be without." Ships being outfitted for attacks on the city were destroyed. The Muslim camp also was inundated with water, adding to the defenders' troubles.

Even though they were outnumbered, the Christians still held the upper hand because the sultan couldn't break their grip on Damietta. But they suffered a serious loss when the wind blew their secret super-weapon—a giant platform built on six big transport ships, filled with an array of attack towers—into the enemy's grasp. Muslim soldiers killed fourteen of the sixteen Christians on board in fighting that broke out after the ship ran aground. Two men managed to jump into the Nile and swim to the other side. An angry John of Brienne treated them like traitors, asking why they did not stay to fight like the others. Both men were hung.

Disease deepened the Christian troops' misery. About one-fifth of the army died from scurvy, suffering from sharp pains in the feet and legs, melting gums, lost teeth, blackened shins. Cardinal Pelagius urged the Crusaders on, telling them they were better off attacking than remaining pinned down on the Nile.

On the night of February 5, 1219, the eve of the feast of the martyr Saint Agatha, heavy rain, hail, and high winds beat down the Crusaders as they prepared to cross the storm-stirred Nile. Cardinal Pelagius had ordered yet another dangerous assault on the enemy camp, one likely to cost many of the Crusaders their lives.

But something very strange happened next. Malik al-Kamil, the sultan of Egypt, vanished. So did his army.

9

Conspiracy Against the Sultan

A turncoat Frank stood on the Muslims' side of the river and shouted in French, "Why do you delay? What do you fear?" The Crusaders listened angrily. Was it a trick? Was he goading them on? "The sultan has fled," the soldier hollered, pledging to give proof if the Crusaders would provide him safe passage back to their side of the river.

John of Brienne wasn't about to take the traitor's word. True, not a single Muslim soldier could be seen defending the riverbank. But faking retreat was a favored tactic of the Muslim warriors, who moved quicker than the more heavily armored Crusaders. John, far more cautious with his soldiers' lives than was the cardinal, sent one of his men, a carpenter named Aubert, across the river to find out more. When the woodworker confirmed that the sultan had indeed retreated, John sent the knight Michel de Viz across as well. He returned to confirm the report once again. John then sent a ship equipped to hurl fire at the enemy. The Crusaders debarked with difficulty. The rough waters were so deep and the bank so muddy that the horses, even without their saddles, had trouble making their way up the east bank. Instead of being slaughtered in the muck, the

Crusaders advanced to find abandoned camps. The fierce Muslim army at al-Adiliya was gone.

The Crusaders were amazed. They found empty tents with the carpets still rolled out, just as the opposing soldiers had left them. Horses, mules, and camels were tied up. The Crusaders quickly seized shields, swords, lances, chain-mail armor, grain, and boats moored on the Nile. Stories passed through the Crusader ranks: Saint George and a small army of knights had appeared miraculously in the night, prompting the fearful enemy to run into the darkness without weapons and provisions. It was obvious, as the Christian chroniclers wrote, that God had struck terror in the heart of the sultan and his men. Mass was celebrated at daybreak, and the military commanders announced to Cardinal Pelagius that the Muslims had fled. With the Templars leading the way, the Christian troops encircled the city of Damietta and built a pontoon bridge over the Nile. The Crusaders now had the upper hand; it looked as if Cardinal Pelagius had been right all along. "Let us all rejoice in the Lord," the Crusaders prayed with him as they celebrated on the Feast of St. Agatha, thanking God for frightening the enemy away.

Sultan Malik al-Kamil had indeed spent the night in a terror-stricken flight along the edge of a canal. But he was not running from the Crusaders; he was fleeing some of his own aides. The death of Sultan al-Adil and the lagging defense of Egypt had offered an opportunity to a leading nobleman, Imad ad-Din Ibn al-Mashtub, to stage a coup.

Imad ad-Din's father, Saif ad-Din al-Mashtub, had been the greatest of Saladin's emirs and a close associate of the hero ruler. Saladin had left his fellow Kurd in charge of the Muslim garrison in Acre when Richard the Lion-Hearted besieged it. The scar-faced hero stayed until it was captured, then escaped and returned to Saladin in an emotional reunion—eluding Richard's subsequent execution of the entire garrison after the surrender.

Saladin had turned over Nablus as a fief to Saif ad-Din al-Mashtub, and after the powerful emir died in November 1192, it passed with its substantial income to his son Imad ad-Din Ibn al-Mashtub. The son, with his impeccable warrior pedigree and the riches he enjoyed as emir of Nablus, was recognized as "noble in his conduct, brave, and possessing a lofty spirit," according to the thirteenth-century biographer Ibn Khallikan. Princes "considered him their equal" and "stood in awe of him." He commanded a regiment in the sultan's army composed of Kurds loyal to him. His father's fidelity to Saladin kept him in good stead with the Ayyubid monarchs who, as al-Maqrizi wrote, considered him to be practically part of the family. Despite such ties, Imad ad-Din Ibn-al-Mashtub conspired against Malik al-Kamil, plotting with emirs and leaders of some of the sultans's own army to replace him with his younger brother Malik al-Faiz. According to the plan, the new sultan would appoint Imad ad-Din as a governor.

It was a desperate time for al-Kamil. With his father dead and the Christian army advancing, poised not only to capture Damietta but to conquer all of Egypt, he now faced treachery in his own family and among his troops. Unable to trust anyone, the historian Ibn al-Athir wrote, the sultan prepared to leave Egypt.

Al-Kamil rode out by night with a small detachment of cavalrymen to protect him, and traveled about fifteen miles, though he had planned on traveling much farther. Imad ad-Din had "stirred up such disorder in the army that al-Kamil had first thought of abandoning Egypt and retiring to Yemen, where his son . . . was governor," according to Abu al-Fida, a Damascus-born historian who wrote early in the fourteenth century.

When daybreak arrived, rumors quickly swept through the Muslim camp outside Damietta. The soldiers, fearful that they had lost their sultan, panicked and fled.

Two days later al-Kamil's brother, Malik al-Mu'azzam, now the sultan of Damascus, arrived in Egypt with troops. Al-Kamil, strengthened by his younger brother's presence, told him about the plot, and together the sultans decided to target Imad ad-Din Ibn al-Mashtub. Al-Mu'azzam rode to the traitorous emir's tent and invited him to go for a ride, saying that his services were needed. The emir asked for time to dress, but al-Mu'azzam refused, forcing al-Mashtub to leave the camp shoeless. After they rode for a time, al-Mu'azzam turned the emir over to a group of soldiers who escorted him away to Syria. He was treated with surprising lenience and was allowed to enter the service of al-Kamil's powerful younger brother, Sultan Malik al-Ashraf. Similarly, the brother who entered the plot, al-Faiz, was spared harsh punishment; he was sent off on a diplomatic mission. According to the thirteenth-century Arab historian Abu Shama, Sultan al-Kamil prostrated himself and kissed the ground before his brother al-Mu'azzam when he returned to the camp.

With the coup defeated, al-Kamil was free to try and rescue the eighty thousand people of Damietta from the Crusaders' chokehold. His subjects were already suffering, but panic swept through the city when word arrived that the sultan had abandoned his nearby camp. In a letter to Pope Honorius III, James of Vitry said there was such a stampede to leave Damietta that nearly a thousand men and women were killed as they tried to rush out the barred gates. No one could get out. With time growing short, the sultan rushed back with his army to a camp several miles south of Damietta at Fariskur. In the first week of March 1219 he launched a series of attacks aimed at putting the cresting Crusaders back on the defensive.

Al-Kamil knew that there wasn't enough food inside the secure walls to last long, and that it would be extremely difficult to defeat the determined Christian army in time to save the besieged people of Damietta from death by disease and starvation. Faced with the likelihood that thousands of his subjects trapped in Damietta would perish, Sultan al-Kamil offered a peace proposal; it would be the first of many. The initial deal that his messengers conveyed to the Crusade leaders offered to grant the Christians control of Jerusalem and surrounding territory if their army withdrew from Egypt. According to Arab chronicles, his father had advised from his deathbed that his sons make just such an arrangement to save Egypt. Under al-Kamil's proposal to the Crusaders, the Muslims would continue to control two key castles located at strategic crossroads in the Transjordan, Al Karak and Krak de Montréal, which posed a threat to the Latin Kingdom of Jerusalem. The proposed truce would last for thirty years—that is, for the rest of the lives of most of the combatants.

John of Brienne, his fellow Frenchmen, and the Western Christians who lived in the Crusader-controlled portions of the Holy Land wanted to take the offer, which largely met the stated goal of the Crusade—to win back Jerusalem. It also meant no further bloodshed and an opportunity for John to truly be the king of Jerusalem.

Cardinal Pelagius, however, opposed the deal, a decision cheered by his supporters from the Italian coastal cities, where merchants were eager to win control of Damietta to expand their trading empires. There *were* valid military reasons to persist in the campaign to conquer Egypt: Jerusalem would presumably be vulnerable to reconquest unless Christian forces could secure a broader region than the sultan offered in his plan. Yet given the intensity of Christendom's ardor for the holy city, the pope's representative could hardly have argued against it. Consider how James of Vitry described the city in *The History of Jerusalem:*

> Jerusalem is the city of cities, the holy of holies, great among the
> nations, and princess among the provinces, by especial prerogative
> called the City of the Great King. She standeth in the midst of the
> earth, in the center of the world, and all nations shall flow unto her.
> She was the possession of the Patriarchs, the nursing mother of the
> Prophets, the teacher of the Apostles, the cradle of our Faith, the
> native country of the Lord, the mother of the Faith, even as Rome is
> the mother of the faithful.

Despite the deep emotions attached to winning Jerusalem, the Christians nonetheless rejected Sultan al-Kamil's peace offer. Pelagius would not be deterred from his mission to strike a heavy blow against Islam by conquering all of Egypt.

As the grim struggle for Damietta unfolded, it became clear to the Crusaders that God was not about to hand them the easy victory Pelagius anticipated. Even though the Christian troops successfully repulsed vigorous attacks in early March, they were obviously vulnerable; the Muslim army had grown much larger with the addition of fresh troops.

Then there was more discouragement. The Crusaders got word that Sultan al-Mu'azzam had pulverized the fabled walls of Jerusalem into rubble, beginning on March 19, 1219, leaving only the gray stone Tower of David standing. Christians saw it as vengeance for the siege at Damietta. "The Muslims then held council as to destroying the noble sepulcher of our Lord, which they had threatened to do in letters," Roger of Wendover wrote, adding that these letters had been sent to the besieged residents of Damietta to lift their spirits.

Though Christians saw the act as revenge, al-Mu'azzam's order to destroy the holy city's walls was a strategic decision to weaken Jerusalem's defenses in anticipation of a Crusader victory. He was prepared to give up Jerusalem to concentrate on defending Damascus, 135 miles northeast of Jerusalem and the center of his domain. Even so, it was a wrenching decision because the destruction of the walls led to mass panic in Jerusalem, where Muslim residents knew that Crusaders had massacred the populace when they conquered the city in 1099.

"There was a terror in the city comparable to that of the last judgment," the historian Abu Shama wrote. People of all ages fled to their sanctuaries for refuge, crowding into the Dome of the Rock and the al-Aqsa Mosque. In a sign of their grief, they ripped their clothing and cut off their hair, leaving piles of it in the holy places. Convinced that the Crusaders were about to arrive, they fled the city in many directions, going to Egypt, the Al Karak fort in the Transjordan, and Damascus. "A great number of the refugees died of hunger and thirst," Abu Shama wrote. "Never had such a terrible catastrophe struck Islam." The chaos continued for seven days.

Meanwhile al-Kamil tried again to free Damietta. On March 31 his forces attacked the Crusaders with an armada of seventy-one ships and a huge army of horsemen and foot soldiers. Muslim troops pierced the wooden ramparts protecting the Crusader camp, with a vanguard of the best knights dismounting their horses to battle savagely against the Christians. They climbed onto the Crusaders' bridge across the Nile and burned part of it, breaking the circle of Christian troops surrounding the city. But the Crusaders, fortified by bread, wine, and water that women in their company bravely brought through the thick of battle, fought back ferociously, using lances, swords, and volleys of arrows. With heavy losses, the Muslim soldiers retreated back to their sultan.

10

Francis Looks East

While men slaughtered one another in God's name beside the waters of the Nile, Francis gathered his growing community of brothers in Italy with new hopes of realizing his dream of preaching the Christian faith peacefully to Muslims and other nonbelievers. An astonishing number of brothers—early Franciscan accounts say there were five thousand—flocked to Assisi for a chapter meeting held on May 26, 1219, Pentecost Sunday. They assembled around the small stone chapel Francis loved so much, St. Mary of the Angels, or the Portiuncula.

As many educated men joined the brothers' ranks, Francis began to feel intimidated by the order's speedy growth. More than ever he found it necessary to insist on the basics of his *Rule,* which required strict adherence to a life of poverty. To that end he had barred the brothers from building a meetinghouse for this event (or any event for that matter). Since there was no shelter, they had to make due with crude lean-tos constructed of matted reeds—hence the gathering was dubbed the Chapter of the Mats. In addition to lacking housing for all these people, the brothers made no preparation to feed such a large crowd either.

Cardinal Ugolino, who was visiting from Perugia, where the Curia was based for a time, was savvy enough to dismount his horse as he drew near to the assembly and walk the rest of the way in the humble style of the brothers. He was so moved by the brothers' sacrifice, it was said, that he cried at what he saw: pious friars sleeping on the ground with stones or pieces of wood for pillows. But radical poverty was evidently chafing at some of the brothers, because a few of the more learned men—those who had studied theology—took the cardinal aside and asked him to convince Francis to model their life on the rules of one of the established monastic orders, such as the Benedictines. Indeed, the learned friars who approached Ugolino were smart enough to know that a request from such a powerful cardinal would really be more an order than a suggestion. Francis, however, was suspicious of university-trained scholars, fearing that book learning could ultimately interfere with simple adherence to the gospel. Intellectual pursuits, Francis believed, would cause excessive pride.

Ugolino spoke with Francis, who listened, then quietly led him by the hand to the brothers' assembly. There Francis scolded the friars. God had dictated to him the form of life the brothers were to lead, he reminded them. That meant that those who opposed the *Rule* were defying divine will. Francis may have been God's fool, but he was no one else's: he warned that God would punish the brothers for undermining not just his *Rule* but God's will. As one early account noted: "The cardinal was shocked, and said nothing, and all the brothers were afraid." The cardinal had been subtly accused before thousands of people of perpetrating an unholy scheme that God would penalize.

At this chapter the friars decided to expand their missionary efforts, not only in Europe but also in Muslim lands. Ugolino, who had opposed Francis's desire to evangelize outside Italy two years earlier, had now been moved by the extraordinary commitment of Francis and his followers and would no longer stand in their way.

Francis, edgy because his brothers seemed to be slipping away from his founding vision even as he prepared for an extended absence in the

East, was eager to get his movement in order before departing for the great adventure of his life, his attempt to convert the sultan of Egypt.

Fully aware that the European missions of 1217 had failed miserably, Francis was ready to pursue a new plan for evangelizing. This time the brothers would carry a letter Ugolino would secure from Pope Honorius to vouch for their orthodoxy. (The pope issued the letter on June 11.) Brothers were assigned to fan out across Europe—with the exception of Germany, which was still judged to be too dangerous. Brother Pacificus, who had gone to France in 1217 in place of Francis, would return. In addition, three missions to the Muslim world were planned. One included Francis's close friend Brother Giles, who had already been to the Holy Land. He was sent to Tunis in North Africa, while six brothers were dispatched to Morocco. And Francis would travel to the East, where the order already had established itself in Acre.

Giles, however, would return rather quickly from his mission. Christians in Tunis forced him onto a boat going back to Italy because they didn't want the brother to rile the authorities with his preaching. Giles's traveling companion, young Brother Electus, stayed behind and eventually was beheaded because of his preaching. According to Thomas of Celano, Electus held a copy of the *Rule* in his upraised hands as he knelt before the executioner.

Fourteenth-century accounts paint an emotional scene as Francis bade farewell to the six brothers posted to Morocco. Particularly telling was the brothers' worry that they were not prepared for the mission. "We are young and we have never been out of Italy," they were reported to have told Francis. "And the people we go to we know not, but we know that they rage against the Christians, and we are ignorant and cannot speak Arabic. . . . They will ridicule us as crazy men and will not listen to us." They asked how they could do God's work without Francis to guide them. Francis told them to trust in God, and all of them plunged into a vale of tears; the young brothers knelt before Francis, kissing his hands and weeping as they asked for his blessing.

Senior churchmen criticized Francis's movement because of the lack of training its missionaries received. "To our way of thinking, this Order constitutes a danger because it sends out not only formed religious, two by two, throughout the world, [but] also imperfectly formed young men who should be tried and subjected to strict conventual discipline for a period of time," James of Vitry wrote in a letter in 1220.

Francis was determined, though, that if his brothers were leaving on perilous journeys, so would he. Brother Jordan of Giano explained in his chronicle:

> The Blessed Father reflected that he had sent his sons to sufferings and labors; and therefore lest, while others were working for Christ, he himself should seem to be seeking his own ease, for he was proud of spirit and did not wish anyone to excel him in the way of Christ but wished rather that he should excel all others, since he had sent his sons to uncertain dangers.

Francis created two vicars to lead the order in his absence: Matthew of Narni was to stay at the Portiuncula, while Gregory of Naples would travel about Italy to monitor the growing number of brothers. Francis designated one of the brothers closest to him, Peter of Catania, to travel with him to the East. Peter, a doctor of law, and the wealthy Assisian Bernard of Quintavalle had been the first two men to give up everything to join Francis. Both were with him in 1208 as he discovered, through random reading of a missal in the Church of San Nicolò in Assisi, the idea that would set the foundation for his order: to give up all possessions. Francis delighted in Peter because he was devoted to poverty and simplicity and deferential to authority even though he was highly educated and sophisticated. With mutual courtesy, they addressed each other as "lord," and Francis eventually would appoint Peter to lead the order.

It was easy for Francis to pick Peter, someone he wholeheartedly trusted, to go with him, but he had trouble deciding on the rest of his traveling companions. According to Bartholomew of Pisa, a Franciscan who published a history of Francis at the end of the fourteenth century, many of the friars tagged along with Francis to seaside Ancona, hoping to travel with him. Francis had to tell the men that the sailors who were to transport him could not take all of them on the ship, which likely was filled with Italian Crusaders. Nor, he told them, did he want to choose some and reject others, since that would only cause division. Instead, Francis beckoned to a little boy who had watched the brothers carrying on. He suggested that the youngster be asked to decide. When the others agreed, the boy selected eleven traveling companions for Francis. All agreed that the choice must have been God's will.

Since this story emerged nearly two centuries after the fact, it must be taken with a few grains of salt. Factual or not, it still captures a larger truth about how Francis planned for dangerous mission work—he left everything to God's will.

Among those who went along with Francis was Brother Leonard, whose father had helped to instigate the war between Perugia and Assisi after his castle, Sasso Rosso, was destroyed by Francis's compatriots (and possibly Francis himself). Also among the chosen was Brother Illuminato, who had grown up a young nobleman close to Assisi and joined the movement in 1210. According to Thomas of Celano, he had been born blind but gained his sight through Francis's prayers. As a result, he acquired a name that meant "enlightened." Another earlier follower who also accompanied Francis was Brother Barbaro, a man so enthusiastic about God that he voluntarily chewed donkey manure to atone for insulting another brother in front of some knights during a stop on the island of Cyprus.

This colorful group set sail on June 24, 1219, the Feast of St. John the Baptist. The galleys used in that era were relatively small, and the swells on the Mediterranean could be huge. Francis had already experienced the perils of sailing when a storm tossed his vessel off course on his first attempt to reach the Middle East. There is no account of Francis's passage in 1219, but a letter that James of Vitry wrote to friends in France about his own journey three years earlier gives a sense of what it was like to sail to the East. Fifteen anchors, he wrote, could barely hold the ship when a storm struck; the front of the boat lifted toward the heavens and then a moment later plunged toward the deep as everyone onboard held fast for their lives.

The route Francis took to Egypt is not known. If he was sailing with Crusaders, he probably stopped off at the island of Rhodes on the way to the mouth of the Nile and an uncertain fate.

With the Muslim forces on the defensive and Damietta besieged, any tolerance the Egyptians had for Christians in their midst had worn very thin. The common people turned violently against Egypt's own Christians, according to *The History of the Patriarchs of the Egyptian Church.*

Egypt's Christians were themselves sharply divided, the result of a theological controversy over the nature of Christ that dates to the fifth century. In 451 the Council of Chalcedon attempted to resolve the debate by declaring that Jesus had a dual nature, divine and human. This failed to end a bitter dispute; and probably more for political reasons than for purely theological ones, most Egyptian Christians eventually coalesced into what became known as the Coptic Orthodox Church, which had frosty relations with the Western church and no love for the Crusaders. Other Egyptian Christians sided with the West.

Damietta had a large Christian community that was mainly Melkite—that is, sympathetic to the West. Few Muslims, however, made a distinction between the various Christian denominations. All Egyptian Christians were suspected as potential enemies. According to Bishop Yohanna Golta, who is today the spiritual leader of Cairo's Coptic Catholics, the Christians of Egypt suffered the mistrust of both sides during the Crusades fought in their homeland. Coptic poetry and song assailed the Crusaders and defended Egypt, he said, and yet Muslim authorities imposed many fatwas against the Copts during the Crusades.

Suspected of being spies for the Crusaders, the Copts were coerced into paying heavy taxes to support the war effort as proof of their loyalty. Looking to wring more money from the churches, Cairo's governor threatened to expose his city's Christian priests to the fury of the crowd unless they met his financial demands. Faced with such threats, the churches and monasteries squeezed the Christians for all they had. Even so, according to *The History of the Patriarchs of the Egyptian Church,* Christians were arrested and sometimes hung by the authorities on suspicion of treason.

The backlash against Egypt's native Christians went beyond the fury of the crowds who gathered in the streets. A contingent of ten thousand soldiers destroyed every church in its path on a march from Cairo to the outskirts of Damietta, according to the Coptic chronicle. And even al-Kamil, appreciated by Egyptian Christians as their most tolerant sultan ever, disappointed Christians when he allowed the destruction of the Church of St. Mark in Alexandria. According to an early Christian tradition, the apostle Mark had established Christianity in Alexandria and was martyred on the site of a chapel later built there. The initial chapel was expanded and rebuilt periodically through the centuries, and Egyptian Christians offered a princely sum to persuade the sultan not to destroy it. But the sultan became concerned that invading Christian troops might seize and use the tower in an attack on Alexandria—and he refused to save the church. The demolition plunged the Christians into anguish, the chronicler lamented.

It was, to say the least, not an auspicious time for Francis to preach the Christian faith to the Muslims of Egypt.

11

"Forbidding War"

B y the time Francis arrived off the Egyptian shore sometime between late July and mid–August 1219, the sweltering summer
heat and the stalemate outside Damietta had made the Christian camp a cauldron of discontent. Cardinal Pelagius, resisting
the objections of John of Brienne, had forced a series of assaults on the
walled city. On July 8, 1219, his allies from Pisa and Venice attacked from
their ships but fled after Damietta's defenders burned the attackers' ladders with the dreaded Greek fire. Sultan al-Kamil sent troops up along
the river to keep the Christian army from rushing in to help the Italians
escape. Pelagius launched another attack two days later, moving forward
a battery of mangonels to hurl rocks at the city walls. The Muslims retaliated. During a lull in the battle, a group of defenders slipped out of the
fortress at night, killed the sleeping Crusaders, and burned their artillery.

On July 13, aware that the spread of disease inside Damietta was weak-
ening the garrison there, Pelagius ordered another attack. It was beaten
back by a torrent of flaming oil. A hellish pattern was established. Since
the Christians lacked enough troops to both launch an attack and defend their base, the sultan could cause havoc repeatedly in their poorly
guarded camp. Yet when al-Kamil ordered a more aggressive attack on the

Crusader camp on July 20, his troops were repelled. Many were killed on both sides.

While the mood in the Crusader camp was dismal around the time Francis debarked along the Nile, al-Kamil was also in increasingly desperate straits. One brave soldier, a man who had come to Cairo from a small village in Syria and found a place in the elite inner circle of the sultan's guards, had managed to swim across the Nile, Crusader ships all around him, and make his way into Damietta to tell the residents that help was on the way. He brought back a message that the people, dying from disease, begged the sultan to help them. Corpses filled the streets, al-Maqrizi wrote, and only a smattering of wheat and barley remained.

Al-Kamil responded by ordering an all-out assault on the Christian camp for July 31, 1219. The Crusaders had dug a protective trench and built a wooden wall around their camp that intimidated and slowed attackers, but this time the Muslim soldiers penetrated, shattering the ramparts and surging through the gap into the Christian stronghold. French knights charged the Muslim soldiers three times without success. "The insulting Saracens then raised a shout, and the alarm of the Christians increased," Roger of Wendover wrote. The Muslims had formed a full battle line of horsemen and foot soldiers within the Christians' battered fortifications, a frightening sight for the stunned Crusaders. The Knights Templars, the disciplined military order with long experience in fighting in the East, coalesced under the leadership of their marshal, who rallied his knights. The order had handbooks specifying a protocol for responding to just such a crisis. Huddled closely together, they concentrated on a weak point in the enemy line and charged. Muslim foot soldiers abandoned their shields and fled, only to be run down and slain by the Templars. The Muslim men faltered in the trench outside the camp, where many were slaughtered. The battle lines took shape again outside the Christian camp; the Muslims held firm and fought into the twilight, then withdrew, leaving behind many mangled corpses. During the battle the Muslim garrison based inside Damietta had come out to burn the many catapults, battering rams, and ladders the Crusaders had built and positioned for the attack Pelagius was planning on the city. So while the Crusaders had repulsed the most alarming counterattack yet, they had lost ground in their siege of the city.

The exact date of Francis's arrival in Egypt is not known, but he probably stepped off a Crusader vessel soon after the July 31 battle. Francis would have landed in time to catch the scent of death in the summer heat. Corpses would have piled up along the ramparts crossed to enter the camp. Even though he had witnessed intense violence on the battlefield at Collestrada, he had never seen anything approaching this horrific sight. He also would have observed the black mood among the soldiers as they set out once more to build attack towers and battering rams for an assault beneath the fiery rain that Damietta's defenders showered upon them every time they approached.

As the summer wore on, it had become clearer that the Crusader army was outnumbered and too small to attack the much larger Muslim force outside Damietta. Time after time the Christians had risked slaughter when they ventured beyond their trenches and ramparts. And it was becoming ever harder to defend their positions against the fierce attacks the sultan had ordered to save the people of Damietta.

John of Brienne and Cardinal Pelagius continued to argue over strategy. They hoped for reinforcements from Emperor Frederick II, but none arrived. John urged that a peace agreement be negotiated with the sultan for the return of Jerusalem, but Pelagius, hoping to conquer all of Egypt, wouldn't hear of it. By force of personality, control of the expedition's purse, ecclesiastical clout, and alliances with key segments of the army, the cardinal always managed to have the last word.

In a letter to Pope Honorius, James of Vitry wrote that many of the Crusaders found the sultan's peace offer worthy and wanted to accept it. But those who supported the deal, he wrote, were not experienced with the duplicity of the Muslim "foxes." The bishop of Acre acknowledged that there was dissension among the Christians but did not mention to the pope that the famed warrior John of Brienne—whose prestige would have carried some weight with Honorius—was among those who favored the sultan's peace proposal.

The turmoil and low morale left a ready role for Francis when he stepped onto Egyptian soil in early August, accompanied by Brother Illuminato and other friars. Francis's zeal for God was sorely needed in the Crusader camp, given the soldiers' steadfast belief that victory lay in winning God's favor. As the founder of a movement that aimed to imitate Jesus as closely as possible, Francis could inspire hope that his sincere goodness would make God smile on the Crusaders. So would his simple appearance. Wherever Francis went, people remarked on the glow of love that emanated from him. And since the Order of Friars Minor had won papal sanction, Francis as founder would have access to the Crusade's leaders—even to the pope's stand-in, Cardinal Pelagius.

Francis would have been tempted to enjoy that role as the hero who had come to save the day by conquering with prayer rather than with the sword. While a young man, he had dreamed of fighting in the Crusades alongside the famed family of John of Brienne, who embodied the romance of chivalry. Now as a religious leader, he was positioned to help John's mission on behalf of the faith at a crucial moment in history.

But if the trauma of his own battlefield experience and imprisonment hadn't already dashed any remnants of his boyhood fantasy about the Crusaders, his first glimpses of life in the Crusader camp would have. Men died slowly of battlefield wounds and rampant disease. All around Francis the class tensions often lurking in medieval life flared. The foot soldiers (commoners who sought to ennoble themselves by taking up the cross) denounced the horsemen (noblemen and wealthy merchants) as cowards. The horsemen jeered at the foot soldiers, making light of the commoners' risk. The hatred between aristocrats and commoners was familiar to Francis from his warrior days in Assisi. He understood the bottled-up anger of the common people. He also knew how it looked from the noblemen's perspective; he had stared down death in a cavalry charge. He knew that the finest armor and a thundering steed were not enough to save a man's life. When he fought in the Battle of Collestrada, Francis saw men hunted like game and hacked apart. He knew the gro-

tesque injuries men suffered in war, and he knew how the wounded suffered. He knew what it meant to linger feverishly in the mud, on the
brink of death.

Francis, in short, saw the nightmares of his youth come alive before
him. Only now, he was seeing war on a far bigger scale than he had
known as a young man in Assisi.

Although the fighting lulled while the two armies staggered with their
losses, there were still some ferocious encounters. On August 6, 1219,
Christian soldiers tried to fill in the moat protecting Damietta, but the
effort failed. One hundred more Crusaders were killed. Pelagius dug deep
into the pope's treasury to outfit four attack ships for his allies from Pisa,
Genoa, and Venice, decking the vessels with as many ladders, ropes, and
anchors as needed. The attackers went forward to the music of trumpets
and reed pipes, banners flying. Muslim troops, who had erected new
wooden towers along the city's walls, halted the attack by burning the
Crusaders' ladders.

Every day Francis had fresh evidence for his belief that warfare released demons. Eight Muslim spies were captured when they tried to
swim across the river. The Crusaders mutilated the men, cutting off their
noses, arms, lips, and ears and gouging out one eye on each. Half of them
were sent back to the Muslim camp; the rest were kept on display. Later
the Muslims sent back a Christian with the same mutilations.

A debate raged through the Christian camp on whether to launch an
all-out assault aimed at breaking the Muslim army or to continue with
the siege until the garrison finally surrendered. Pelagius was quietly planning yet another attack. Fearing spies were all around, he revealed his
plans to only a few loyal clerics and trusted knights. The cardinal was
concerned that if that word got out, opposition to his plan would mount
among the Crusaders who thought it far better to wait for the enemy to
starve, James of Vitry wrote in his letter to Pope Honorius.

When Pelagius tipped his hand, John of Brienne and other French
commanders allied with him urged the cardinal to continue the siege in-

stead of attacking. The military leaders had seen the condition of people who tried to escape the walled city and run for their lives. "Their swollen and famished condition plainly showed the suffering of their fellow citizens," according to Roger of Wendover. It was clear that Crusaders' lives could be saved if the Christian army waited out the siege. But Cardinal Pelagius, allied with the seafaring Italian Crusaders and the military orders such as the Templars, insisted on attacking. The entire force readied itself for an assault by land and river planned for August 29, 1219, the Feast of the Beheading of St. John the Baptist.

Francis retreated into his prayers and contemplated the coming battle. Deeply distressed, he prayed through that hot night—perhaps reflecting on the fate of the beheaded baptizer. Francis had been born with the name John, and he had a great devotion to the saint, considering his to be the most important of all the saints' feast days. Deep in prayer, Francis believed that Jesus spoke to him. And by morning on the day of the planned battle, his prayer experience had led him to conclude that the Crusaders would be making an enormous mistake if they attacked. Grieving, he wondered what he could do and went to speak with one of his traveling companions.

"If the battle happens on this day the Lord has shown me that it will not go well for the Christians," Francis said. The brother Francis spoke to, not named in early accounts, would have known how grave this prediction was, believing that if God disapproved of the battle, many Christians would die.

Francis continued. "But if I say this, they will take me for a fool, and if I keep silent, my conscience won't leave me alone," he said. "What do you think I should do?"

Ever since his conversion, Francis had shown no concern about being looked upon as a fool. But if he spoke up now at the last moment—if he told the soldiers, their leaders, and the cardinal himself that Jesus had warned against the battle—it could unleash a wave of anger and even violence against him. The last thing the Crusaders wanted to hear as they offered their prayers on the morning of battle was a holy man's warning that God was not on their side—an ill omen for sure. After just a few weeks in the Crusader camp, Francis chafed at playing the cheerleader role expected from clergy and the religious; a voice inside told him not to follow the pack of presbyters who prayed on the battle's sidelines for victory. Announcing his conviction that the battle was already lost was nearly seditious because of the threat it posed to the troops' morale.

The brother Francis spoke with knew he was not the kind of man who feared the consequences of doing what was right. He simply offered Francis's teachings back to him. "Father, don't give the least thought to how people judge you," he said. "This wouldn't be the first time people took you for a fool. Unburden your conscience, and fear God rather than men." The comment comes in the voice of someone who had known Francis for a long time, going back to the antics of his conversion in Assisi. It could well have been Peter of Catania, Francis's longtime friend and confidant.

If Francis went forward with his warning, he would be inserting himself into the middle of a political controversy that divided the leaders of the Crusade. It would be very difficult for him because of his belief that conflicts among the "princes of this world" were fed by a pride and arrogance that led to violence—the very behavior he had sought to escape through his new life. He would have preferred to avoid opposing the cardinal's wishes; he had always prized obedience and shrunk from confrontation with the church hierarchy, hoping to reform the church's leadership with his example rather than through polemics. But despite his emphasis on obeying church authorities, he wrote in the *Earlier Rule* and in his *Admonitions* that a brother should heed his own conscience rather than a prelate's misguided order—and should be willing to suffer the consequences.

So his companion's response confirmed for Francis that he had to follow his conscience. Still, it would not be easy to announce, in essence, that God opposed plans that the headstrong Cardinal Pelagius had masterminded. Through his very bearing Pelagius seemed to assume he spoke for God. As papal legate, the cardinal was to be treated with the same respect as the pope, the Vicar of Christ.

Pelagius played this role to the hilt. In an era when princes of the church were only beginning to wear scarlet robes, Pelagius was ahead of his time in adopting garb that would show off his prestige and might. Draping himself in a color meant to symbolize the blood of the martyrs,

Pelagius displayed an obvious love for the trappings of power. A decade earlier his triumphal entry into Constantinople on horseback had disgusted the Greeks, who were seething over the Crusaders' brutal sacking of their capital in 1204. Even his spurs were gold. As the bishop of Albano, a town just ten miles from Rome, Pelagius played a powerful role in the courts of Innocent III and his successor, Honorius III—so much so that Albano was transferred from the pope's own diocese to become Pelagius's domain. Pelagius epitomized church authority. It is no surprise that Francis, who had made obedience a cornerstone of his ministry, was reluctant to disagree publicly with the cardinal.

Nonetheless he began to preach vigorously against the battle, shouldering the risk that he would be labeled a security threat. "The saint leapt to his feet, and rushed to the Christians crying out warnings to save them, forbidding war and threatening disaster," Thomas of Celano wrote. "But they took the truth as a joke. They hardened their hearts and refused to turn back." The soldiers' words aren't recorded, but the foulmouthed jeers and taunts of a surly mob of men pumped for battle are easy to imagine. The barefoot little holy man who looked and talked like a heretic was an easy target for their scorn. Francis, arguing vociferously, was a force to be reckoned with. But the soldiers had long been warned by preachers of the Crusade to reject those who told them it was against God's will to do battle. "When people falsely assert that you are not allowed *for any reason whatever* to take up the physical sword or fight bodily against the Church's enemies, it is the devil trying to attack the fabric of the Order and by means of these people to destroy it utterly," James of Vitry once said in a sermon to the Templars, who spearheaded the attacks on the Muslim army at Damietta.

A later chronicle added that the leader of the army—evidently John of Brienne—heard the commotion and took it as a further sign that he should press for a truce with the Muslims to avoid more slaughter. But the angry foot soldiers shouted down Francis, described in one chronicle as "a despicable and unknown friar." Cardinal Pelagius, though disturbed that the rabble had taken over, was going to get his way.

H istorians have long debated the meaning of the passage in which Thomas of Celano told of Francis's objection to the coming battle. Was Francis "forbidding war" or merely opposing battle on "this day"? It poses the question of whether one of the greatest Christian saints opposed the popes' war, the Crusade.

Historians who argue that Francis supported the war stress that Celano quoted him as saying, "If the battle happens on *this day*," it will go badly. But James M. Powell, a historian at Syracuse University who is a leading expert on the Fifth Crusade, has written that there is a deeper meaning to the phrase "this day," rooted in the religious thought of the time. Proponents of the Crusades made much of a Scripture passage declaring that it was the "acceptable time" to achieve salvation. It traces back to the Book of Isaiah, which declares that the time had come for Israel's liberation:

Thus says the Lord:
In a time of favor I answer you, on the day of salvation I help you,
To restore the land.

The Second Letter to the Corinthians picked up on this: "Behold, now is a very acceptable time; behold, now is the day of salvation." The hope that it was the "acceptable time"—a time of God's favor—lay at the heart of the papal call for Crusades to wrest the Holy Land from Muslim domination. "For it was entirely in the power of almighty God, if he had so wished, to prevent that land from being handed over to hostile hands," Pope Innocent III wrote in his letter in 1213 that formally called for the Crusade. "And if he wishes he can easily free it from the hands of the enemy, since nothing can resist his will." That time had come, according to Innocent. The sign he cited came from the passage in the Book of Revelation that associated a powerful beast with the number 666. This "beast," according to Innocent, was Muhammad. "The end of this beast is approaching, whose number, according to the Revelation of St. John, will end in 666 years," the pope wrote (1236 would be 666 after the Prophet Muhammad's birth in 570).

The Crusades had been cast in religious terms from the beginning, when Pope Urban II rallied Christendom in 1095 with the war cry "God wills it." Bernard of Clairvaux, preaching in the twelfth century, also used the theme that it was the acceptable time before God for a Crusade, as Powell points out. Likewise, the Christian writers who witnessed the Fifth Crusade, Oliver of Paderborn and James of Vitry, time and again saw the Crusaders' successes and defeats in terms of whether they had been virtuous or sinful. It was all in God's hands, they wrote repeatedly.

When Francis told his confidant that he opposed the battle on "this day," he disputed the major justification given for the Crusade for nearly 125 years—that "God wills it." Francis had essentially warned that it was not the "acceptable time"—and he believed that God had told him so.

Francis's manner of expressing opposition to the Crusade was not new. He paralleled the more intellectual arguments of Joachim of Fiore, the famed Calabrian scholar whose biblical prophecies were sought out by popes and kings at the end of the twelfth century. The failure of Richard the Lion-Hearted to win Jerusalem in the Third Crusade had convinced Joachim that the Crusade violated God's will. Interpreting passages in the Book of Revelation, the abbot came to favor peaceful conversion as an alternative to warfare against Islam. When Pope Innocent III called for the Fifth Crusade in 1213, he seemed to be responding to Joachim, who had died eleven years earlier, by justifying his cause with passages from the Book of Revelation. There is no evidence that Francis knew Joachim's writings at this point in his life, but these ideas were in the air, part of the era's apocalyptic mind-set.

Nor did Francis mean that while it was a mistake for the Crusades to attack on "this day," it would be acceptable to God to do battle on an ensuing day. God's favor was not something to be poured out at will; it could be won only through genuine reform and holiness—a holiness that Francis believed was lacking in his greedy, violent time. To Francis,

August 29, 1219, was not the "acceptable time" for battle, nor was any other day.

"He's saying that to go out at any time is to violate the will of God," said the Rev. Michael Cusato, director of the Franciscan Institute at St. Bonaventure University, North America's leading Franciscan research center.

Further evidence for Powell's argument comes from Dutch scholar Jan Hoeberichts, who notes that Thomas of Celano, writing in Latin, had Francis forbidding *bellum,* or war, and not just *pugnam,* or battle. Francis opposed the war, not just a particular battle.

The debate over whether Francis opposed the Crusade should not, however, come down to this single, much-debated passage. The best evidence can be found in the broader context of Francis's well-demonstrated revulsion at warfare and his penchant for peacemaking. Any ambiguity in this key passage about Francis's outspokenness should be resolved against that background.

In speaking out, Francis had taken to heart his unnamed companion's advice to follow his conscience in spite of the church teaching that the Fifth Crusade was God's will, a fight to be spurned only at the risk of one's soul. As noted earlier, conscience was important to Francis. A friar should obey a church leader, but "if the prelate ... commands something contrary to his conscience, even though he may not obey him, let him not, however, abandon him."

Despite his desire to serve the church, Francis felt that he had to speak out against its war. The initial reason given for the fighting was undercut by Sultan al-Kamil's offer to return Jerusalem to the Crusaders. Francis's weeks in the Crusader camp had given him the chance to observe how economic motives spurred the merchant-backed armies from Pisa, Genoa, and Venice to lobby for war over peace.

All of this shocked Francis's conscience to the point that he was willing to oppose even the papal legate, Pelagius. By calling for a halt to the battle on "this day," Francis entered a debate that was raging among the Crusade leaders: he had sided with John of Brienne and others who favored a stop to the warfare so that a peace treaty could be negotiated with Sultan al-Kamil. His warning immediately became fodder for the ongoing internal political dispute among the Christian army's leaders. John of Brienne seized on Francis's premonition as one more reason to accept the sultan's offer. He could see as well as anyone the sword hanging over the Crusaders' heads as they prepared to charge the stronghold of an army many times larger than their own to win over what already had been offered.

It was to no avail.

Having dismissed Francis—and having said their prayers—the troops moved south in an orderly line of battle on both land and river on the morning of August 29, 1219. The crusaders were still "disagreeing amongst themselves" as they left camp, Roger of Wendover wrote. Oliver of Paderborn, who was an aide to Pelagius, made light of all objections by noting that "scarcely any were to be found who would remain in the custody of the camp."

Francis, vehemently opposed to the battle, stayed behind. He would not join Pelagius, Patriarch Ralph of Jerusalem, and the clergy attached to the army as they headed for the battlefield accompanied by the True Cross.

When the Christian army advanced, Muslim soldiers encamped between saltwater Lake Manzala and the Nile took down their tents and feigned retreat. To the Christians, it looked as if God were about to deliver an easy victory. The Crusaders moved forward, but soon found to their alarm that there was no source of fresh water. They tasted the water in a trench the Muslims had dug, but it was salty. Leaders of the Christian army engaged in a long debate about what to do next. Many of the foot soldiers lagged behind, suffering from thirst and heat that blazed from the sky above and glared from the sand below. They struggled with the weight of their armor and weapons. According to a letter that James of Vitry wrote to the pope, the leaders decided to fall back. At the same time some of the infantrymen—the same soldiers who had pushed for an attack—panicked as they became more and more dehydrated.

Under the sizzling August sun, the Christian soldiers slumped. Without water, the foot soldiers couldn't dilute the wine they carried into battle, as was their custom. Parched, they had no choice but to drink their wine undiluted. Their chain mail, their swords and shields and helmets became crushing burdens. The heat and thirst were so terrible that those who stood their ground became woozy and collapsed without ever having been wounded. The sun scorched the knights' armor, heating it like iron pots hung over a fire.

Seeing the Christians' indecision, the Muslims surged. Italian foot soldiers at the center of the Crusaders' line had bulged forward, leaving an opening for the Muslims to attack one flank. As James of Vitry solemnly informed Pope Honorius in a letter, the enemy soldiers seemed to suddenly be on all sides, shooting arrows, thrusting with spears and lances, clubbing with maces and hurling fireballs. Meanwhile John of Brienne was occupied fighting Bedouins who had driven off the women assigned to carry water from the Nile to the Christian soldiers. Cypriot knights on the right flank quickly discovered that the sultan's army had merely faked a retreat; they fled as the enemy charged. The Italian foot soldiers, once so eager for battle, ran away. Then knights from various nations fled on their horses, and even some of the vaunted knights from the Hospitalers of St. John retreated. Pelagius and the patriarch of Jerusalem shouted to the troops, begging them to turn around and fight. Some knights charged forward, only to be surrounded and slaughtered.

Back in the emptied Christian camp, Francis worried about what would befall the troops and asked one of his brothers to get up and look. The brother came back to tell Francis he saw nothing; the battle was several miles to the south.

The anxious Francis later asked his companion to look for a second time to find out what was happening. Perhaps because of the trauma of his own battlefield experience, he did not go to see for himself. Once again the brother returned to say he saw nothing.

Meanwhile some of the foot soldiers abandoned their swords and jumped into the river, where the enemy—fresh, lightly armed, and riding on horses accustomed to the heat—hunted them down, sloshing through the shallows to kill them one by one.

John of Brienne fought back furiously to protect his army's retreat. In a scene reminiscent of the gory feats described in the popular epic *Chanson de Roland,* he allegedly stood up to a gigantic, club-wielding "pagan" who was slaying Christians all over the field and cleaved him in two, from the head down, with one stroke of the sword. Knights from the military orders—the Templars, Hospitalers, and Teutonic knights—and various counts and knights from France and Pisa joined him, slowing the enemy charge. But the pursuit continued all the way to the threshold of the Crusaders' camp, with the knights trying to protect the horde of Christian soldiers fleeing back across the protective trench and wooden palisades. John, who'd had so many misgivings about the battle, was scorched and nearly killed by Greek fire.

Francis asked his brother to look a third time to see what was happening. "What a sight!" Thomas of Celano wrote. "The whole Christian army was in retreat fleeing from the battle carrying not triumph but shame. The massacre was so great that between the dead and the captives the number of our forces was diminished by six thousand."

Other chronicles placed the number of dead Crusaders between 2,000 and 4,300, including the loss of hundreds of elite knights protecting the rear and an entire galley carrying 200 men. Two French bishops; the chamberlain of France and his son; the French nobleman Milo of Beauvais and his brother Andrew of Nanteuil; and many other aristocrats were among the thousand Christians captured. They were taken to a prison in a castle that belonged to the sultan. From among the disciplined Templars—the last Christians to return through the ramparts to camp—thirty-three men were killed.

Francis grieved over the loss of so many. He especially mourned the loss of the many Spanish soldiers because they had fought courageously. While he opposed the war, he had enormous compassion for the soldiers.

If he was angered that so much destruction had occurred despite his warning, his early biographers didn't mention it. But in a rare expression of outrage, Thomas of Celano assailed the authorities for the carnage. "Let the princes of the world know these things and let them know that it is not easy to fight against God, that is, against the will of the Lord," he wrote. That statement, which condemned the military and religious chieftains who allowed the devastation, may well have reflected Francis's outlook. He didn't blame the foot soldiers who had denounced him, but he held the leaders responsible for the carnage.

That criticism of the "princes of this world" gives an insight into Francis's concept of peace. It was not limited to inner serenity or one-to-one interactions with people he met. At Damietta he intervened in a politically charged dispute in the Crusaders' camp—whether to accept the sultan's peace treaty—and was proven right. His objection to the battle was cast in the language of faith; for Thomas of Celano, it was a sign of Francis's prophetic power. But prophecy and politics were welded together. The Christians' major political decisions in the Crusades were always preceded by the great prophetic question, Is God on our side? Francis declared that the answer was no. To weigh in, on one side or the other, even in religious terminology, was a political act.

Francis wasn't finished. He had an idea to prevent yet another bloodbath. If the Crusade leaders would not seek peace, *he* would.

12

The Saint and the Cardinal

After his victory Sultan al-Kamil sent the good news to Cairo by carrier pigeon. His subjects rejoiced, decorating the streets in celebration. They celebrated more when al-Kamil sent hundreds of Christian captives to be paraded through the capital and then thrown in a dark prison. But the sultan's exultation was tempered by the fact that the Nile River had flooded later than usual; the canals and ditches used to irrigate Egypt's fields of wheat and corn were dry. Prices rose so high that Cairo's residents were unable to buy food. Meanwhile the plight of the encircled citizens of Damietta remained no less desperate, since the sultan's troops had been unable to drive the Christian army away.

Sultan al-Kamil decided to try his peace offer again, hoping that the Christians' defeat on August 29 would chasten the Crusade's leaders. He met resistance among his own allies, but the captive Christian noblemen he brought before him were relieved to hear the sultan's plan. Al-Kamil chose two of the Christian knights he held prisoner to deliver his message. The first was Andrew of Nanteuil, whose brother Milo, a bishop-elect in Beauvais in northern France, was also a captive. The second was John of Arcis, a seasoned warrior known for his bravery on the battlefield.

The two men were dispatched back to the Christian camp in early September to deliver the proposal to John of Brienne. When they entered the king's tent, Andrew did the talking. He spoke approvingly of the sultan's offer, which once again would give the Crusaders control of Jerusalem and the lands lost to Saladin. In addition, al-Kamil pledged to return the rest of the True Cross and release all Christian prisoners held throughout the region, he told the king and other Crusade leaders. Andrew pointed out that the sultan even sweetened his earlier proposal by agreeing to pay tribute to keep two key castles used to protect Muslims traveling to Mecca. The sultan, he said, would also pay to rebuild the shattered walls of Jerusalem.

John argued strongly in favor of the deal that Andrew of Nanteuil presented, and an English earl and French and German noblemen agreed with him. Pelagius rejected it, contending that after two years of warfare and long suffering through heat and flood, the Christian soldiers were close to capturing Damietta. All the clergymen present—an array of bishops and archbishops—backed the cardinal, as did the Templars and the commercially conscious contingents from Pisa, Venice, and Genoa. Pelagius insisted that reinforcements were expected—Emperor Frederick II had not yet sent troops—and continued to envision himself conquering not only Damietta but all of Egypt, dealing Islam a powerful blow.

Andrew of Nanteuil and John of Arcis were returned to the sultan to reject the deal. It was a grim mission for these men, since it meant going back to prison. Sent to their cells to await an audience with the sultan, they broke the bad news to their fellow captives, who mourned over their prolonged captivity. Then the two knights met with al-Kamil, who also was disturbed at what he heard. The sultan, still wanting to broker peace, kept sending messengers to the Christian camp, and the back-and-forth of negotiation continued for several weeks until September 26, creating a brief period of relative calm after the intense summer of fighting.

In the Crusader camp, as the debate over war and peace continued, Francis decided to act. This was the "acceptable time" for him to take a bold stand. For years, Francis had dreamed of converting a Muslim leader to bring peace between Christianity and Islam. Francis decided that he and Brother Illuminato would venture out of the relative safety of the Crusaders' fortifications to meet the Muslims in their own camp. Moreover, Francis planned on insisting that he be taken to the sultan himself. Illuminato, having witnessed the bloody results of the Christians' defeat on August 29, must have blanched at the idea. Francis had to reassure him: "Trust in the Lord, brother."

Francis understood the risks. Having been traumatized by his earlier experiences as a soldier and prisoner of war in Perugia, he would have known that death or imprisonment were likely outcomes of his plan to cross enemy lines during wartime. But with Cardinal Pelagius once again rejecting peace, he decided there was no other choice.

Francis, however, felt a deep loyalty to church authority and decided to seek permission for his journey from the cardinal, whose bejeweled clothing and hunger for power were the antithesis of the friar's humble way. He might have slipped out of the camp, but that would have risked suspicion that he was spying for the enemy. A meeting with Pelagius would be no small matter, since Francis already had argued so strenuously against the cardinal's battle plans and then made himself conspicuously absent when prelates and priests prayed before the True Cross during the battle on August 29. Furthermore, if Francis flouted the papal legate's authority, he would in effect be contravening the authority of the pope, Francis's protector.

The scrawny little friar who stood before Pelagius served as a living reminder of the cardinal's disastrous decision to launch an attack that his experienced military commander opposed. Pelagius was not the kind of man who could easily accept that he was wrong. When Francis had tried to avert the Crusaders' attack on August 29, he called into question in a not-so-subtle way Pelagius's ability to lead the war. Moreover, by insisting that God had told him to speak out against the attack, Francis had claimed a divine inspiration that the cardinal lacked.

With these tensions in the background, Francis and Illuminato approached Pelagius. The story of this touchy encounter between the future saint and the cardinal was recorded in *The Chronicle of Ernoul,* a secular French Crusader chronicle written in the late 1220s; it was evidently too controversial to be included in the early Franciscan biographies.

When Francis and Illuminato asked the cardinal's blessing for their plan to visit the sultan, Pelagius quickly rejected the request. "The Cardinal told them that as far as he was concerned, they would go there neither with his blessing nor under his orders, for he would never want to give them permission to go to a place where they would only be killed," the chronicler wrote. "For he knew full well that if they went there, they would never come back."

Francis responded that Pelagius would carry no blame for anything that happened to him and Illuminato "because he had not commanded them, but only allowed them to go." The cardinal reiterated that he was not about to be the one responsible for sending to his death the founder of a religious order close to the papal heart. These rejections only made Francis press all the more for the cardinal's approval.

The Chronicle of Ernoul hints that Pelagius's refusal had a darker side, a concern that went beyond protecting Francis's well-being or his own reputation in Rome. "Sirs, I do not know what is in your hearts or in your thoughts, whether these be good or evil," Pelagius said, in essence questioning the friars' loyalty. Francis pointed to the great good that could be accomplished if Jesus' message were preached to the sultan. Bit by bit, the cardinal relented. "If you do go, see that your heart and your thoughts are always turned to the Lord God," the cardinal said. Shortly thereafter the cardinal agreed to let the duo go to the sultan, washing his hands of the matter by saying, "All this is to be your sole responsibility, because certainly I shall not be the one to send you to your certain death."

A s Francis and Illuminato began the dangerous journey across enemy lines, they steadied their nerves by singing the Twenty-third Psalm. "The Lord is my shepherd," they chanted. "There is nothing I shall want."

The words of the psalm expressed their situation perfectly, for they were trusting the divine shepherd to lead them to peaceful pastures: "Even though I go through the valley of the shadow of death, I fear no evil, for you are with me." They carried no letter or token that might be used to protect them when they encountered enemy soldiers. They had no weapons to fight back or shield to ward off arrows. They were protected only by the "shield of faith," as James of Vitry put it. As they made their way across their very own valley of the shadow of death, Francis knew well that warfare had unleashed the worst in men's hearts. By this time neither the Crusaders nor the Muslims were content simply to slay the enemy. Spies were mutilated in ghastly ways. Severed heads were hurled and piled as a warning of the brutality to come. War had unleashed the demons. Francis knew there was a strong chance he could be killed.

D id Francis *want* to die? Bonaventure's account gives that impression: "The thought of death attracted him." If Francis were killed while trying to preach the faith to the infidel, he would be guaranteed salvation as a martyr. But Francis's march to the sultan's side was more than a saintly suicide mission. While he was not averse to risk—his *Earlier Rule* tells the brothers to "make themselves vulnerable to their enemies"—he had not come all this way to die but to further the peacemaking he began in the first days of his ministry. "He had a vision," says the Rev. Michael Cusato, director of the Franciscan Institute. "Further bloodshed was not a part of it."

Hugh of Digne, a gifted Franciscan writer who tried to recover the order's authentic tradition in the 1240s, put it this way in his commentary on the order's *Rule:* "Because of the desire for martyrdom, one should not act precipitously but in fact prudently. For we should strive for the death for Christ and [yet] flee in an ordinate manner." Martyrdom was not to be courted; Hugh urged friars to be willing to sacrifice all for Christ but to be prudent as well by extricating themselves from a violent situation rather than seeking death.

From the outset of his ministry, Francis had discovered that peaceful submissiveness was his best weapon when dealing with a more powerful force, whether it was his aggressive father, assorted street bullies and robbers, or the papal court. Now he was bringing that approach into the valley of the shadow of death, and with each step he took he reminded himself, "I shall not fear evil because you are with me."

13

The Saint and the Sultan

T he day began when Francis and Illuminato left the palisaded Crusader compound to cross the Nile. They needed to get to the east bank of the river before heading south to reach the sultan, about eight miles away at his camp in Fariskur. The easiest way across the river was to cross a bobbing pontoon bridge that the Crusaders had built over a series of boats lashed together on the surging Nile. The poet Henri d'Avranches offered a much more dramatic scenario, however, claiming that they crossed in a small boat under bombardment:

> What manly courage in a man to cross that great river
> In a tiny skiff! Alone and unarmed he moves towards
> The weaponed and hostile host, through darts, through
> Unquenchable "Greek fire," through a thousand mortal perils!

Henri was drawing on his poetic license; by the time Francis set out for the enemy camp in late September, fighting had waned while the Crusaders considered the sultan's peace offer. The two coarsely clad friars passed within sight of triple-walled Damietta, where conditions were so desperate that the gates had been braced and barred to prevent the city's desperate residents from fleeing. The countryside south of Damietta had once been a pleasant place with orchards, rows of crops, and pastures, land made fruitful by the river's annual surge. In quieter times fishing boats trawled the waters. Now it was different. Only days before, terrified Christian soldiers had fled across this landscape, running from the charging enemy's swords, arrows, and balls of fire. By the time Francis and Illuminato passed through, Muslim troops already had combed the battlefield to seize booty and ambulatory prisoners. Grisly signs of the August 29 battle lingered. Butchered corpses or body parts, now putrid in the heat, remained. Many decayed in the bottom of the protective trench surrounding the Crusader camp, where fighting was most fierce. Others would have dotted the landscape. Dead horses rotted. Stretches of farmland were burned black. It was a landscape from hell, far worse than the body-littered battlefield where Francis was taken prisoner as a young man.

As Francis and Illuminato approached Fariskur, Muslim sentries confronted them. It would not have taken them long to reach this point—only a few hours if they were walking steadily. They most likely had set out in the cool of daybreak, so it was still morning. What happened next is up for debate.

At least fifteen sources from the thirteenth century refer to Francis's visit with Sultan Malik al-Kamil, but the accounts diverge, often sharply. As the decades passed, increasingly embellished versions gradually transformed the event from a surprisingly peaceful encounter into a violence-tinged clash of civilizations. We see that process even in a small detail in the plot, the initial experience Francis and Illuminato had with Muslim sentries.

According to Bonaventure, soldiers "fell upon them like wolves upon sheep and seized them fiercely," savagely beating the two brothers with whips, then insulting and chaining them. The poet Henri d'Avranches was florid: "[Francis's] flesh is livid, his blood pours out;/Violet is his body from violence, and rose-red his wounds."

Earlier accounts by James of Vitry and *The Chronicle of Ernoul* were far more restrained. As *Ernoul* put it: "When the Saracen sentinels saw them coming they thought that they were messengers or perhaps had come to renounce their faith. When they met them, they seized them and led them to the Sultan."

In describing Francis's encounter with the Muslim soldiers, Bonaventure and Henri d'Avranches strained to draw comparisons to the arrest of Jesus on the Mount of Olives and his initial torture. Bonaventure, in particular, wanted to fit Francis's story into a broader theological framework. James of Vitry and the author of *The Chronicle of Ernoul* provide the more reliable accounts. They were closer to the events, since both participated in the Fifth Crusade, and neither was trying to sculpt the facts to promote Francis as a great saint.

In any case, Francis stated his business to the Muslim soldiers by declaring himself a follower of Jesus and asking to see the sultan. Faced with that announcement, the soldiers drew the logical conclusion that Francis and Illuminato were sent as messengers to convey the latest Christian response to the sultan's peace proposal. There may have been some initial confusion; Brother Jordan of Giano wrote in the 1260s that Francis, unable to speak the soldiers' language, cried out, "Sultan! Sultan!" as he was pummeled. After that, it appears, the sentries warily escorted Francis and Illuminato into the camp.

While various accounts disagree on the particulars, all agree on one thing: Francis was taken before Sultan Malik al-Kamil, preparing the way for a unique historical event. Artists have sought through the centuries to depict this scene—a bearded sultan in his flowing robes and turban, and Francis in his brown tunic. Thomas of Celano gives a sense of what the man standing before the sultan looked like:

He was a most eloquent man, a man of cheerful countenance . . .
he was of medium height, closer to shortness; his head was moderate
in size and round, his face a bit long and prominent, his forehead
smooth and low; his eyes were of moderate size, black and sound; his
hair was black, his eyebrows straight, his nose symmetrical, thin and
straight; his ears were upright, but small; his temples smooth. His

speech was peaceable, fiery and sharp; his voice was strong, sweet, clear, and sonorous. His teeth were set close together, even, and white; his lips were small and thin; his beard black, but not bushy. His neck was slender, his shoulders straight, his arms short, his hands slender, his fingers long, his nails extended; his legs were thin, his feet small. His skin was delicate, his flesh very spare. He wore rough garments, he slept but briefly, he gave most generously. And because he was very humble, he showed all mildness to all men, adapting himself usefully to the behavior of all.

Francis had met two popes, much of the Curia, and the king of Jerusalem, so he was familiar with "princes of this world." Powerful men such as the sultan did not cow Francis. "He had no fear of anyone's status, rather he spoke calmly to the wise and the uneducated, to the great and the small," Brother Julian of Speyer wrote in the 1230s. The future saint and the sultan were roughly the same age; al-Kamil was thirty-nine and Francis a year and a half younger. Francis would have begun with the same greeting he used everywhere—"May the Lord give you peace"—at once a friendly, down-to-earth embrace of the person he addressed and a prayer for the transformation of a violent world. He began all his preaching that way, and it would have been more appropriate now than ever. Sultan Malik al-Kamil returned the friars' greeting and then, according to *The Chronicle of Ernoul,* "asked if they wished to become Saracens or perhaps had come with some message."

The idea that Francis and Illuminato had shown up before the sultan to "become Saracens" is not as outlandish as it might sound; soldiers on both sides of the Fifth Crusade converted. The sultan's own experience with Egypt's Christians also had taught him that some wanted to convert; he had dealt personally with several cases involving Christian monks who became Muslims. Still, it must have appeared to him more likely—considering the timing of Francis's visit and his greeting of peace—that the two friars arrived with a new message from the Christian camp in response to the sultan's peace initiative.

Al-Kamil might have noticed the similarity between Francis's greeting and the familiar Arabic greeting of peace, *as-salamu alaikum,* or "peace be upon you." The Qur'an even urges the benefit of the doubt for those who use a greeting of peace: "Say not to those who greet you with peace, 'you are not a believer.'" And perhaps the sultan was struck by Francis's directness; his own Christian subjects would likely have embedded any statement to the sultan in flowery praise. Francis preached "using no words of flattery," Thomas of Celano wrote.

The early accounts do not explain how the language gap was bridged. Al-Kamil had brought imprisoned Western priests into his court to teach Western languages, so it is possible he understood Francis. Absent that, translators would have been available. Francis's dramatic gestures and sonorous voice should not be underestimated as communication tools either.

Francis and Illuminato quickly brushed aside the sultan's suggestion that they wanted to convert, responding that "they never would want to become Muslims, but that they had come to him as messengers on behalf of the Lord God, that he might turn his soul to God."

There is a subtle and interesting twist in Francis's response. Al-Kamil thought Francis was a messenger for the leaders of the Crusade, but Francis invoked the name of God in his response, not of Cardinal Pelagius or John of Brienne. In *The Chronicle of Bernard the Treasurer,* an Old French chronicle dated to 1230 and based on *Ernoul,* the two friars declare: "We are ambassadors of the Lord Jesus Christ." Whatever the actual words, Francis did not agree with the violent means of the Crusades, and his response to the sultan implied as much without explicitly stating it. Francis saw a divide between God's will and the war. He knew which side he wanted to be on, and he declared it to the sultan: he was God's ambassador, not the pope's. After opening the encounter with a well-received greeting of peace, Francis had managed to separate himself from warmongering Pelagius and the other leaders of the Crusade without blatantly disavowing them.

According to *The Chronicle of Ernoul,* Francis continued to speak of conversion:

If you wish to believe us, we will hand over your soul to God,
because we are telling you in all truth that if you die in the law
which you now profess, you will be lost and God will not possess
your soul. It is for this reason that we have come. But if you will give
us a hearing and try to understand us, we will demonstrate to you
with convincing reasons, in the presence of the most learned
teachers of your realm, if you wish to assemble them, that your law
is false.

Francis subtly announced his peaceful intent right away: "*If* you wish
to believe us," he said, asking only to be heard. Still, no matter how gentle
Francis was in delivering this invitation, it is a wonder that al-Kamil did
not dispatch his soldiers to deposit the two friars with the other prisoners. After all, the war was ongoing. Whatever Francis said, it delighted the
embattled sultan immediately; he "became sweetness itself," as James of
Vitry wrote.

Why did the sultan hold court with these two Christians? Intellectual
curiosity was one possible motive, but the time was hardly right for the
sultan to indulge his scholarly interests. More important to al-Kamil was
the possibility that Francis might provide a bridge to peace with the
Christians. Even though the Crusaders had suffered heavy losses, the sultan's situation was still dire. The remaining residents of Damietta had be-
seeched him to save their lives. In Cairo the populace had turned out to
defend the city against an expected Christian attack. And at Fariskur the
sultan was pushing a peace agreement while planning his battlefield strategy should the talks fail. Even al-Kamil's triumph in the battle fought on
August 29 had failed to send the Christian army home, and it was always
possible that the massive Crusader reinforcements rumored to be en route
would actually arrive. Ordering Francis's death would have only further
inflamed the Crusaders at a time when the sultan was trying to negotiate
peace.

As a stalwart Sunni Muslim who founded religious schools, al-Kamil
was not about to convert to Christianity. In listening to Francis, he was

honoring his faith's tradition of respect for holy Christian monks. He told Francis that his religious advisers had to be present.

According to James of Vitry, the sultan became very attentive as Francis preached to him and his followers. The bishop did not elaborate on this astonishingly peaceful scene of a monk preaching the Christian faith to the enemy's monarch in the middle of a war.

Later accounts, however, turned this scene into a potential battle to the death. In *The Chronicle of Ernoul* the unnamed "two clerics" respond to the sultan that if they fail to demonstrate with solid arguments that Islamic law is false, "then you can have our heads cut off." Under this scenario, the sultan's religious advisers were ushered into his tent. Once they found out that al-Kamil was going to let Francis preach, they warned him that this would violate Islamic law. "If there should be someone who wishes to preach or speak against our law, the law commands that his head be cut off," *The Chronicle of Ernoul* quotes them as saying. "It is for this reason that we command you, in the name of God and the law, that you have their heads cut off immediately, as the law demands."

The *Ernoul* chronicle, written within a decade after the Fifth Crusade, contains valuable details. But it is the rough work of an untutored warrior who did not even know Francis's name, much less what he stood for. Told through a warrior's eyes, it miscasts Francis as a willing combatant—a fellow soldier.

Bonaventure made the encounter even more confrontational. He wrote that Francis urged the sultan to build an enormous fire. "I will go into it with your priests. That will show you which faith is more sure and more holy," Francis supposedly said.

"I do not think that any of my priests would be willing to expose himself to the flames just to defend his faith, or suffer any kind of torture," the sultan was said to have replied. Francis supposedly offered to walk into the fire himself if the sultan and his people converted to Christianity, but the sultan refused that as well.

At this point we need to look closely at James of Vitry's account:

We have seen the founder and master of this Order, the one whom all the others obey as their superior general: he was a simple unlettered man, loved by God and men; he was called Brother Francis. Spiritual fervor and ecstasy moved him to such excesses that, having arrived at the army of the Christians before Damietta in Egypt, with no fear whatsoever, fortified solely with the "shield of faith," he set out for the camp of the sultan of Egypt. The Saracens arrested him on his way. "I am a Christian," he said; "bring me to your master!" And so they brought him to him. On seeing the man of God, the sultan, that cruel beast, became sweetness itself, kept him with him for a few days and with a great deal of attention listened to him preach the Faith of Christ to him and to his followers. But in the end he was afraid of seeing some of his soldiers whom the effective words of this man would have converted to the Lord go over to the army of the Christians. He, therefore, had Francis led back to our camp with many signs of honor and with security precautions, but not without saying to him: "Pray for me, that God may reveal to me the law and the faith that is more pleasing to him."

The French bishop had made a close study of Francis, his order, and the entire subject of converting Muslims. He was more than willing to portray Muslims as ogres but did not in this case. He also was willing to portray Francis as reckless but did not depict him as dangerously confrontational when encountering the sultan. He wrote shortly after the events took place. All of this makes his account more credible than the later ones, particularly Bonaventure's.

Under Bonaventure's scenario, Francis essentially proposed a trial by ordeal, a practice the Fourth Lateran Council had condemned in 1215. These trials had great appeal to the medieval mind. A defendant would submit to torture: walking across a fire or heated metal, or submerging an arm in boiling water. If he came through the ordeal without being seriously injured or killed, it was assumed that God had demonstrated his innocence.

This colorful scene of Francis standing beside a blazing fire, with a horrified Illuminato close by and the concerned sultan before him on a marble throne, is the enduring image of the encounter between saint and sultan. Giotto di Bondone, drawing on Bonaventure's life of Francis, painted it in works that appear in the Basilica of St. Francis in Assisi and in the Basilica of Santa Croce in Florence. Many other artists have followed suit.

While it made for great art, the scene is not historical. Even Bonaventure's account does not contend that a fire actually was burning—it says the sultan turned down Francis's suggestion to build a fire. Writing more than forty years after the event, Bonaventure was the first to claim that Francis had proposed this combat with the sultan's advisers. Such a colorful story would not have eluded Celano, the imaginative Henri d'Avranches, or other chroniclers writing closer to the event if it had had any basis in fact.

Furthermore, the violence of this proposed trial by ordeal contradicts everything Francis wrote and said about loving his enemies, the bedrock of his conversion from soldier to preacher of peace and penitence. Francis, the former soldier, was drawn from the early days of his conversion to a key verse in the Sermon on the Mount: "But I say to you, love your enemies, and pray for those who persecute you." He used it five times in the small collection of his known writings. He elaborated on it in his *Earlier Rule,* instructing:

> Remember the words of our Lord, Love your enemies, do good to those who hate you. Our Lord Jesus Christ himself, in whose footsteps we must follow, called the man who betrayed him his friend, and gave himself up of his own accord to his executioners. Therefore, our friends are those who for no reason cause us trouble and suffering, shame or injury, pain or torture, even martyrdom and death. It is these we must love, and love very much, because for all they do to us we are given eternal life.

Some experts believe this passage was a parting testament that Francis delivered before leaving for the East. It is the real voice of Francis, contradicting the one imposed in accounts written after his death. It is not the voice of a man who would have goaded his enemy to walk into fire. Furthermore, it is unlikely that Francis would have disobeyed the command of the Fourth Lateran Council by proposing a forbidden trial by ordeal.

While it may not be great history, Bonaventure's account of this scene serves a theological purpose. He depicted Francis as a new Elijah, a man of God who defeated the prophets of Baal by calling upon the Lord to ignite a fire beneath his sacrifice of a bull. The prophets of Baal, unable to do the same by calling on their pagan gods, were sent to their death after losing this competition with Elijah. That parallel appealed to Bonaventure, who cast Francis as a new messenger of the word of God. But Francis offered a different path that eluded Bonaventure; he wanted to approach the sultan and his advisers as friends.

While the challenge to an ordeal by fire conflicts with what is known about Francis, it does fit quite nicely as the mirror image to an important story that Muslims tell about how the Prophet Muhammad established relations with Christians. This story dates back to a time when Muhammad had been successful in bringing Islam to most of the Arabian Peninsula. He wrote a letter to leaders of the large Christian community in Najran, located in southern Arabia near Yemen, giving them the choice of either becoming Muslims or paying a special tax. A delegation of Christians traveled to Medina to meet with Muhammad and prayed with him in the mosque. They told the Prophet that they already were *muslims,* that is, people who had submitted to God. But Muhammad responded that they would have to change their belief that Jesus was divine and stop worshiping the cross if they were to call themselves by that name. Finally, Muhammad challenged the Christians to the *mubahala*—to meet at a designated place and pray that God's curse be called upon themselves if they were lying. The fearful Christians decided that if Muhammad brought his family to the showdown, it meant he was confident that he had God's favor and would prevail. When Muhammad did indeed show up with his family, including his daughter Fatima, the Christians of Najran quickly

Giotto di Bondone's *Saint Francis of Assisi before the Sultan* in the Basilica of Santa Croce in Florence is based on the dubious account in Bonaventure's *Major Legend of Saint Francis.* Note the sultan's aged religious adviser making his exit. *Copyright © Erich Lessing/Art Resource, New York*

refused to take the challenge and agreed to pay an annual tax. Versions of the story vary, but in one ancient account Muhammad was said to have commented that had the Christians accepted the challenge to call down God's curse, fire would have poured down on the valley where they lived.

In Bonaventure's account, Francis's actions paralleled those of Muhammad. The question, then, is whether Francis really did offer to walk through fire or whether it is a fiction that sprang up to meet some need at the time Bonaventure was writing *The Major Legend.* Given Francis's commitment to loving his enemies, it could not be a true story.

Similarly, some of the thirteenth-century accounts portray the sultan's religious advisers as bent on doing violence to Francis and Illuminato. This aggressive tone clashes with accounts of other incidents in which Muslim rulers were reluctant to execute Christians for preaching against Islam, doing so only when Christian preachers repeatedly forced the issue by deliberately assailing the name of the Prophet Muhammad. Those who were executed tended to be more interested in achieving martyrdom than in persuading an audience. The Islamic scholar Seyyed Hossein Nasr has said that in claiming the sultan's advisers wanted to execute Francis, *The Chronicle of Ernoul* picked up on an old theme: that a monarch himself was good but his advisers were evil.

The Christian chroniclers probably were exaggerating the Muslim religious leaders' reaction against Francis, since it would have taken a great deal of provocation for Muslim authorities to execute a Christian preacher. But possibly some of the sultan's supporters came on strong because they felt that al-Kamil had a track record for being too lenient with Christians. And of course, the fear that Francis and Illuminato were enemy agents in a war killing thousands upon thousands of their countrymen could have inflamed the sultan's advisers.

Bonaventure, having presented Francis's challenge to trial by ordeal, insisted that the sultan's advisers sneaked away to avoid the competition. He wrote that the sultan "caught a glimpse of one of his priests, an old and highly esteemed man, who slipped away the moment he heard Francis's proposal."

There was in fact an aged, highly esteemed holy man who advised Sultan al-Kamil on religious matters—Fakhr al-Farisi, a respected mystic and authority on the law. But al-Farisi was far from the type of adviser who would encourage the sultan to decapitate Christian preachers. The Persian-born al-Farisi was influenced by Sufism, a mystic approach to Islam known for its tolerance of other faiths. He followed the teachings of Mansur al-Hallaj, the great tenth-century ascetic, teacher, and poet of mystical union with God. Al-Hallaj, a Sufi born in Persia, was in many ways a Jesus-like figure, to the point that some accounts say the authorities crucified him in Baghdad in 922.

Three centuries later al-Farisi was known in Cairo as a defender of al-Hallaj and his legacy. As a powerful speaker who could evoke strong emotions, he had won the sultan's respect. The Sufi influence in the sultan's court was also reflected in al-Kamil's devotion to the verses of the famed

Sufi poet of love Ibn al-Farid. According to one story, the sultan was so taken with the mystical poet's work that he tried to lure him into his court by offering him a huge sum of money, which al-Farid refused.

"Al-Farid is the greatest Sufi poet of the Arabic language," says Seyyed Hossein Nasr. "...Any person who is a lover of al-Farid must have a very great love for God, and cannot be a ruthless person. The two cannot combine, unless the love of al-Farid is just a show."

Sufis were intrigued by Jesus; al-Farid, among others, wrote about him. Rather than focus on Muslims' opposition to the Christian understanding of Jesus as God, they tended to look at him more as a model for how to live. The Sufis viewed Jesus (or Isa in Arabic) as a wandering preacher dressed in a wool tunic, accompanied by John the Baptist. "The Sufis always had an openness to other religions," Nasr says, adding that they sometimes had Christian and Jewish disciples under their direction.

Francis's Christianity in many ways paralleled the Sufi interpretation of Islam. Both dwelt on sacred scriptures that emphasized God's transforming love and presence in the world. Both rejected worldliness in favor of ascetic poverty, repentance, and fasting. And both were orthodox, if unconventional. It should be stressed that Sufism was not some separate sect, but rather an influence within Islam.

The medieval Christian chronicles—and some modern commentators too—presented the sultan's kindly attitude toward Francis as a break with Islamic law. "I am going to act against the law, because I am never going to condemn you to death," *The Chronicle of Ernoul* quoted al-Kamil as telling Francis and Illuminato. "For that would be an evil reward for me to bestow on you, who conscientiously risked death in order to save my soul for God."

It doesn't ring true that al-Kamil, who established Islamic schools and was devoted to the memory of the great Sunni legal scholar Imam al-Shafi'i, would announce publicly his intent to violate the law. "He didn't see himself outside of his own religious tradition," says Fareed Z. Munir, a professor of religious studies at Siena College in New York State, who has studied the sultan's perspective on the encounter. "Actually, he saw himself as actively involved in his own religion by allowing for an audience for Saint Francis."

Influenced by Sufism, al-Kamil would have believed he was acting within Islamic law in listening to Francis and Illuminato, so long as they refrained from criticizing God or the Prophet Muhammad. The Qur'an does not prescribe or even refer to the death penalty for blasphemy, according to Mohammad Hashim Kamali, author of *Freedom of Expression in Islam* and a leading international expert on Islamic law. In a discussion on the law of blasphemy, Kamali cites two passages in the Qur'an that would suggest tolerance in the situation the sultan faced:

> And you shall certainly hear much that will insult you from those
> who received the Scripture before you and from the polytheists. But
> if you persevere patiently and guard against evil, this will be the best
> course with which to determine your affairs.

And:

> Among the followers of the Book, many would wish that they could
> turn you back to infidelity after you have believed—because of their
> envy after the truth is manifest to them. But forgive and overlook
> until God accomplishes His purpose.

With a prominent Sufi as his religious adviser, al-Kamil would have seen the friar in the light of his interest in Sufism and the Muslim tradition calling for respect for Christian monks. In their rough, patched tunics, Francis and Illuminato would even have looked like Sufis, since the very name of the Muslim holy men came from the Arab word for wool, the scratchy material used to make their robes. Like Francis, they also wore a cord rather than a belt. Perhaps the appearance of these scruffy wanderers reminded al-Kamil of what he had heard about Jesus and John the Baptist. So as James of Vitry wrote, the sultan and his court listened attentively to Francis.

———

Francis was a dynamic preacher. Rather than imitate the logical, analytical style of argument taught to priests, he came across like the fiery street-corner orators who held court in the piazzas of the politically charged Assisi of his youth. He preached from the heart. Thomas of Celano gave an engaging account of how he addressed learned people such as the sultan and his advisers:

> Although the evangelist Francis preached to the unlearned people through visible and simple things, in as much as he knew that virtue is more necessary than words, nevertheless among spiritual men and men of greater capacity he spoke enlivening and profound words. He would suggest in a few words what was beyond expression, and using fervent gestures and nods, he would transport his hearers wholly to heavenly things. He did not make use of the keys of philosophical distinctions; he did not put order to his sermons, for he did not compose them ahead of time.

Celano wrote that Francis spoke to crowds of thousands as confidently as if he were speaking to a close friend, and to individuals with the fervor he showed to a mass of people. Sultan al-Kamil would no doubt have enjoyed his style of preaching, but theirs was likely at least a two-way conversation rather than the solo performance the Christian chroniclers describe. Al-Kamil was fond of such exchanges; he enjoyed debate with the group of learned men with whom he sat every Friday night. He lodged Muslim sages and grammarians in the Citadel, his residence and fortress in Cairo, just so they would be available. He even set up beds so that they could converse with him in the night on law, language, and religion. And so the sultan and his followers probably parried with Francis in much this same style. Even some of the Christian accounts hint of a give-and-take rather than a one-way conversation with Francis doing all the talking. "With great steadiness he withstood the sultan and with great eloquence he neutralized the arguments of those railing against the Christian faith," Julian of Speyer wrote in the 1230s. The contemporary concept of interreligious dialogue didn't exist at the time, but this was nonetheless a dialogue—a peaceful exchange of ideas about two competing religions.

In a tent populated with brilliant, sophisticated religious thinkers and poets, Francis held his own. So much we can infer from James of Vitry, who noted that the discussions went on for several days, a good indication that the conversation had multiple participants. Unfortunately, we have no detailed record of the historic exchange. What can be said for sure is that in the worst of times, a Christian and a prominent Muslim engaged in reasoned public discussion about their religious differences.

And for at least several days and possibly longer, Francis and Illuminato were treated as honored guests in the Muslim camp. As James of Vitry wrote, they were even permitted to preach to the Muslim soldiers. He mentioned this in passing, but it is astonishing. While Cardinal Pelagius and the Christian military leaders a few miles to the north were busy building weapons of war for the next assault—and while Muslim troops prepared their own attacks on the Christian camp to which the two friars would return—Francis and the enemy soldiers were treating one another like friends. Perhaps even more surprising is that the sultan and his military leaders would let the persuasive, engaging Francis anywhere near their troops. One wonders if the sultan thought it might help build a consensus for peace in his own ranks if his military leaders saw a more human side to the enemy.

Francis had ample time to view Muslim religious practices, especially the call to prayer. His later writings give evidence that he was deeply impressed to see the soldiers stop their work, face southeast toward Mecca, and prostrate themselves before God. According to Seyyed Hossein Nasr, a story has circulated orally among Muslims that the sultan gave Francis the key to his private prayer room.

That Francis was able to preach for several days or longer implies that he dwelled on subjects that Islam and Christianity have in common and avoided direct criticism of Muhammad or Islam. James of Vitry wrote that Muslims listened to friars who came to the East willingly, so long as they did not dishonor Muhammad in their preaching. When they did charge that Muhammad was evil, the bishop of Acre wrote, they barely escaped with their lives. Francis, on a mission of peace, evidently took the peaceful path.

The few details recorded of the back-and-forth between Francis and al-Kamil are unreliable. One story says that al-Kamil challenged Francis about why the Christians invaded Muslim lands when the Bible quotes Jesus as telling them not to pay back evil for evil. He may well have raised that issue, but Francis's supposed response is not feasible. According to the story, he responded that the invasion was justified because "you blaspheme the name of Christ and alienate everyone you can from his worship," adding that if the sultan recognized Jesus as redeemer, "Christians would love you as themselves." The story was attributed to Bonaventure, who in turn was said to have learned of it from Illuminato. But if Francis really said this quote, it means he didn't believe his own writings about loving his enemies. The quote advocates eradicating Muslims for blasphemy— whereas the sultan had protected Francis from any penalty under Islamic law. It also advocates forced conversion—the antithesis of Francis's attempt to emulate Jesus by sending out his unprotected brothers, two by two, on mission. The fact that this quote was circulated some four decades or so after Francis's death demonstrates that the saint's ideas about nonviolent relations with Muslims were soon to be edited out of the story and disregarded even within his order.

An accompanying story claims that the sultan set before Francis a carpet with images of crosses on it, then invited him to walk across it and approach him. Francis was given a choice of disrespecting the sultan or the cross. According to this story, Francis walked across the carpet, then said: "Thieves were also crucified along with our Lord. We have the true Cross of our Lord and Savior Jesus Christ; we adore it and show it great devotion; if the holy Cross of the Lord has been given to us, the cross of the thieves has been left to you as your share. That is why I had no scruple in walking over the symbols of brigands."

The comment is interesting in light of the fact that part of the peace negotiations between al-Kamil and the Christian leaders concerned the return of the chunk of the True Cross that Saladin's soldiers confiscated in their victory in 1187. There was concern in the Christian camp that al-Kamil did not really have this piece of the True Cross, and Francis's comment appears to reflect that. Whether this scene—supposedly provided by Illuminato some forty years after the fact, well after he contributed anecdotes to other collections of stories on Francis—actually occurred is difficult to judge. If it did, it suggests a certain level of gamesmanship in the exchange with Francis that the sultan might have encouraged.

Before Francis's departure, the sultan offered him lavish gifts. This seems to have been the sultan's way of showing appreciation to those he admired. As noted earlier, one story has it that he offered a thousand dinars to his favorite poet, Ibn al-Farid, and even wanted to allow the Sufi mystic writer to be buried in the domed mausoleum he built for the legal scholar Imam al-Shafi'i—the same burial place where al-Kamil laid to rest his mother. The poet declined, further stimulating the sultan's admiration for him.

So it is not surprising that al-Kamil offered his largesse to this Christian Sufi—perhaps as a test of sorts to see if Francis was genuine. According to Thomas of Celano, the sultan offered him many gifts, trying "to bend Francis' mind toward the riches of the world. But when he saw that Francis most vigorously despised all these things as so much dung, he was filled with the greatest admiration, and he looked upon him as a man different from all others." *The Chronicle of Ernoul* said the gifts Francis turned down included "great quantities of gold, silver, and silk garments." Bonaventure wrote that al-Kamil persisted, urging Francis to accept the gifts for the Christian poor or churches. But Francis would not accept them even on that basis.

The idea that Francis rejected the sultan's wealth appealed greatly to the early Franciscan writers, and as a result some experts have dismissed this scene as fanciful. Surely the sultan was able to tell, if only from Francis's shabby appearance, that he was not interested in acquiring precious metals. But in extending this offer, al-Kamil gave the rest of his court a visible sign of his approval for Francis. "He wanted to offer the saint silver and gold to show a part of his appreciation for the man's holiness and poverty," says Mahmoud Ayoub, a scholar of Islam at Temple University who is a leading expert on Christian-Muslim relations.

Francis did, however, apparently agree to accept a token of their extraordinary meeting: an ivory horn, which is now displayed in a room of relics accessible through the lower level of the Basilica of St. Francis in Assisi. Such horns were used to announce battle or other major events. According to an inscription later added to the horn, Francis used it to call people to hear him preach.

The Christian accounts insist that Francis had deeply affected Sultan al-Kamil. This notion tended to be exaggerated over the years as writers embellished on the earlier versions. Thomas of Celano, the first Franciscan to write of the encounter, said simply that the sultan "was deeply moved by his words and he listened to him very willingly." Jordan of Giano, a Franciscan chronicler, wrote that Francis was "honorably received" and "treated kindly" but gave no further indication of how the sultan reacted except to note that Francis "could not harvest any fruit." Bonaventure gilded the story in his *Major Legend of Saint Francis,* quoting al-Kamil as saying he dared not convert to Christianity because his people would revolt. In a sermon he preached in Paris on the Feast of St. Francis, October 4, 1267, he went even further. After telling the story of how Francis offered to walk through fire to prove the truth of Christianity, Bonaventure added that the sultan replied that he was afraid to convert. "I could not dare do that, for fear my people would stone me," Bonaventure quoted him as saying. "But I believe that your faith is good and true." Bonaventure then added: "And from that moment the Christian faith was imprinted on his heart." Subsequent accounts, to be described later, elaborated further with fanciful claims that al-Kamil converted to Christianity on his deathbed.

This is hagiography, devoted to showing Francis as miracle worker, and should not be taken as a historical record. Perhaps the hagiographers should have been content with the miracle that Francis and Sultan al-Kamil had found a way of talking peacefully in the middle of a gruesome war. For that was the real wonder of their encounter. In a letter home James of Vitry treated his readers to a surprising exchange between the feared enemy monarch and the zealous friar: "The Sultan, the ruler of Egypt, privately asked him to pray to the Lord for him, so that he might be inspired by God to adhere to that religion which most pleased God."

The early Franciscan accounts say that Francis was disappointed not to have converted the sultan, and that must be true. By the time he was ready to leave the sultan's camp, there would have been signs that the fighting was going to resume. His attempt to achieve reconciliation by preaching a gospel of peace was on the way to failure. It was time for the sultan to send Francis and Illuminato away.

On one level, the remark James of Vitry recorded reads as if al-Kamil privately expressed belief in the Christian God and wanted Francis to pray to that deity in his behalf. In that sense, the remark might have consoled Francis in his disappointment. But a closer look shows that al-Kamil was praying the prayer of every good Muslim: that he would do God's will.

This intriguing close to their days of discussion is difficult to assess because James of Vitry was a fervent advocate of the Crusade and a scathing critic of Muslim beliefs. But the comment does ring true because the sultan is heard to remark that he hoped to do what pleased God. The Dutch scholar Jan Hoeberichts ties this remark to the widespread use in the Arab world of the phrase *inshallah,* or "God willing." The sultan's authentic voice is heard in this passage that the Crusade preacher wrote. It is sophisticated, subtle, and filled with respect—and even love—for Francis. Al-Kamil had seen the worst face of Christianity: the face of invaders pressing forward, wielding the True Cross like a weapon, even after a reasonable peace had been offered. He knew the avarice of the Christian merchants with whom he once negotiated trade treaties and who now hoped to seize a city where they had found business to be profitable. Francis had shown Sultan al-Kamil what it meant to be a true Christian, a holy person who truly believed Jesus' call to love the enemy. As the Qur'an states:

> They are not all alike. Of the People of the Scripture there is a
> staunch community who recite the revelations of God in the night

season, falling prostrate (before Him). They believe in God and the Last Day, and enjoin right conduct and forbid indecency, and vie with one another in good works. These are the righteous . . . God is Aware of those who ward off [evil].

It would have been scandalous for Christians if one of their chroniclers wrote that the sultan had a similar influence on the saint. Instead, the Christian accounts mostly present a businesslike Francis who insisted on going back to the Crusader camp when he couldn't complete the desired transaction, whether it was his martyrdom or the sultan's conversion. But as time passed, Francis would reveal himself in writings and comments that reflected his respect—and even love—for the sultan.

While the Crusaders would not accept Jerusalem from the sultan in a peace treaty, al-Kamil granted Francis and his brothers the right to go there to visit the Holy Sepulcher without paying tribute. Sultan al-Kamil then dispatched Francis and Illuminato to the Christian camp under his protection. Muslim soldiers returned the two friars reverently, "with many signs of honor," as James of Vitry wrote.

But before leaving, Francis told the sultan that while he would not accept his gold, silver, or silk, he would take a meal. It is a strange request coming from Francis, who had no problem with going hungry. But Francis must have had something else in mind besides slaking his hunger before the trip back to the Crusader camp. He always tried to imitate Jesus, who sought to realize the kingdom of heaven on earth through table fellowship—by dining with people society despised. "The Sultan gave them plenty of food to eat," according to *Ernoul*.

Given how attentive and hospitable the sultan had been over an extended period of time, he likely took part in the meal instead of merely catering it. Such hospitality is traditional in Egypt. It is not surprising that other Christian accounts failed to pick up on this meal. Years later Cardinal Ugolino, by then elevated to the papacy as Gregory IX, castigated Emperor Frederick II for the offense of eating sociably with Muslim leaders. This scene of Francis peacefully breaking bread at a banquet with Sultan Malik al-Kamil, his supposed enemy, could not differ more from the fictitious image that has come down through the ages to capture their encounter: two tense antagonists separated by a threatening bonfire. Their meal ought to have been the enduring image of the encounter between the saint and the sultan, painted in bright colors on cathedral walls.

14

"Evil and Sin"

The attack came swiftly after Francis returned to the Crusader camp.

On September 26, 1219, Sultan Malik al-Kamil launched a squadron of galleys that drifted north on the Nile to deposit waves of soldiers outside the Christians' compound. The Muslim forces set up mangonels that lifted huge rocks into the Crusader camp. They rolled tree trunks forward to fill the deep trench that had stymied their past attacks on the Christians. The Crusaders had used the month-long truce to build up their ramparts, but the Muslim troops attacked "with their usual barbaric ferocity and violence," Oliver of Paderborn wrote. When newly arrived French troops who had just debarked from ten armed Genoese galleys stood their ground, the sultan's men were forced to withdraw. After that al-Kamil took increasingly desperate steps to free the dying people of Damietta. He advanced yet another peace proposal; he bribed Christian soldiers; and on the night of November 3 he sneaked several hundred men, carrying food and provisions, through the marshes in an attempt to get supplies into the city.

Cardinal Pelagius readied his final assault on Damietta, its tripled walls and twenty-eight towers intact despite months of bombardment and the deaths of most of the garrison to disease. Scouts sent ahead of the troops found a people in ruin; they were able to cross the city's moats, burn their way through wooden gates, and scale the walls without being opposed. The city's disease-ridden residents looked on as the intruders raised the Crusader flag on a tower, carrying out what once had seemed a mission impossible.

The next day more Crusaders scaled the walls and arrived triumphantly in the city, facing no opposition. According to Roger of Wendover, the Christian soldiers

> found the streets strewed with the corpses of the dead, and were met by an intolerable stench from them and the most squalid-looking human beings. The dead had killed the living; husband and wife, father and son, master and servant, had perished from the stench of one another. And it was not only the streets which were full of the dead, for corpses were lying about in houses and bedchambers; boys and children had asked for bread, and there was no one to break it for them; infants hanging at the breasts of their mothers were rolling over the bodies of the dead; the pampered rich died of hunger.

Francis entered Damietta, but we have no record of how he reacted to the inhumanity of this macabre scene—a city of eighty thousand in which three thousand survivors remained, lingering near death. We can only imagine how such horrors would have affected a man who grieved even over the fate of fish, birds, and worms. It is unlikely that he would have shared the triumphalism of the Crusade chronicler Oliver of Paderborn, who wrote that God himself had taken the city: "Damietta was captured without treachery, without resistance, without violent pillage and tumult, so that the victory may be ascribed to the Son of God alone."

Arab chronicles contradict Oliver's version of the conquest. Abu Shama, a thirteenth-century teacher and historian from Damascus, wrote in *The Book of the Two Gardens* that Damietta's residents had negotiated an agreement with the Crusaders after finally concluding that Sultan al-Kamil would be unable to save them. The pact, reached in the presence of

Christian priests, would have allowed residents to leave with whatever belongings they could carry. Without respect for their sworn oath, Abu Shama wrote, the Crusaders raped women in the night and massacred or enslaved the inhabitants at will. The sheikh at the city's grand mosque, Abou'l-Hassan, widely respected for his virtue, charity, and devotion to the poor, was left unscathed and lived to tell Abu Shama the story of Damietta's fall.

The History of the Patriarchs of the Egyptian Church portrayed the fall of Damietta as a terrible embarrassment to Sultan al-Kamil, who did not know that the city had surrendered until his soldiers encamped near the Nile saw crosses and the Crusaders' flags erected on the mighty towers. The chronicle noted there were conflicting reports on the number of survivors, and indicated that those who didn't flee—primarily the common people—were captured.

Disease continued killing residents who had survived the siege and the city's capture. James of Vitry, as the bishop of Acre, baptized many infants—but noted that more than five hundred of them "passed to the Lord" after receiving the sacrament. Most of the captured soldiers, he said, were sold into slavery because it was too expensive to feed them.

The Crusaders had sworn under penalty of excommunication that the spoils taken from Damietta would be divided among the victors. Greed won out, and only a small portion of the goods fleeced from the coveted trading port—gold, silver, silk, expensive clothing, pearls, amber, gold thread—was ever turned in to be redistributed. "The greediness of the eyes made many thieves," Roger of Wendover wrote.

While the early Franciscan biographers did not sully the popes' war by depicting the Christian soldiers' debauchery in Damietta, the French Crusader chronicle *L'Estoire de Eracles Empereur* spoke volumes about Francis's intense dismay in a few swift sentences. Written shortly after he was canonized in 1228, it noted that "Brother Francis . . . came into the crusaders' camp of Damietta, performed many good works and remained till the city was captured. He saw how evil and sin started to increase among the people at the camp and detested it." The chronicler contrasted Francis's virtue with the sinful behavior of the Crusaders in Christian-controlled Damietta, which included robbery, larceny, and murder. Once the city was taken, the Crusaders' refrain seemed to be "We have no more need of God's help," the chronicler complained.

While Francis was repulsed by what he saw, church officialdom rejoiced in the victory. Pelagius enjoyed the pope's support more than ever. Honorius likened him to Joshua, for whom the walls of Jericho tumbled down. Meanwhile, *Eracles* added, the hatred between John of Brienne and Cardinal Pelagius grew. They squabbled over whether Damietta should be added to John's kingdom of Jerusalem, as he insisted, or come under papal jurisdiction. This led to open warfare in the streets of Damietta, with Italian Crusaders contending that John of Brienne and the French had stolen away their fair share of the city. The official dedication of a cathedral to the Blessed Virgin—previously the home of Egypt's second oldest mosque, built nearly six centuries before—had to wait until February 2, 1220, while a semblance of peace was restored.

Francis most likely stayed for that event and prayed in the newly dedicated church, a grand structure that had 170 white marble columns that supported arch-covered passages edging a large open courtyard. Pointed arches made of brick lined the top of the thirty-one-inch-thick exterior walls. Pathways were made of marble cut into small, angular white and gray pieces and set strikingly against a black background. The Crusaders built altars dedicated to the Virgin Mary, Saint Peter, the Holy Cross, and Saint Bartholomew, who was honored because the enemy's tower on the Nile had been captured on his feast day. A brick tower that had served as the mosque's minaret rose more than a hundred feet above it all.

During this time Francis founded a small convent in Damietta. Although there was ample opportunity to preach to the Muslims who survived the siege of Damietta, Francis, shaken after seeing the devils of greed and violence seize control of men who had pledged themselves to the cross, wanted no part of it. He left soon after the church was dedicated, as quickly as the winds and weather allowed.

An account from the fourteenth century said that the sultan had given Francis the right to preach to Muslims and free passage to visit the holy places in Jerusalem. Although far from certain, it is quite possible that he took advantage of this gift from the sultan to visit the Church of the Holy Sepulcher in Jerusalem. But this visit is noted only in the writings of Angelo Clareno, a friar who wrote *A Chronicle or History of the Seven Tribulations of the Order of Brothers Minor* in the 1320s, more than a century after Francis left Damietta. It's hard to accept that he alone picked up on such an important moment in Francis's life while all of the accounts from the previous century missed it. The earlier Franciscan biographers had duly noted Francis's pilgrimages to the tombs of Saint Peter and Saint James. Why would they leave out Francis's reaction to Christianity's most revered shrine?

There is a plausible explanation that makes Angelo Clareno's version worth considering, even if it cannot be confirmed. In 1217 Pope Honorius III had barred Christians, under pain of excommunication, from visiting any shrines under Muslim control. He specifically forbade visits to the Holy Sepulcher, and he had his missive posted at the major ports where pilgrims departed for the Holy Land. So it is unlikely that the earlier accounts, which were aimed at establishing Francis's standing as a saint, would have mentioned that he visited Jerusalem. Angelo Clareno, a Franciscan dissident embittered at what he saw as the order's departure from the founder's ideals, was willing to include such a tradition.

Francis eventually arrived in Acre, a Crusader stronghold that was a sort of Wild West of the East. Its bishop, James of Vitry, wrote that the city had more than its share of murderers, robbers, pirates, whoremongers, apostate monks, "nuns that are common harlots," women who left husbands and lived in brothels, and men who ran from faithful wives and took others. "Wicked people such as these in the West crossed the Mediterranean Sea, and took refuge in the Holy Land, where, as they had only changed their climate and not their character, they defiled it by numberless crimes and shameful deeds," he wrote, adding that some were exiled to Acre as an alternative to a criminal sentence. James denounced the local clergy as corrupt men who came to blows in the streets, and complained that even the nuns were disobedient to their superiors.

Francis appears to have spent several months in Acre, preaching occasionally in Christian-controlled areas. He also was trying to recuperate from illness, having developed a painful eye infection that would slowly destroy his vision.

During these months in Acre the jarring news reached Francis that five of the six brothers he had dispatched to Morocco at the chapter meeting in 1219 had been beheaded because of their preaching there. Illness had forced the leader of the group, Brother Vitale, to drop out of the mission in Spain. Brother Berard, an Umbrian nobleman whom Francis had brought into the order in 1213, had learned some Arabic and taken the lead in preaching to Muslims. The brothers were ejected from Seville, which was then under Muslim control, and were sent by Muslim authorities to Sultan Abu-Jacob in Morocco. After the monarch released them to an influential local Christian, the friars once again preached in public. Upon catching Berard in the act, the sultan had the five brothers arrested and shipped to the port city of Ceuta, to be sent home. Once there the friars managed to return and continue preaching. Sultan Abu-Jacob turned the men over to a powerful local Christian, Dom Pedro, a leader in the sultan's army. Dom Pedro was eager to quiet the controversy and avoid touching off persecution of the Christian population. But he couldn't control the friars, who again preached in public, choosing a spot where they thought the sultan would pass. They got their wish for martyrdom. After defying their judge by continuing to preach, the friars were tortured. The sultan himself beheaded them on January 16, 1220. The five martyrs—Berard, Peter, Adjuto, Accursio, and Otto—would be canonized in 1481.

Francis grieved at the loss of these young men but had mixed feelings about their insistence on being martyred. While he valued their devotion, he knew that the brothers had confronted a Muslim ruler in a way he had avoided: they had approached an enemy more as provocateurs than as friends. Perhaps Francis recalled that before they left, the young men had spoken of their fears and lack of preparation. In a tearful scene the brothers had wished aloud that Francis would go with them. Had Francis gone to Morocco rather than to Egypt, the five brothers would not have been permitted to pursue such an insistently self-destructive course. Francis realized he needed to do more to teach his brothers about how to evangelize in non-Christian lands.

During this time Francis got more disturbing news. While he was sitting down to dinner with his friend Peter of Catania, Stephen, a lay brother, arrived as a surprise guest from home. Embarrassed and apologetic, Stephen spilled out the story of why he had ventured all the way from Italy without permission from a superior.

Back home, he said, rumors were rampant that Francis had died in the Crusade. Stephen didn't believe it. He wanted Francis to know that during his absence terrible changes were being made in the order—disturbing enough for Stephen to bring the news directly to Francis in the East. The vicars Francis had appointed, Matthew of Narni and Gregory of Naples, had tampered with the order's *Rule,* challenging Francis's basic beliefs concerning poverty and humility. They had allowed houses to be built for the brothers, violating Francis's rule that the order own no property. Furthermore, the brothers would use a new building in Bologna as a place of study, challenging Francis's insistence that the order not be turned into a scholarly monastic community.

Another of Francis's principles was trampled when one of the brothers, Philip, persuaded the pope to allow critics of the Poor Ladies—the order Clare of Assisi began after she embraced Francis's life of poverty—to be excommunicated. Francis opposed seeking such privileges from church authorities. To make matters worse, the vicars also tampered with the *Rule* by requiring further fasting from meat, an extra penance possibly imposed on the friars to mitigate the decision to begin acquiring property for the order.

The news probably didn't surprise Francis. Even before he had sailed for Egypt, he had been losing control of the growing order. If what Brother Stephen said was true, the Friars Minor was fast turning into a standard-issue religious order. This only increased Francis's fear that the friars would be more susceptible to the temptations of money and power.

Stephen unfurled the new rules that had been legislated in recent months. Francis read them as dinner was placed before him. Jordan of Giano noted in his chronicle that Francis was about to eat meat, thus violating the new rule adopted in his absence. "My lord Peter, what shall we do?" Francis asked Peter of Catania, questioning whether they should eat the meat set before them or obey the new rule that forbade it. Peter reminded Francis that he was the boss: "Ah, my lord Francis, whatever pleases you, for you have the authority." There was a pause, then Francis said, "Let us then eat, according to the Gospel, what has been placed before us."

According to a chronicle written in the 1270s by Brother Thomas of Pavia, a former Franciscan provincial minister in Tuscany who as a young man had met Brother Stephen, Brother Philip's gambit to control the fate of Clare's monasteries incensed Francis. "When the blessed Francis learned of this, he . . . cursed Philip as a destroyer of the Order," Thomas wrote. "Indeed, Brother Stephen said that he had heard Saint Francis pronounce these words: 'Until now the ulcer has been confined to the flesh and so there remained a hope for a cure; but now it has penetrated to the bone and it will surely be incurable.'"

Ailing and angry, disappointed by the evil of the Crusaders at Damietta and by the doings of his brothers in Italy, thwarted in his attempt to make peace by converting the sultan, Francis hastened home. He still had much to say.

The Outsider

S ailing into the most frustrating years of his life, Francis arrived amid the canals of Venice in the spring or summer of 1220. In the months and years that followed, he found himself more and more marginalized within the order he founded. Powerful and learned men such as Cardinal Ugolino had begun to organize and reshape the Order of Friars Minor, positioning it to grow dramatically. We need not consider the historical debate over whether Ugolino acted with good intentions or deliberately compromised Francis's vision—he may have done both. The point is that Francis, having lost control of the order during his absence, lacked the full authority to act on the insights he gained during his trip to the East. He harbored dramatic new plans for sending out friars to live peacefully among Muslims, but he had trouble getting his order to remain true even to the essentials of his vision for it. He had become an outsider.

Leaving Venice, Francis traveled west to Verona and then headed south to Bologna. He learned that a new building in the university city was known as the "house of the brothers"—that is, it was owned by the brothers in violation of Francis's explicit warning against possessing worldly goods. Francis ordered the house closed immediately. "Not even the sick remained but were cast out with the others," Thomas of Celano wrote, adding that the person who told him the story was among the sick people who were ejected.

Angelo Clareno, who stressed Francis's anger at the changes in the order, later told a more detailed story that he said came from a brother who saw Francis preach in Bologna. In that account, Francis headed straight for the place where his brothers lived and saw that a house had been built that violated the level of poverty he expected from his brothers. Francis quickly walked away and went to stay at the house of Dominic's Order of Preachers, which had established itself in the university center so that members could become better educated. Given the competition between the two orders, it was a great rebuke for Francis's friars. One of Dominic's men, Clareno went on to say, told Francis that his brothers were despondent and tried to convince him to return, giving them a chance to repent. After some coaxing Francis agreed, only to wind up cursing a highly respected brother and doctor of law, Brother Pietro Stacia, whose teachings contradicted the purity of the order's *Rule*. Francis was so angered that he refused to pardon the friar even years later, according to this account.

The evicted brothers appealed to Cardinal Ugolino, who happened to be in the region at the time, probably trying to drum up more troops for the Crusade. Ugolino provided a detour around Francis's objections by declaring that he, and not the brothers, owned the building; the friars' vow of poverty had not been broken. He made the announcement while preaching in public, a not-so-subtle way of telling Francis from the authority of the pulpit that he had to back off. The friars had the cardinal's permission to return. The future pope knew the way to power. In short order, Ugolino showed the friars, the public, and Francis who was in charge.

Despondent, Francis made his way back to Assisi to call a special chapter meeting in September 1220. He was amazed, according to one account, to find that a large house of stone and mortar had been built close to the Portiuncula, the little Chapel of St. Mary of the Angels, in his absence. The people of Assisi had constructed it in a well-intentioned effort to help the friars, who slept beneath straw roofs in huts made of branches and mud. Francis was outraged—the humble Portiuncula was supposed to embody the simple, apostolic life of poverty he wanted for his brothers. During the chapter meeting he climbed to the tiled roof and ordered other brothers to join him in destroying it. They were heaving tiles to the ground when some knights and officials from the commune of Assisi arrived and asked him to stop. Trying to assuage the incensed Francis, they told him that the local government owned the house, not the order. Francis relented, having demonstrated his anger.

In another affront, a week before the chapter meeting Pope Honorius III had issued a bull that required newcomers to the Friars Minor to serve a year in novitiate before professing their final vows—one more step toward reining in the order's free-spirited ways. More and more, Francis's roughly drawn plans were being redrafted.

Angry, frustrated, and disappointed, Francis, who always had a knack for the dramatic, gave up his position as head of the Friars Minor. "From now on I am dead to you," he told the brothers assembled at the Portiuncula. He presented Peter of Catania to them as their new leader and bowed to him to show his obedience. His anger during this time was featured with particular prominence in some of the later accounts. According to the fourteenth-century *Mirror of Perfection,* Francis, feeling ill, sat up in his sickbed after relinquishing his leadership post and cried out: "Who are these who have torn my Order and my friars out of my hands? If I come to the General Chapter, I will make my intention clear!"

The heat of his anger continued to burn in the chill of December, when Brother Stephen found that Francis still had not cooled off about Philip's attempt to commandeer the cloistered Poor Ladies. (Cardinal Ugolino helped Francis in this instance by getting the pope to rescind the privilege Francis opposed.) Francis and Stephen were on a journey in Umbria when Stephen spilled the fact that while Francis was in the East, he had gone to one of Clare's monasteries on Brother Philip's order. Francis was outraged; he had insisted that the brothers avoid any role in the Poor Ladies. Stephen had not acknowledged in Acre that he played a part in the scheme. Stephen begged for forgiveness, but Francis required repentance as well. He ordered him to dive, clothed, into a river on the roadside. Stephen did so, then emerged from the water wet and shivering in the December cold and walked another two miles with Francis to their destination.

Ill, shunted aside, and frazzled by his exposure to so much violence and death in Egypt, Francis suffered in a way he hadn't in years. He wrestled with "a most serious temptation of the spirit," a recurring sadness that Thomas of Celano wrote left Francis "filled with sorrows" for several years. Separating himself from the other brothers, he prayed and meditated, trying to overcome his gloominess.

Francis is often depicted as a merry jester, but there were some long shadows in his life, dating back to his imprisonment in Perugia. He once told a companion: "If the brothers knew how many trials the demons cause me, there would not be one of them who would not have great pity and compassion for me."

It was a poor time for Francis to announce the insights he had gained into Islam. But although occupied with the battle within his order and slowed by a melancholy that made him feel far from God, Francis still pondered the meaning of his visit to Sultan al-Kamil. He may have left the East, but it had not left him. Feeling like a stranger at home, he longed to go back. According to the chronicle of Richer of Sens, a Benedictine monk in northern France who wrote in the late 1250s and early 1260s, Francis had hoped to return to the East after securing permission from the sultan to preach. "But because it is not proper to the laborer or traveler, but to the will of God to direct the course of a person, he was detained by some obstacle or other and did not return," the monk wrote.

Isolated within his own order and too ill to return to Egypt, Francis turned to writing letters and a new *Rule.* One of his most interesting documents, known as *A Letter to the Rulers of the People,* was written "to all magistrates and consuls, to all judges and governors all over the world and to everyone else who receives this letter." He started the letter with much the same message he'd had one of his brothers deliver years earlier to Emperor Otto IV, when he passed by their hovel outside Assisi: "Consider and realize that the day of death is approaching." With the deaths he'd seen in Egypt still fresh in his mind, Francis called on the world's rulers to repent for their sins. It was a blunt message, but he was courteous as he entreated members of the ruling class to change their ways: "I therefore beg of you with all the respect I am capable of that you do not forget God or swerve from his commandments because of the cares and anxieties of this world which you have to shoulder. For all who forget him and turn away from his commandments shall be forgotten by him."

Here Francis reiterates the idea that led him to object to the Crusade before the catastrophic battle on August 29, 1219: the Christian rulers were not doing God's will. A year later Francis's view had not changed. In a new letter he switched from directly addressing the world's rulers to speaking about them in the third person: "When the day of death comes, all that they thought their own will be taken away from them. The more wisdom and power they enjoyed in this life, the greater the torments they will have to endure in hell." After that jeremiad Francis instructed sinful rulers to repent. The first step was to receive the Eucharist, which in itself would have required them to be free of serious sin. He followed with an extraordinary request:

> See to it that God is held in great reverence among your subjects;
> every evening, at a signal given by a herald or in some other way,
> praise and thanks should be given to the Lord God almighty by all
> the people.

Francis was obviously taken by the *adhan,* the call that he heard when soldiers in the sultan's camp were summoned five times a day to turn toward Mecca in prayer. He was not content simply to admire this practice; he wanted to bring that same intensity of devotion to the Christian world. Just as Muslims listen for the call of a muezzin, Francis wanted Christians to await a signal from a "herald." He was insistent, telling the rulers, "If you refuse to see to this, you can be sure that you will be held to account for it at the day of judgment before Jesus Christ, your Lord and God."

Francis was no stranger to periodic prayer throughout the day. What impressed him, then, were the universality and the public nature of the Muslim prayer. The world could be transformed if all people submitted to God's will, and Francis saw a seed for that in the prostrate Muslim soldiers, his supposed enemy. The most extraordinary aspect of the letter is not that a Muslim prayer practice impressed Francis, but that he sought to create parallel prayer routines of praise and thanksgiving in the Christian and Muslim worlds. Late in his life, in a letter to be read at a general chapter meeting of the order, he wrote, "At the sound of his name you should fall to the ground and adore him with fear and reverence." Francis's words reflected his ardent desire to transform the world by converting not only Muslims but his fellow Christians as well. If all the world's people bowed peacefully in prayer, Francis was saying, the new era of peace could not be far off, *inshallah*.

This was not a fleeting idea for Francis; he sounded the same theme in a letter to the heads of his order's provinces. He wanted the custodians, as these ministers began to be called, to remind people in every sermon of the importance of receiving the Eucharist. And he told them: "May you announce and preach His praise to all nations in such a way that praise and thanks may always be given to the all-powerful God by all people throughout the world at every hour and whenever bells are rung." This wish seems to have been based on the Muslim prayer practices Francis witnessed in Egypt; an otherwise similar letter he wrote before going to Egypt, known as *Exhortations to the Clergy,* did not ask priests to arrange such prayers. He also was determined to see his vision realized, invoking "holy obedience" in his letter to the order's custodians to command that they carry out his wishes.

Francis's order buried these letters, which did not surface until long after the saint's image was sculpted. The missive to the world's rulers was not discovered until the seventeenth century, when Luke Wadding, a Franciscan historian, found it. Paul Sabatier, the French Protestant historian who modernized the study of Francis, found the letter to the custodians in 1902. Despite the importance these letters held for Francis, his early biographers made no mention of the saint's call for universal public prayer. It did not matter that Francis directed that the letters be widely dispersed. That was not done: the letters were evidently an embarrassment to the order.

I n the midst of writing a new version of the *Rule* in 1221—later known as the *Earlier Rule*—Francis remained under strong pressure from disgruntled brothers to change the order's direction and adopt the more comfortable trappings of monastic life. Compounding the problem, Francis had developed startling ideas about peacefully approaching Muslims and wanted to incorporate them into the *Rule,* which had to be submitted to Pope Honorius for his approval.

In revising the *Rule,* Francis wanted to teach his fellow friars the art of prudence so they would not be so eager to seek martyrdom in the provocative manner of the five brothers whom the sultan of Morocco had executed. Their deaths had inspired other zealous friars to seek the same fate. Among them was Ferdinand, a Portugese academic who had studied with the Augustinians in the Convent of Santa Cruz in Coimbra, Portugal. After the five brothers' remains were brought to the convent, Ferdinand was inspired by their example. When some Franciscan friars stopped by the monastery for food, Ferdinand decided to join them in hopes he too would become a martyr. He took the name Anthony and became a renowned preacher, today remembered as Saint Anthony of Padua. Even Clare of Assisi, Francis's good friend and herself the founder of an order devoted to the life of poverty, was so stirred by the deaths of the five brothers that she hoped at one point to leave the cloister and seek martyrdom.

Francis saw another way. He inserted into the *Rule* a carefully written chapter instructing "missionaries among the Saracens and other unbelievers." Drawing directly from his own experience in journeying to the sultan's camp, Francis started chapter sixteen of the *Earlier Rule* with the Scripture passage he had recalled as he walked south along the Nile: "Behold I am sending you like sheep in the midst of wolves; so be shrewd as serpents, and simple as doves." By comparing his missionary brothers to sheep in the threatening company of wolves, Francis recognized the danger they faced. But the same quotation also offered the brothers tools for responding to the danger: they were to be "shrewd" and yet simple as doves.

In response to church authorities alarmed at how poorly prepared some of the friars were for dangerous missionary assignments, Francis required that brothers seeking such work get approval from the minister of their province. But he was reluctant to throw obstacles in the path of those who wanted to serve, writing, "The minister, for his part, should give them permission and raise no objection, if he sees they are suitable; he will be held to account for it before God, if he is guilty of imprudence in this or any other matter."

The heart of Francis's instruction for approaching Muslims followed:

> The brothers who go can conduct themselves among them
> spiritually in two ways. One way is to avoid quarrels or disputes and
> to be subject to every human creature for God's sake, so bearing
> witness to the fact that they are Christians. Another way is to
> proclaim the word of God openly, when they see that is God's will,
> calling on their hearers to believe in God almighty, Father, Son, and
> Holy Spirit, the Creator of all, and in the Son, the Redeemer and
> Savior, that they may be baptized and become Christians.

With these words Francis spoke out in the midst of a Crusade to establish a new way for Christians to encounter Muslims: to live in peace, "to avoid quarrels or disputes." Even as Francis wrote his proposal, Crusaders were hunkered down on the Nile, preparing to thrust deeper into Egypt. It may have looked terribly idealistic at the time, but Francis's approach jibed with his long-held beliefs that the best way to change others' behavior was to lead by example. The way to win over Muslims, in his view, was through a true Christian witness of peace and not through contention or violence.

It was also a startling correction for his own brothers, some of whom were seduced by the glory ascribed to the five brothers martyred in

Morocco. Francis wanted his brothers to be a model of peace, not disputation. Unlike Pope Innocent III, who assailed the Prophet Muhammad's character when declaring the Crusade, Francis wanted his brothers "to be subject to every human creature for God's sake." The idea that Christians should "be subject" to Muslims was revolutionary.

Francis also offered a second, traditional path, telling his brothers that they might preach the Christian faith "when they see that is God's will." That too is a surprising statement because it means Francis thought there were times when preaching the Christian message was *not* God's will. This indicates that a process of discernment—an effort to determine God's will—was required. The brothers were not to feel, as the five Moroccan martyrs apparently did, that the only acceptable course was to preach at all costs. Nor did Francis leave it to ecclesiastical authorities to decide the acceptable time for preaching. The individual missionary was to discern God's will through prayer or some sign.

Whichever course they chose, the brothers were instructed to proceed without violence of any kind and to be willing to accept the consequences. They were to go "spiritually" among the Muslims. "No matter where they are, the friars must always remember that they have given themselves up completely and handed over their whole selves to our Lord Jesus Christ, and so they should be prepared to expose themselves to every enemy, visible or invisible, for love of him," Francis wrote in the *Earlier Rule*. Francis clearly wanted to send brothers out to live among the Muslims, not to die among them. In the end, Francis sought perseverance, not combativeness: God would work through the brothers' quiet example. "By your patience, you will win your souls," he wrote, adding, "he who has persevered to the end will be saved."

Francis's unvarnished words in the months after his return from the East show that he was never the man Bonaventure would depict: a harsh, impatient figure who appeared before Sultan al-Kamil only to seek martyrdom. While it is true that the *Earlier Rule* expected missionary brothers to be prepared to die, it was not a manual for self-destruction. Instead, it showed that Francis believed it was God's will that he and his friars embody Jesus' message to love the enemy.

As he brought the new *Rule* before the brothers for their approval at the Pentecost Chapter in May 1221, Francis tried to temper and channel their enthusiasm for martyrdom. When a history of the five martyred brothers was brought to Francis, he mourned the friars' loss but forbade a public reading of the celebratory account. In doing so, Francis rejected many possible advantages that the brave but foolhardy conduct of Brother Berard and company presented: the deaths were a ready-made recruiting advertisement and a sign to church authorities of the order's orthodoxy. "Everyone should glory in his own suffering and not in that of another," Francis said.

Having guided his brothers as best he could, Francis sent them out once more, sheep in the midst of wolves. The Pentecost 1221 chapter meeting concluded with his request that the brothers return on mission to Germany, despite the ferocious reception that some had received there earlier. Jordan, who prayed that he would never be sent to Germany, wrote that ninety men stepped forward, "offering themselves to death." Jordan blithely ignored Francis's warning about celebrating the martyrdom of the five friars and could think only of how disappointed he'd been not to have met them. So he made it his business to start introducing himself to the ninety men who wanted to go to Germany, figuring that he would meet a future martyr. But as Jordan wrote, one of the brave brothers dragooned him into the group, and he wound up going on the mission to Germany despite his fear of being killed there.

Jordan survived to tell the story, and the fledgling order expanded its missionary effort. But like Jordan of Giano, many of the brothers didn't understand Francis's vision for it. Distressed in body and spirit, cast aside in his own order, Francis had little success in bringing the brothers to his revolutionary ideas on how to relate to the Muslim world.

Not long afterward some interesting news arrived from Egypt.

16

"Kamil"

While Francis struggled with his order, pondered what he had learned about Islam, and tried to suggest a startling new way for Christians to interact with Muslims, Sultan al-Kamil fought for his life as the war in Egypt built toward its climax. Sending out emissaries to seek help, the sultan worked ceaselessly after the fall of Damietta to convince the rest of the Muslim world that the Christians had to be stopped before they conquered Egypt. It was a hard sell because an emerging enemy to the east posed a new danger: Genghis Khan's brutal Mongol warriors had swept into Persia. According to the early fourteenth-century historian Abu al-Fida, the Islamic world had never seen such a vicious foe—the invaders massacred adults, sacked mosques, burned the Qur'an, and took children into slavery. "Never, since the establishment of Islam, had Muslims been subjected to such a test," Abu al-Fida added, referring to simultaneous attacks by Crusaders and Mongols.

Another historian, Ibn al-Athir, described the dilemma Muslims faced from two sets of enemies, one from Asia and the other from the West. "All the provinces in Egypt and Syria were on the point of being conquered," he wrote. "The people feared the Franks, and they waited morning and night for some calamity. Fearing the enemy, the Egyptians hoped to flee into exile. But they couldn't; the enemy surrounded them on all sides. If al-Kamil had let them be their own masters, they would have abandoned their cities and let them turn to ruins."

Al-Kamil's adversary, Cardinal Pelagius, was more determined than ever to conquer all Egypt. Poised to attack from his new headquarters in occupied Damietta, the cardinal saw Genghis Khan's invasion of the Muslim world as divine assistance. "He is believed to be the executor of divine vengeance, the hammer of Asia," his aide Oliver of Paderborn wrote.

Pounded from all sides, al-Kamil had to steady his own people. Some were so frightened that they sent bribes to the Christian captives held in Cairo in hopes they would be treated well after the Crusaders triumphed. Al-Kamil fortified Cairo, pressing into service all the men except the old or crippled. Meanwhile he begged for help from his brothers, sending a stream of letters carried by messengers on his swiftest camels. Al-Mu'azzam, the sultan of Damascus, was ready to return with his troops to Egypt, but first had to rouse a powerful younger brother, Malik al-Ashraf, to join him. Al-Ashraf, building an empire in what is now southern Turkey and northern Syria, already had rejected entreaties from a representative of his brother al-Kamil. Al-Mu'azzam had to visit him in the ancient city of Harran to persuade him to bring an army to Egypt.

When the brothers arrived with troops in August, a delighted and relieved Sultan al-Kamil mounted his horse to greet them with honors at al-Mansura, or "the Victorious," the military camp that he had built into a city during a lull in the fighting. Al-Kamil had a huge army now—one account estimated there were 40,000 horsemen alone—and was ready to move forward. Even so, he made one more peace offer to the Christians.

But after many months of delay and bitter infighting, Cardinal Pelagius was eager to attack. Seeing all of Egypt before him and a large army standing by, he pressed ever harder for the Crusaders to resume fighting. He repeatedly called the military leaders together to rouse them with speeches and public sermons. They resisted. Even mercenary troops refused to budge, despite the money they had taken from the cardinal to fight. "Certain of them were excommunicated," Oliver of Paderborn wrote. Others returned their pay rather than battle the far larger Muslim force. Even the Italian soldiers, who had supported Pelagius in the past, were not eager to attack now that they controlled the coveted port city of Damietta. In a sermon Pelagius warned that those delaying the attack faced God's judgment. His frustration is reflected in his aide Oliver's scathing view: "No one can describe the corruption of our army after Damietta was given us by God . . . Lazy and effeminate, the people were contaminated with chamberings and drunkenness, fornications and adulteries, thefts and wicked gains."

Pelagius and Oliver of Paderborn missed the point. With Sultan al-Kamil offering to turn over Jerusalem, the Crusaders no longer had any reason to risk their lives by charging into the teeth of a much larger army that was determined to defend the homeland. Through their inaction the military leaders had quietly rebelled against Cardinal Pelagius. Given a choice between drunkenness, fornication, and larceny or fighting an unnecessary war on unfamiliar terrain under Pelagius's incompetent leadership, much of the army chose the former.

The master of the Templars, Peter of Montaigu, who had fought bravely in numerous battles, sent home a sober assessment of the Crusaders' prospects. The sultan was "waiting with such an immense army that the crusaders, by proceeding further, would incur the greatest danger," he wrote to a bishop. Similarly, James of Vitry wrote a letter to the pope noting that the troops were reluctant to attack because they were outnumbered.

When Emperor Frederick II sent a contingent of fresh troops that arrived in May 1221—the month of Francis's Pentecost Chapter—Pelagius readied a new assault. The sultan's camp, which lay between the Christians and Cairo, was the target.

Pelagius bolstered his case for an attack by seizing on a book of supposed prophecy that was turning into a sensation in the Crusader camp. No one knows where the book originated or whether it was truly an ancient document. Rumors had it that the text was a recent fabrication, but many Crusaders believed it had been written centuries before. Written in Arabic, it cited predictions that Saint Peter had allegedly made to a follower named Clement. Some Syrian Christians in the army translated this "Book of Clement," an apocalyptic history of the world, for the Crusade leaders. "It was said that the law of Muhammad would endure only six centuries, that it will be destroyed in the month of June and that its destroyer would come from Spain," according to an anonymous Christian chronicle. "The legate, who was born in that country, had much confidence in this book." Other predictions in the book excited the Crusaders: that kings arriving from the East and West would seize Jerusalem during a year in which Easter fell on April 3, as it would in 1222.

Two years earlier Cardinal Pelagius had refused to heed Francis's prophetic warning before a disastrous battle. This time he had found prophecy more to his taste: such tales were used to justify launching men into battle and were believed in no less fervently than the shadowy intelligence sources and satellite photos used today.

In preparation for an attack, the cardinal ordered a three-day fast, gathered a host of prelates who had come to Crusader-controlled Damietta, unsheathed the remnant of the True Cross, and led a procession barefoot past the city's three walls, out the gates, and to the soldiers' camp beside the rising river Nile. That was July 6, 1221. John of Brienne, who had gone back to Acre after arguing with Pelagius, returned when Pope Honorius III called him to task in a letter. The pope had lectured the king of Jerusalem on how odious it would look if he failed to show up for a battle in which other men risked their lives to win back Jerusalem for him. Any further dissent was neutralized when Pelagius went about the camp excommunicating all who dared to oppose his attack plan.

John of Brienne warned Pelagius that the Crusaders were unfamiliar with the canal-crossed delta that lay before them. If they managed to approach Cairo, he said, they would have to fight not just an army but an entire people. If they conquered Egypt, the Crusaders would be unable to defend it.

Nonetheless the Crusaders advanced the eight miles south from Damietta to Fariskur, the riverside encampment from which al-Kamil had fled after the capture of Damietta. Some six hundred ships protected the Christian army's right flank. Four thousand archers marched forward ahead of some five thousand knights arrayed behind them, row after row.

Forty thousand foot soldiers secured the left flank. Clergymen and women carrying water trailed the army.

Al-Kamil struck at the Christian force with thousands of horsemen who assaulted the infantrymen, shooting arrows as they rode swiftly past on their fast horses. The Christian foot soldiers held their ground; the two armies exchanged volleys of arrows for several days until the Muslims withdrew. They fell back and yielded up Sharamsah, a town a dozen miles farther down the Nile, with its fields of barley, its orchards, and its fleeing women and children. Al-Kamil ordered the destruction of his beautiful riverfront palace there to prevent the Crusaders from using it.

By now some Christian leaders were beginning to realize the full size of the Muslim army that was forming about sixteen miles south on the Nile near al-Mansura, where the sultan's men encamped at the juncture of two arms of the great river. An alarmed Queen Alice of Cyprus wrote to Pelagius of the peril the Crusaders faced as Muslim reinforcements arrived. The heads of the Templars and Hospitalers, military orders that never shied away from a fight, counseled their field commanders to find a safe place for the troops. But as Oliver of Paderborn wrote, "Sane counsel was far removed from our leaders."

Sultan al-Kamil, aware of the threat the Mongol attack posed, still wanted to end hostilities with the Christians quickly. He renewed the peace offer, shocking John of Brienne, who knew how weak the Crusaders' position was. Even Oliver of Paderborn, aide to Cardinal Pelagius, conceded that John was wise to urge that the offer be accepted. But it was too late. Even if Pelagius had been inclined to accept, both the pope and the emperor had insisted previously that there be no peace treaty without their approval.

The Crusaders dug trenches in a soggy neck of land that was surrounded by water while the Muslims threw up bulwarks and erected siege engines on the opposite side of a Nile tributary. Al-Kamil's strategy called for his troops to isolate the Crusaders from their supply line to Damietta, where a big garrison was stationed. To do that, he took control of the river, capturing Christian galleys that had sailed back up to Damietta to bring back food to the Crusaders. Meanwhile he took advantage of the Crusaders' ignorance of the Nile's complexities. When the Christian leaders took their position, they had ignored a canal that entered the river from the west; it seemed too shallow to be of any strategic use. But as the river rose, the canal deepened enough for al-Kamil to sneak ships behind the Crusaders, cutting off the supply line from Damietta and leading to destruction of many of the invaders' ships. It's possible that al-Kamil had his ships taken apart, carried by camel, and reassembled in secret.

The Crusaders were trapped. The sultan threw up a pontoon bridge to send a mass of soldiers who blocked an escape overland. Even messengers could not get out of the Christian camp. The Crusade leaders, having made a series of disastrous decisions at Pelagius's instigation, puzzled and debated. The troops had food for twenty days under semi-starvation rations, they had no way of knowing when the emperor's reinforcements would arrive, and the Nile was rising. Leaders of a Bavarian contingent that the emperor had sent persuaded the others that the Crusaders should fight their way back to Damietta.

On the night of August 26, 1221, the Christian troops prepared to retreat under cover of darkness, but some of the German soldiers made the terrible mistake of burning their tents. The sultan's army, alerted by the fires, readied an attack on the fleeing Christians. Meanwhile many of the Christian soldiers had gotten drunk. Unwilling to leave behind their supplies of wine before retreating, they imbibed. Some drunken soldiers fell prostrate to the road. Others stumbled while boarding ships and drowned. Stores of arrows, camels, mules, clothing, tents, and silver vessels were all lost in the sloppy nighttime departure. Troops "wandered through the darkness of the night like sheep astray," according to Oliver.

A heavily armed fortress ship carrying Cardinal Pelagius slipped away from the other Christian vessels protecting it, carried by the rising river's swift current. It brought with it much of the Crusaders' remaining food and medical supplies, which had been stored on board. Muslim galleys surrounded a ship carrying German soldiers, setting it on fire and killing those on board. On another vessel three hundred priests whom Pelagius had permitted to flee lost their lives.

Following that night of horror, daybreak brought the swift Muslim cavalry. At the same time Ethiopian foot soldiers allied with the sultan launched a strong assault. The Ethiopians marched through the marshes to attack the Crusaders. Once again John of Brienne took on the dangerous task of picking up the pieces in a disastrous battle he had opposed in the first place. Joined by the Templars and Hospitalers, the military orders, he pushed the oncoming Ethiopians back until a fierce onslaught of arrows put the Crusaders on the defensive. Thousands were killed on both sides.

The Crusaders' troubles were far from over. The next night al-Kamil sent a detachment of soldiers across the canal to the camp the Christians had vacated. Once there they opened sluice gates used to manage the river's annual flooding. That unleashed a flood on the already impaired Crusaders, miring them in muck as they waddled away in the dark. As the mud deepened, even horses were hindered. "Our people were in water up to their legs and waists, to their great misery and suffering," one recently arrived nobleman wrote home. Before making his exit, Cardinal Pelagius was said to have cried out to John of Brienne to tell him, "for God," what to do. John responded that Pelagius had destroyed the Christian army and lost all. With the Crusade checkmated, Peter of Montaigu, the leader of the Templars, raised his banner to call a halt.

It was time to talk peace.

Christian emissaries to the sultan offered to extract their force from Egypt and give up Damietta in return for peace. By that time the Christians had rejected peace offers from the sultan many times—even just before the most recent, ill-advised attack. Only days before al-Mu'azzam and al-Ashraf had joined their older brother in a reluctant offer to return all the lands that their exalted uncle Saladin had seized in 1187. Now an argument broke out among al-Kamil's allies, with some contending that the trapped Christians should be obliterated

Al-Kamil pleaded with his allies to accept the peace deal. They countered that the noblemen who had come to them seeking peace should be seized and exchanged for Crusader territory, such as Acre. But al-Kamil knew that after more than three years of fighting, his troops were weary. Even though it was possible to kill every last Christian wriggling in his net on the Nile, he realized many of his own soldiers would die. And with Damietta well defended, many more would die there as well.

An uneasy truce persisted during the tense negotiations. On August 29, 1221—the Feast of the Beheading of St. John the Baptist, and exactly two years after the massacre that Francis had predicted—the Crusaders lined up for battle, deciding they couldn't take their soggy misery any longer. According to Oliver of Paderborn, the Muslim forces fell back slightly on orders of the sultan. Nightfall averted a battle, Oliver wrote, implicitly praising al-Kamil by adding that "wise men" knew it would have been treacherous to fight while peace talks were being conducted.

The Crusaders surrendered the next day, "that we might be filled with bread," as Oliver of Paderborn put it. Pelagius's aide was unrepentant, insisting unrealistically that if the army had attacked earlier, before the river rose, the outcome would have been different. The terms of the treaty called for prisoners on both sides to be released; return of the True Cross; and the return of Damietta.

Despite the Crusaders' desperation, the Christian leaders who had remained behind in securely fortified Damietta refused to give up the city without a fight. The prestigious heads of two military orders, Peter of Montaigu of the Templars and Hermann von Salza, master of the Teutonic Knights, were sent to persuade them. James of Vitry, ever the Crusade preacher, argued hard against surrender. So did newly arrived noblemen sent by Emperor Frederick II. Fighting broke out among the Christians; John's house in Damietta was attacked. Meanwhile al-Kamil rightfully worried that the garrison at Damietta would refuse to give up. And he knew that the longer it held out, the more likely it was that reinforcements would arrive.

The sultan bided his time. Hostages had been exchanged to ensure that the negotiations were not a trap: John of Brienne and Cardinal Pelagius were among twenty top-tier Crusade leaders ushered into the sultan's camp. For his part, the sultan handed over his fifteen-year-old son and a number of his friends as well as his sister's son. They were taken to a Crusader ship anchored on the Mediterranean.

Sultan al-Kamil showed an extraordinary level of kindness to John of Brienne and the other hostages, according to *The History of the Patriarchs of the Egyptian Church*. He threw a banquet for the war-weary Christian hostages and the churchmen and aristocrats taken prisoner two years earlier, holding court in a vast, high-roofed tent as he received his brothers, al-Mu'azzam and al-Ashraf. The Crusaders were astounded at the reception they got.

Sultan al-Kamil and John of Brienne became such great friends that some whispered that the Crusade leader—who had risked his life time and again during the long battle—was in collusion with the Muslims.

In the midst of the feast al-Kamil set out, John of Brienne wept. The sultan quickly asked why, and John responded that he was thinking of his soldiers, who were dying of hunger. It was not unusual, during such occasions in the Crusades, for the aristocrats on both sides to treat one another with great courtesy. But al-Kamil distinguished himself by providing generously for the starving soldiers who were ensnared along the Nile. He sent them an ample bounty of bread, pomegranates, and melons. He also opened the way for merchants to visit the Christian camp to trade food. For fifteen days Sultan al-Kamil fed the Christian army.

After the leaders at Damietta and the newly arrived Crusaders there angrily accepted the surrender, hostages were released. Al-Kamil provided the Christian army with passage out of Egypt, selling ships at what a Christian chronicle said was a fair price. When the Muslim governor of Damietta tried to stop the Crusaders from taking home the impressive masts that remained from some of their battered ships, the Christians complained to al-Kamil. He insisted that the Christians be given their masts. Al-Kamil also built a bridge over the Nile to speed up the Christian army's withdrawal.

With the Crusaders gone, Sultan al-Kamil entered the city of Damietta on horseback on September 8, 1221, accompanied by his troops and family. A huge force of Christians had arrived in Egypt that same day, but it was too late; Damietta had been surrendered. Once it was a city of eighty thousand people; now the sultan saw a ghost town that had been emptied by war and disease. After so many months of desperation, the victory was an enormous relief to the Muslim forces. They celebrated all day and through the night, filling the empty streets of Damietta with blazing lights and music.

The departing Christians were left to explain the inexplicable. The sultan, whom they had labeled a "cruel beast " and a "perfidious" Muslim, had spared their lives and treated his would-be destroyers with kindness. How was that possible? They were not slaughtered, as Jerusalem's inhabitants were when the Crusaders conquered the city in 1099. *The Capture of Damietta,* the pro-Crusade account that Oliver of Paderborn wrote, closed on an extraordinary note. Sultan al-Kamil was likened to a gracious father who saved the trapped Crusaders, visited them in their misery, heard their complaints, cared for their sick, and excelled all other noblemen with his wisdom.

> The Sultan was moved by such compassion toward us that for many days he freely revived and refreshed our whole multitude . . . Who could doubt that such kindness, mildness and mercy proceeded from God? Those whose parents, sons, and daughters, brothers and sisters we killed with various tortures, whose property scattered or whom we cast naked from their dwellings, refreshed us with their own food as we were dying of hunger, although we were in their dominion and power. And so with great sorrow and mourning we left the port of Damietta, and according to our different nations, we separated to our everlasting disgrace.

That high praise echoed a letter that Oliver of Paderborn, Crusade architect and future cardinal, wrote to the sultan in 1221 after peace was made. "Truly," he wrote, "you are justly titled with the name 'Kamil,' which means 'perfect,' because you govern wisely and, by your virtue, surpass all princes."

———

Sultan al-Kamil's kindness toward the invaders can be explained entirely in strategic terms; it made political sense to get the enemy out of his country as quickly as possible and to avoid a protracted battle to take back Damietta. But Francis would probably not have viewed these events in political or diplomatic terms. Like Oliver of Paderborn and other fellow Christians, he would have seen God's hand behind the sultan's compassion. For Francis, already deeply affected by his encounter with the sultan and Islam, it would have confirmed a belief in the value of engaging Muslims peacefully.

Francis, who had an instinct for the grand gesture, could not have overlooked that with the war's end, tableaux of peace had replaced scenes of horrific death: Muslims fed the starving Christians whom they once had fought; prisoners were freed from their dungeons; the wounded were healed; the leaders of opposing armies sat together at banquets. To Francis, such scenes would have harkened back to the ultimate tableaux of peace prophesied in the Book of Isaiah: lions grazing beside lambs; cows and bears living as neighbors; a baby playing by a cobra's den.

Unfortunately, we have no record of how Francis responded to news of the Crusade's conclusion. Did he view the sultan's humane concern for the Crusaders as fruit that had grown from the seed his preaching planted? The answer is not known.

Even so, intriguing signs suggest that Francis, longing to return to the East, held the sultan deep within his heart.

17

Weeping

In the last years of his life, Francis's yearning for peace intensified. Thomas of Split, a Croatian churchman who studied law and theology in Bologna, witnessed this firsthand on August 15, 1222, when he saw the ailing Francis preach in the city's main piazza. With a huge crowd gathered, Francis spoke more in the emotional style of a political orator than a preacher:

> The whole tenor of his words concerned itself with abolishing
> hostilities and renewing agreements of peace . . . God gave his words
> such efficacy that many factions of the nobility among whom the
> monstrous madness of long-standing enmities had raged
> uncontrollably with much bloodshed, were led to negotiate peace.

Francis's speech proved so inspiring that the various warring factions soon entered peace talks. Thomas, writing years later in his *Historia Salonitana,* recalled with surprise that Francis carried so much influence even though he was filthy in his appearance. While he had been treated like a subversive in the early years of his movement, many now saw him as a living saint.

Even so, in the last years of his life he was stymied time and again as he struggled to ensure that his vision for an order devoted to peace and poverty outlived him. In 1221 he set out once again to write a *Rule* that would be supported within his order and gain papal approval. It never did. The rambling, passionate document was not formal enough to suit church authorities; it urged the brothers to "be subject" to Muslims, and the strict poverty it required may have been too demanding for a substantial number of friars. Thereafter, Francis rewrote the document with Cardinal Ugolino, who understood what the pope expected.

By the time Honorius III at last gave formal papal approval to the *Rule* on November 29, 1223, Francis's revolutionary words on reaching out to Muslims had vanished. No longer were the brothers encouraged to live peaceably among Muslims, preaching through example rather than word. No longer were they instructed to "be subject" to Muslims. Francis's inspiring discourse had been chopped down to a brief legalism: if any brother was inspired by God to "go among the Saracens" and other nonbelievers, he "must ask permission from his provincial minister. The ministers, for their part, are to give permission only to those whom they see are fit to be sent." The long and effusive *Earlier Rule* of 1221, written in Francis's voice, had sought to stir the brothers to join in his dream to reach out to Muslims peacefully. In place of inspiration, the *Later Rule* offered bureaucracy—where to file a request for transfer.

Hugh of Digne, a highly respected Franciscan who wrote in the 1240s, said in a commentary on the *Rule* that the final version did not go as far in emphasizing the gospel-based nonviolence that Francis stressed. He also noted that Francis's earlier instruction on the two ways for approaching Muslims had been deleted. Hugh leaves no doubt which of the two methods—to "be subject" to Muslims and win them over through peaceful example, or to preach the Christian faith—was to be preferred. He noted: "As the saint encouraged in the first Rule: 'Let all the brothers preach with their deeds.'"

Hugh, who was concerned that the Franciscan order had veered away from its founder's ideals, evidently was so respected that he was able to speak bluntly to the Curia about such matters. *The Chronicle of Salimbene,* written by a Franciscan friar in the 1280s, praised his eloquence and learning, saying that he spoke to the pope and cardinals as if they were children.

It is not clear exactly who was responsible for eliminating Francis's innovative approach to the Muslim world from the *Rule.* Perhaps it was Cardinal Ugolino; as a Crusade preacher and later as architect of a new Crusade while serving as pope, he was not one to encourage Christians to "be subject" to Muslims.

That does not mean the approved *Rule* contradicted Francis's vision. This much-streamlined version starts with an exhortation for the brothers "to observe the Holy Gospel." For Francis, that summarized all the friars had to do for a holy life. He may well have been satisfied that Jesus' call in the New Testament to love enemies would govern his missionaries. To Francis, that was all the law they needed. Even so, his specific plan for approaching Muslims had been stricken from the most important document in his order's history, the *Rule* of 1223.

B y late 1223 plans already were under way for a new Crusade. A springtime summit had been held in Ferentino, a hilltop town southeast of Rome. The major players were there: the aged Pope Honorius III, Emperor Frederick II, John of Brienne, Patriarch Ralph of Jerusalem, and leaders of the military orders. Frederick once again vowed to take part in the Crusade. It also was agreed that the red-haired, green-eyed emperor—a brilliant but cruel man who was at home speaking Arabic, Greek, and Latin—would marry John of Brienne's daughter, known as Queen Isabella II, making him heir to the kingdom of Jerusalem. This seemed to solve one of the political problems that undermined the Fifth Crusade: Frederick, having failed to keep his Crusade vow in the past, now stood to add to his holdings if the Christians conquered Jerusalem—an enticing incentive for the monarch. The next Crusade was to be launched in June 1225. The newly motivated Frederick was again the Christians' great hope; the entire Fifth Crusade had been spent waiting for him and his army to put in an appearance. The new campaign likewise depended on his commitment to the fight.

I n the summer of 1224, as the call for a new Crusade went out across the land, Francis went to the mountain hermitage of La Verna in Tuscany. It was a rugged, isolated spot ideal for the solitude he craved. Francis had decided to observe the "Lent of St. Michael," a forty-day period of fasting that began with the Feast of the Assumption on August 15 and ended with the Feast of St. Michael the Archangel on September 29.

Thus began the most celebrated episode in Francis's life, the miracle in which his Franciscan biographers said he received the wounds of the crucified Jesus, the stigmata. For Thomas of Celano, Bonaventure, and other early Franciscans who told Francis's story, this event explained all others in his life: why he had taken sick in Spain instead of preaching to the sultan in Morocco; why Sultan al-Kamil had spared him. Francis had been unable to achieve martyrdom, as Thomas of Celano wrote, because God was "reserving for him the prerogative of a singular grace." To Bonaventure, the stigmata were Francis's destiny: "The memory of Christ Jesus crucified was ever present in the depths of his heart like a bundle of myrrh, and he longed to be wholly transformed into him by the fire of love."

Over the centuries Franciscans have continued to meditate on the mystical experience Francis had on the mountain of La Verna. And in recent times some Franciscan scholars have proposed a link between the most revered event in their order's history and Francis's deep concern for Sultan al-Kamil after news arrived that another Crusade was being planned. Father Michael Cusato, director of the Franciscan Institute at St. Bonaventure University, writes:

> Given this news [of Crusade preparations], I am convinced that
> Francis went with a few of his closest companions to the hermitage

of La Verna profoundly discouraged, perhaps even depressed, over the events about to unfold. Once again, unable or unwilling to resolve human problems peacefully and fraternally through dialogue and mutual respect, the leaders of the Christian world were mobilizing their military might to engage in actions which would inexorably lead to yet more bloodshed and death. More personally still, Francis stood in danger of seeing the death of a man he had come to view as an *amicus* and, even more importantly, as his *frater:* someone he had come to know and apparently respect during that famous encounter with him under the tent in Damietta.

According to the fourteenth-century work *The Little Flowers of Saint Francis,* Francis gradually entered deeper into contemplation in his mountain retreat, reaching a sort of trance in which he was oblivious to physical surroundings. He removed himself from the brothers who accompanied him to secluded La Verna, praying alone in a small shack on a craggy overlook reachable on a footbridge. Francis instructed his beloved friend Brother Leo to approach the bridge once a day with some bread and water. From the bridge, he was to announce in Latin the opening prayer of the Liturgy of the Hours, "O Lord, open my lips." If Francis gave the response, "And my mouth shall declare Your praise," Leo was to cross the bridge and say morning prayers with Francis.

As the Feast of the Exaltation of the Cross arrived on September 14, Francis meditated deeply on Jesus' passion. This feast is closely tied to the True Cross, the wood that Cardinal Pelagius and Patriarch Ralph of Jerusalem had treated not as a source of salvation but as a weapon during the Crusade that Francis witnessed. Its roots go back to the fourth century, when what was believed to be the True Cross was discovered, and to the seventh century, when Christians celebrated the return of the cross after Persian invaders seized a portion of it. From his mountaintop perch, the physically feeble Francis poured himself into reflection on Jesus' suffering on the cross. It was a dark time for Francis, who was two years away from death and weakened by disease—scholars today believe he suffered from trachoma, an eye disease, as well as malaria and possibly leprosy.

Thomas of Celano later enfleshed this intense experience when he described how Francis saw a seraph, a vision of what appeared to him as a man with three pairs of wings, fixed to a cross. After this worrisome vision, Celano wrote, came the stigmata: "The marks of the nails began to appear in his hands and feet, just as he had seen them a little before in the crucified man above him . . . his right side was as though it had been pierced by a lance."

When an anxious Francis emerged from this searing vision, he asked Brother Leo to bring him a pen and paper so that he could write out a prayer. As Father Cusato and others have pointed out, the prayer Francis penned resembled the Muslim meditation on the Ninety-Nine Most Beautiful Names of God, which pious Muslims pray using a set of beads. These ninety-nine names come from descriptions of God in the Qur'an: the Compassionate, the Merciful, the Sovereign, the Holy, the Peaceful, the Mighty, the Creator, the Forgiver, the Provider, the Generous.

Francis, evidently affected by prayers he learned about while in the East, wrote:

> You are holy, Lord, the only God,
>   and your deeds are wonderful.
> You are strong.
>   You are great.
>   You are the Most High,
>   You are almighty.
>   You, holy Father, are
>   King of heaven and earth.
> You are Three and One,
>   Lord God, all good.
>   You are Good, all Good, supreme Good,
>   Lord God, living and true.

You are love,
  You are wisdom.
  You are humility,
  You are endurance.
  You are rest,
  You are peace.
  You are joy and gladness.
  You are justice and moderation.
  You are all our riches,
  And you suffice for us.
You are beauty.
  You are gentleness.
  You are our protector,
  You are our guardian and defender.
  You are courage.
  You are our haven and our hope.
You are our faith,
  Our great consolation.
  You are our eternal life,
  Great and wonderful Lord,
  God almighty,
  Merciful Savior.

After writing his praises on one side of the parchment, he turned it over and wrote a blessing from the Book of Numbers:

God bless you and keep you.
May God smile on you, and be merciful to you;
May God turn his regard towards you
and give you peace.

Francis drew the head of a man at the bottom of the parchment, as if the figure were lying flat on the ground and looking straight up. And then he drew the letter *tau,* a large T rising from the figure's mouth. Finally he wrote words that appeared on both sides of the vertical line in the *tau.* The meaning varies, depending on whether the T sound is included. According to Cusato, the phrase can be viewed as *fleo,* "I weep," or *fleo te,* "I am weeping for you." (Francis would have used imperfect Latin grammar in the latter case.) Francis then entrusted the parchment to Leo, telling him to guard it carefully for the rest of his life.

Heavy on symbolism and light on explanation, the famous parchment is something of a puzzle. Leo treasured it, folding it and wearing it around his neck. The apparent wordplay deepens the mystery. Many scholars have taken it as an attempt on Francis's part to ease some concern that Leo had by blessing him and drawing his picture. Father Cusato found that the answer to the puzzle is hiding in plain sight: in the face Francis drew.

Scholars have debated whether it is meant to represent Brother Leo or Adam. But according to Father Cusato, the face Francis drew on the parchment represents none other than Sultan Malik al-Kamil. The bearded figure appears to be wearing a turban, and the map of Egypt appears to be behind him, the northern coastline slanting up toward Jerusalem. As Father Cusato noted, the "talking head" was not uncommon in vernacular medieval literature—it was often a skull, telling a tale of the woes of the afterlife. In some medieval stories, Jesus called back the dead from the afterlife to let them confess faith in him.

The parchment, then, is less a blessing for Brother Leo than a heartfelt prayer for God to protect Sultan al-Kamil and bring him peace. The drawing places the sultan in the shadow of the *tau.* As noted earlier, the *taw* was an important symbol in the Book of Ezekiel, a sign of God's protection. The prophet had a vision in which God sent out executioners to kill the idolatrous people of Jerusalem; God also sent a holy man, dressed in linen, to mark the worthy on the forehead with the *taw.* Only those marked with the *taw* were to be spared. It was a favorite sign of Francis, who yearned to save people through his call to peace and repentance. Used here, it may well be a call for the sultan to receive God's protection, possibly by converting to Christianity to avoid a new Crusade.

This means that Francis's mystical vision of the suffering Christ included a very socially conscious concern about suffering and safety for others. A new war could devastate the sultan and, by extension, his people. Francis himself would not reveal the full story of the communications he believed he had received during his vision at La Verna, even to his closest friends among the friars.

It may seem unlikely to some that he had depicted Sultan al-Kamil—unless one gets the chance to view the famous parchment that Brother Leo treasured. The parchment, on display in a room of relics accessible through the lower level of the Basilica of St. Francis in Assisi, is about the size of the cover of a small paperback book. The small portrait on it is much more vivid when viewed in person, rather than in photographs, which reproduce poorly because of the cracked, aged surface of the parchment. The head Francis drew clearly wears a turban, a three-tiered headpiece.

Francis wept through his last years. He stayed inside a dim cell in the Poor Ladies' convent at San Damiano, the Assisi church where he believed he had heard Jesus' call, unable to cope with the light of day because of a disease that made his eyes ache and tear. Mice scurried about him, keeping him from sleeping. But from these doldrums he composed in his native Umbrian dialect the famous poem "The Canticle of Brother Sun," praising God for the beauty of "Sister Moon and Stars," "Brother Fire," and "Sister Earth, our mother."

The poem, forerunner to all literature written in the Italian vernacular, would come to figure prominently in Francis's last attempt at preaching peace. Even in his sickness and isolation, he learned from his friars about an angry political dispute in which Bishop Guido had excommunicated Assisi's mayor, Bernardo. The mayor responded by ordering a boycott on all business and legal dealings with the prelate. This quarrel reminded Francis of the strife that consumed Assisi during his youth when a previous mayor was excommunicated. What really seemed to bother Francis was that his brothers had done nothing to reconcile the antagonists. He had done his best to set an example for peacemaking, but as he prepared for death, he could see that the message had not gotten through to many of his followers. He reproved some of the brothers for standing by without trying to create peace between the two men.

Francis decided to act in the only way he could at this time. His first step was to write a new verse for "The Canticle of Brother Sun" that fused his love of the Creator and creation with his greeting of peace:

> Praised be by You, my Lord, through those who give pardon for Your love,
>   and bear infirmity and tribulation.
>   Blessed are those who endure in peace
>   for by You, Most High, they shall be crowned.

Francis, barely able to see, painted one more tableau of peace with his words. He told one of his brothers to ask on his behalf that the mayor and other officials go to the bishop's residence. Then Francis sent two more brothers with instructions to sing "The Canticle of Brother Sun," with the new verse, to the bishop and mayor. "I trust in the Lord that He will humble their hearts and they will make peace with each other," he said.

The brothers did as he said, telling the leaders that Francis had asked them to listen to this song. Tears formed in Bernardo's eyes, and he knelt at Bishop Guido's feet. The bishop, a combative man known for provoking political and legal battles to extend his wealth and power, asked the mayor for forgiveness.

The scene is remembered today in tableaux on the walls surrounding the bishop's palace, which faces a piazza in front of the Church of Santa Maria Maggiore, a Romanesque church that was already old in Francis's time. But the point Francis was trying to make seems to have been lost on his brothers at the time. He wanted to convince them of their duty to be peacemakers. He showed them how it was done: as the original performance artist for peace, he wrote, produced, and directed a presentation orchestrated to move the hearts and minds of the bishop and mayor. The friars took the reconciliation of mayor and bishop as a miracle that proved

Francis's power of prophecy—rather than as a practical lesson in how to create harmony.

Aware that his plans for the friars were being undermined, Francis wrote his *Testament,* or will, to declare once more the vision he believed he had received from God. In this closing statement he explained that his life had changed when he learned to love lepers. What once "seemed bitter to me," he wrote, had become "sweetness of soul and body." He discovered the guiding principle—to love all—when he overcame his disgust and embraced a leper. Francis tried his best in the *Testament* to make clear that those who thwarted his vision for the friars were opposing God. "No one showed me what I had to do, but the Most High Himself revealed to me that I should live according to the pattern of the Holy Gospel," he wrote. Francis added: "The Lord revealed a greeting to me that we should say: 'May the Lord give you peace.'"

Francis's message was clear: God had enlisted him and his friars to bring a message of peace to all—to the outcasts, the marginalized, the enemy—just as Jesus did. In the final hours of his life Francis forgave his friars all they had done to anger him and asked two of them to sing "The Canticle of Brother Sun" for him. Then he requested a reading of the Passion in the Gospel of John. His was, by all accounts, a happy death. But even before he died on October 3, 1226, his wishes were being undone.

The peace that broke out among Sultan al-Kamil and his brothers after their victory over the Crusaders was short-lived. Tensions rose to the point that by 1226 al-Mu'azzam and al-Kamil were on the verge of going to war with each other. With the sands shifting beneath his feet, Sultan al-Kamil sought help from an unlikely ally: Emperor Frederick II, who was planning a new Crusade.

Facing excommunication if he failed to go on Crusade, Frederick had gathered an army in Apulia in southern Italy and set out for the East in September 1227, with the stated aim of conquering Jerusalem. Within three days he returned to port, claiming he was sick and needed time to convalesce. This led to an angry clash with Pope Gregory IX, the former Cardinal Ugolino, who was elected to the papacy after Honorius III died on March 18, 1227. The new pope, a nephew of Innocent III, insisted that the illness was a ruse. In an angry letter that followed, Pope Gregory blamed Frederick for the great bungle of the Fifth Crusade—the decision to pass up Sultan al-Kamil's offer to hand over Jerusalem. Overlooking the role of Cardinal Pelagius at Damietta, the pope claimed that the Crusaders would have recovered Jerusalem in return for Damietta "had they not been several times forbidden to do so by the letters of the emperor."

Frederick responded with a letter of his own, sealed in gold and sent to the kings of Europe. The pope had reached his quick judgment out of greed, he told them, implying that Gregory had turned on him to gain advantage in the long battle between popes and emperors over land in Italy. And he warned his fellow monarchs that they could be the next to face the pope's avaricious wrath.

"He is making treaties with the sultan and other Saracens, and shows kindness to them, but open hatred to the Christians," Gregory retorted in another letter, dubbing Frederick an "agent" of Muhammad.

A dizzying whirl of events followed. Thousands of soldiers went home because they thought Frederick had abandoned the Crusade. An incensed Pope Gregory called off the Crusade, but Frederick soldiered on, setting out once again for the East. Then Gregory excommunicated him for being disobedient and launched an army to attack his holdings in southern Italy.

Emperor Frederick II, much like Sultan al-Kamil, found himself vulnerable. Neither monarch was prepared for a full-scale war against the other. And both men were wily negotiators with an unusually keen understanding and appreciation for the other's culture and religion. Their diplomatic dance began before Frederick set sail. Al-Kamil sent the talented and sophisticated emir Fakhr ad-Din Yusuf to woo the emperor at his palace in Sicily. Fakhr ad-Din was like a brother to the sultan—closer, actually, given the dysfunctional relations within the royal family. The influential emir had grown up close to the seat of power in Damascus, debating philosophy and theology at a very high level. His mother had nursed al-Kamil in his infancy. (Born in 1184, he was four years younger than the sultan.) And al-Kamil called on him and his highly respected brothers to handle the most sensitive diplomatic tasks. One of these was for Fakhr ad-Din to befriend the emperor, who spoke Arabic.

Frederick already had shown a fascination with the ways of his Muslim subjects, whose families had settled in Sicily when it was under Islamic control from the ninth to eleventh centuries. The two men exchanged gifts and shared their interests in science, religion, and philosophy. As they got beyond pleasantries, Fakhr ad-Din convinced Frederick that it was possible to befriend the sultan and agree on a treaty that would allow both of them to achieve their aims—provided that the emperor would ally with al-Kamil against his brother al-Mu'azzam. He persuaded Frederick to send Count Thomas of Acerra, his top envoy, to the sultan. The count brought along many gifts, including horses and a gold saddle encrusted with jewels. Al-Kamil responded by sending Frederick the finest goods he could find, worth double those he had been given—including an even more impressive gold saddle. From these exchanges, an agreement—but not yet a signed treaty—emerged by which Sultan al-Kamil would turn over Jerusalem to the Christians, so long as he could count on Frederick to aid in battles with his brothers.

The problem with this unlikely alliance was that in the end al-Kamil didn't need it. On November 11, 1227, his brother and rival al-Mu'azzam died of dysentery in Damascus. He was buried in the Citadel there. That put Damascus within al-Kamil's grasp, and he pursued it. Frederick became a hindrance to his plans. After the emperor arrived in Acre with his troops, Fakhr ad-Din kept him tied up in negotiations for months while al-Kamil sought control of Damascus. Al-Kamil made sure to welcome Frederick with exotic gifts, including camels, monkeys, and elephants as well as silk, gold, and silver. The insatiably curious Frederick had plenty of questions about mathematics and philosophy and posed complex problems; al-Kamil referred them to specialists in his court.

Both leaders risked losing face at this point. As the emperor pointed out in a letter to the sultan, the Christian world had great expectations that its most powerful monarch would win back Jerusalem. He confided to al-Kamil's envoy that he didn't even care all that much about Jerusalem—he just wanted to save his reputation.

Al-Kamil's reputation was at risk too. He had repelled the Fifth Crusade valiantly and was running Egypt efficiently during peacetime. But loss of the holy city of Jerusalem and other lands that Saladin, his uncle, had conquered would be sure to provoke an angry reaction and strengthen his rivals. On the other hand, he was eager to avoid war.

The deal hammered out amid those concerns was aimed at saving both monarchs' reputations. Frederick would get Jerusalem, but just for ten years. Muslims would continue to have control over the Dome of the Rock and the al-Aqsa Mosque, which were built atop the remains of the old Temple, and villages surrounding Jerusalem. Christians would control Bethlehem and Nazareth, but many other towns, such as Hebron and Nablus, would remain under Muslim control. And Frederick agreed that he would defend the sultan from attack, even from fellow Christians.

In the end, tolerance and diplomacy triumphed over bloodshed. There were many pragmatic reasons for the Treaty of Jaffa, which was reached on February 11, 1229, but they do not fully explain why both men opted for peace. Both rulers were cunning, but the unusual appreciation each had for the other's religion and culture put this matchup on a different plane from all other negotiations between Muslims and Christians during the Crusades. Each man had a level of comfort with the other's culture that allowed him to see it was possible to make a deal instead of going to war.

The treaty, for all it says about the sultan and emperor, reveals even more about the difficulty of achieving compromise when a powerful religious symbol such as Jerusalem was at stake. An uproar arose immediately as both Christians and Muslims opposed the treaty, castigating the rulers. "That painful event humiliated and distressed Muslims beyond all description," the historian Ibn al-Athir wrote, beseeching God to return possession of Jerusalem quickly. Muslims wept openly in Jerusalem, in Damascus, and in other centers of Islam. As a sandstorm of protest blew his way, al-Kamil tried to defend his reputation, insisting he had given away little and that Muslims would still control the places that were holy to them.

Pope Gregory, already at war with Frederick in Italy, complained bitterly that the emperor had dared to enter the Church of the Holy Sepulcher while excommunicated and had even crowned himself king of Jerusalem in a ceremony in Christendom's holiest place—and then assailed the pope from the main altar. Patriarch Gerold of Jerusalem excoriated Frederick for his deal with the sultan, "his dear friend." It was clear that the emperor had kept the patriarch out of the loop. "What more shall I say?" the prelate complained in a letter to the faithful. "After long and mysterious conferences, and without having consulted any one who lived in the country, he suddenly announced one day that he had made peace with the sultan."

Gregory renewed his accusation that Frederick was too close to the Muslims, both on personal and diplomatic levels. "In his palace at Acre, he had eaten and drunk with Saracens, and introduced Christian dancing women to perform before them, and, as was said, that they afterwards had connection with them," he wrote with some delicacy. The pope expressed outrage that the treaty required Frederick to ally with Sultan al-Kamil even against Christians. And he complained that the legal format of the treaty seemed to owe more to Muslim law than to Christian custom.

Islam intrigued Frederick, to be sure, to the point that some Muslim observers thought he might secretly have been one of their own. Frederick got Sultan al-Kamil's permission to visit the Haram al-Sharif, the Noble Sanctuary built on the platform of the Temple in Jerusalem. He much admired the Dome of the Rock and al-Aqsa Mosque, according to al-Maqrizi, and even walked up the steps of a *minbar,* or pulpit. He threatened to gouge out the eyes of a priest he saw approach the mosque with a Bible in hand, telling him that the Muslim holy places had to be respected out of deference to Sultan al-Kamil, who had opened the churches. When Frederick noticed that the muezzin had not announced the call to prayer at the appointed hour, he asked why. Informed that the muezzin had been silenced out of respect for him, Frederick insisted that the call to prayer go forth. He had come to Jerusalem to hear that call, he said.

Both men weathered the storm, although Frederick suffered the indignity of trying to slip out of Acre early in the morning, only to have early-rising butchers throw animal innards at him. But the excommunicated emperor was able to spite the pope by boasting far and wide that he alone had freed the holy city from Muslim rule.

Sultan al-Kamil prospered in his remaining years, free from the wrenching decisions he had to make during the battle for Damietta. At the age of fifty-seven he conquered Damascus. After feeling a cold coming on, he visited the baths to warm himself in the waters there but became feverish and nauseous. He died on March 9, 1238, having ruled Egypt as viceroy and sultan for some forty years.

Al-Kamil was praised even in the Christian world, and Emperor Frederick II wept at his death. According to the monk and chronicler Matthew Paris:

> The most powerful sultan who, being about to die, liberally
> bequeathed rich revenues and large sums of money to the sick
> Christians who remained in the house of the Hospitalers, and had
> liberated a great many confined prisoners, and performed many
> other deeds of charity, breathed forth his spirit, to the grief of many.
> For he was, although a pagan, a truth-speaking, munificent man, and
> (as far as the rigors of his faith and the suspicion of his neighbors
> permitted it) a merciful man to Christians. When the Roman
> emperor Frederick heard of this, he lamented his death with tears,
> for a very long time, for he had hoped, as the same sultan had
> promised, that he would receive baptism, and that Christianity
> would by him, at some time or another, receive a great increase of
> prosperity.

The Christians' notion that Sultan al-Kamil longed to convert was embellished in later accounts. Well after both Francis and the sultan were dead, stories circulated among the Franciscans that their founder had promised to send friars to al-Kamil on his deathbed so that he could be baptized. According to this fanciful tale, which first appeared in the fourteenth century, the dying sultan put guards at his gate to usher in the friars when they arrived. The brothers baptized the sultan, saving his soul.

PART THREE

UNCOVERING
THE
STORY

18

The Story Changes

The true story of Francis, the sultan, and their peaceful exchange was buried. It did not serve the purposes of popes who continued to drum up support for a string of ill-fated Crusades. Nor did it fit the needs of Francis's order at a time when it had to fight off a heresy scandal. As the story was retold in the Christian world, Francis's thirst for peace and the sultan's noble treatment of the Crusaders at the close of the Fifth Crusade were downplayed and then forgotten; Francis was turned into a soldier who used the gospel as a weapon. The sultan became a malevolent foe.

As we follow the story of Francis and the sultan in art and literature through the decades of the thirteenth century and then from one century to the next, we'll see how it was manipulated. It is part of the larger story of how church politics reshaped the account of Francis's entire life, leading to a defining work in which Bonaventure portrayed Francis as an ethereal "angel of peace" but eliminated the flesh-and-blood details of nearly every instance in which he actually tried to make peace. The Francis who yearned to transform the world with a message of peace was lost. So too was the true story of his encounter with Sultan Malik al-Kamil.

INNOCENT III·

GREGORY IX

Marble relief sculptures of Pope Innocent III and his nephew Pope Gregory IX, the former Cardinal Ugolino, are among the figures of twenty-three "lawgivers" depicted in the House of Representatives Chamber in the U.S. Capitol. Pope Innocent III, by Joseph Kiselewski; Pope Gregory IX, by Thomas Hudson Jones. *Copyright © 1950 by Architect of the Capitol*

F rancis's legacy was profoundly influenced by the election of Cardinal Ugolino as Pope Gregory IX in 1227. A brilliant Vatican insider, Gregory warred relentlessly against those he targeted as enemies of Christendom. He formalized the Inquisition, pursued yet another Crusade vigorously, and warred with Emperor Frederick II over landholdings. Gregory had no interest in portraying Francis as a peacemaker who wanted to "be subject" to Muslims. And it was under Gregory's watchful eye that Francis's "biography" took shape. The pope canonized the friar in 1228 and commissioned Thomas of Celano to write his earliest biography, effectively taking control of Francis's legacy.

With Gregory as his patron, Celano could not possibly have presented the truth about Francis, the Crusade, and Islam. Within a year of Francis's death, the pope pressed the Friars Minor into recruiting for the Crusade, which Francis had not done. Pope Gregory and Brother Elias, a despotic but highly organized minister general from 1232 to 1239, enthusiastically pushed to send missionaries to the Muslim world, including Tunis and Aleppo. Francis had done the same, but to Gregory, these missions had a quasi-military purpose. Sounding like a prelate from the *Chanson de Roland,* he issued a bull in 1238 to the Franciscan and Dominican orders stating that converting Muslims by preaching was akin to subduing them with weapons.

With Francis dead, Pope Gregory could easily ignore his wishes. In 1234 he gave the friars the job of accepting money from men who wanted to buy their way out of their Crusade vows. This may have helped the Vatican treasury by channeling the money through honest hands, but it flew in the face of Francis's insistence that his brothers not handle cash. "The friars, no matter where they are or where they go," he wrote in the *Earlier Rule* of 1221, "are forbidden to take or accept money in any way or under any form."

Celano's *The Life of Saint Francis* was presented to Gregory in the latter part of 1228 or in 1229. Shaped to the pope's preferences, it offered no hint at the ideal that Francis had revealed seven or eight years before in his *Earlier Rule:* his hopes for living among Muslims peacefully. It had to be concealed; the pope did not need to tell the world, as he pursued a new Crusade, that the great Saint Francis thought Muslims could best be approached with love.

Until his death in 1241 Gregory continued to play a central role in reshaping Francis's legacy. Trying to resolve a feud within the order, he issued bulls that watered down Francis's vision for a life of radical poverty lived in strict adherence to the gospel. This only served to feed the bitterness between the friars who wanted to stay true to Francis's vision—the "Spirituals," as some of them came to be known—and those who wanted to adapt as the order grew to have tens of thousands of friars.

I n 1244, against this historical background, the order's general chapter in Genoa decided to have Thomas of Celano write a new life of Francis. The first biography had met an institutional need at the time by explaining Francis's greatness as a saint. But it failed to include the mother lode of anecdotes available from the brothers who had walked beside Francis in his amazing journey. This time Celano wrote not for the pope but for the order's minister general, Brother Crescentius, and for his fellow friars.

Although Gregory was dead, Celano still faced a delicate political task as he wrote a new life of Francis. The Spirituals in the order wanted him to capture Francis's complete abandonment to a life of poverty, supporting their calls for a strict observance. Crescentius, meanwhile, was a stern critic of the rebellious Spirituals; he stressed that the friars must be obedient to the order's leadership at the time.

Celano's *The Remembrance of the Desire of a Soul,* completed in 1247, focused less on miracles than on stories from Francis's close friends in such collections of anecdotes as *The Legend of the Three Companions.* It created a more human Francis and filled out some important details in the saint's story, including his imprisonment after fighting in the war between Perugia and Assisi.

Francis's experience as a soldier became an important point for Celano, who compared the friar to the great Saint Martin of Tours, a man who opposed military service and gave away his belongings to the poor. In this account God spoke directly to the young Francis in a dream, telling him not to go to war in Apulia. This, for Celano, marked the beginning of his conversion: "He refused to go to Apulia, and he strove to bend his own will to the will of God. Accordingly, he withdrew for a while from the bustle and business of the world and tried to establish Jesus Christ dwelling within himself."

A close reading of Celano's second biography indicates just how much papal politics had prevented him from truly telling Francis's story in the first. Celano wrote that the second biography included new details of Francis's conversion, noting in his introduction that they were not included in the earlier work because "they had not come to the notice of the author." But the first life of Francis contains an indication that Celano knew about the saint's battlefield experience and imprisonment in Perugia, even if he had not mentioned them directly. "Stirred by the venom of the serpent of old," he had written, "suddenly the divine vengeance, or better, the divine unction, came upon him . . . visiting upon him mental distress and bodily suffering." In his first book Celano wrote about the *result* of Francis's imprisonment without ever mentioning the actual internment in Perugia.

At the time the first biography was being written, Pope Gregory IX had found refuge in Perugia; he had been driven out of Rome by supporters of Emperor Frederick II on Easter Monday in 1228. Celano would have had ample opportunity to find out that the Perugians had massacred Francis's army and broken him in a harsh imprisonment. Brother Elias, who provided Celano with much information for the first biography, could have informed him about that. But to include such details about Perugia, a crucial papal ally, while it was protecting the pope, would have been impolitic. Instead, Celano only hinted at the story of Francis and the war with Perugia in the first biography.

Political considerations may also have influenced Celano's account of

Francis's sojourn in Egypt in the second biography—especially the story in which Francis tried to stop the Crusaders from heading into a disastrous battle. As noted earlier, whether Francis objected to the war or simply to attacking the Muslim camp on that particular day is open to debate. By the time Celano presented his work to the order in 1247, the Muslims had recaptured Jerusalem and King Louis IX of France was preparing a new Crusade aimed at Damietta. So the story of Francis's warning during the battle for Damietta nearly three decades before was timely. But for Celano to state directly that Francis had opposed the entire war would have been too obvious a prophecy against Louis's Crusade.

J ust as Celano's second life of Francis was delivered in 1247, Brother Crescentius, who was unpopular with the dissident friars, departed as minister general. Soon afterward conflict cascaded through the order Francis founded, leaving it so vulnerable to powerful enemies that its survival was in doubt. Bonaventure, a mystic and a brilliant theologian, stepped forward to save the order—and in the process to rewrite the story of Francis, particularly concerning his encounter with the sultan.

At first the future after Crescentius's departure looked promising. The minister general's replacement, John of Parma, was a beacon for those who wanted to return the order to the purity of Francis's vision. The chronicling friar Salimbene enthusiastically described John as a handsome, gentle, articulate, and pious man who was a learned theologian but lived in simplicity. He was a scholar who washed vegetables in the kitchen, traveled on foot to all of the order's provinces, avoided high church office for himself, and did not cozy up to prelates and princes.

He would seem the perfect minister general, but Salimbene recognized one problem: Brother John was heavily influenced by the teachings of Joachim of Fiore, a Calabrian abbot famed for his biblical prophecies. Popes and kings had sought out Joachim during his lifetime—Richard the Lion-Hearted did not set out on the Third Crusade in 1190 until the abbot told him the Book of Revelation predicted a victory over Saladin. After the Third Crusade ended without the conquest of Jerusalem,

Joachim reinterpreted Revelation to see the Muslim enemy as resurgent. In practical terms, this meant abandoning warfare and finding a better way to win the battle with Islam—such as peaceful conversion.

Joachim's prophecies continued to grow in popularity after his death in 1202 and started to influence the friars as early as the 1220s. One prediction in particular stirred the hearts of the friars who wanted to restore the ascetic glory of Francis's time: Joachim prophesied that two new religious orders (later seen as the Franciscans and Dominicans) would lead the world into a new age of the Spirit.

A mid-thirteenth-century work that was erroneously attributed to Joachim fanned the friars' rebellion. The treatise, called the *Super Hieremiam,* severely criticized the popes for launching Crusades. Some friars came to believe that Saint Francis was the angelic herald of the new age of the Spirit, his arrival foretold in Revelation 7. It was thought to be the time of peace the prophet Isaiah predicted, when swords would be beaten into plowshares. For some brothers, this treatise demonstrated that God would not favor any further Crusade. Salimbene wrote that two fellow friars who followed Joachim had predicted to him in 1247 that the Crusade of Louis IX in Egypt would end in disaster, as it did three years later when Muslim forces captured the future Saint Louis and much of the French nobility and massacred many soldiers.

"These two laughed and made fun, saying that if he did go it would turn out badly for him—as indeed did take place," Salimbene wrote.

One of these brothers, Gerard of Borgo San Donnino, a close friend of John of Parma, was said to have been preaching in Constantinople in 1250 when he stopped, looked at the sky, and began to weep. According to a story recounted in Angelo Clareno's fourteenth-century chronicle, he told the crowd before him that King Louis IX had just been captured—and it turned out to be precisely the time when that occurred. The story, whether true or not, shows that a strain of prophetic opposition to the Crusade ran through the rebellious faction of friars.

Gerard had come from southern Italy to study and teach at the University of Paris. He had stepped into a cauldron, for the established theologians of the time as well as the parish clergy and some bishops bitterly opposed the Friars Minor and Saint Dominic's Preachers, who seemed to usurp them at every step—even at the university. Gerard plunged into controversy in 1254 by writing *The Introduction to the Eternal Gospel,* which took Joachim's ideas to extremes. The clergy would no longer be needed in the new age of the Spirit, he declared. Instead there would be barefoot monks committed to the life of the apostles. Gerard maintained that Joachim was the angel referred to in Revelation 14:6, a figure who would come from on high to announce the "eternal gospel" to people of all nations. For Gerard, the "eternal gospel" was not the writings of Matthew, Mark, Luke, and John but their replacement—Abbot Joachim's books of prophecy.

It was a very rash move, given that the atmosphere at the University of Paris already was poisoned against the Franciscans and Dominicans. Powerful enemies there set out to destroy the two orders. The friars' purpose, these jealous scholars claimed, was to tear down the hierarchical structure of the church and to replace the established political order as well. Some of the church's most prominent thinkers essentially called on the pope to scuttle the two great orders. One notable Franciscan master at the university, Brother Bonaventure, stood up to that scholarly smear job. His Dominican friend, Thomas Aquinas, joined him.

Gerard's heretical book, which Pope Alexander IV condemned in 1255, gave enemies of the friars plenty of ammunition. Gerard had essentially replaced the church hierarchy with Franciscans and the Bible with Joachim's writings. John of Parma, head of the order, quickly stepped in to bar friars from writing books without permission. But it was too late for him as well; as a committed follower of Joachim, John of Parma took the fall no less so than Gerard. The pope pushed him to resign as minister general. Then he was put on trial for heresy. Gerard of Borgo was stripped of his power as a priest, according to Salimbene; then he and an associate, Leonard, were tried on heresy charges.

The judge in these cases was no one less than the future Saint Bonaventure, who was named the order's new minister general at John's urging. The ensuing saga had huge consequences for the biography of

Francis that was handed down through the centuries—including the story of his encounter with Sultan al-Kamil. It shows that while Bonaventure has a deserved reputation as a humble, mystic sage, he was ready to go to extremes to restore the order's credibility by purging any hint of heresy or disobedience.

Bonaventure swiftly found Gerard and Leonard guilty of heresy, then sentenced them to life in prison. One can imagine his feelings toward Gerard, whom he would have known at the University of Paris. While Bonaventure had been fighting off the scholars who tried to push the Franciscans and Dominicans out of the university, the imprudent Gerard had given the orders' enemies an easy shot at them.

Running the heresy trial of the venerable John of Parma must have been a very difficult task for Bonaventure, a younger man who owed his appointment at the University of Paris to John. Like John, Bonaventure had a great interest in the teachings of Abbot Joachim. Nor did John endorse the ideas in Gerard's heretical book.

According to Angelo Clareno, a Spiritual Franciscan leader, John of Parma said that Bonaventure agreed with him when they spoke privately. But in open sessions with the brothers—where John had many enemies, especially among those in leadership positions—he would give the impression that he opposed John. Angelo wrote that John was afraid that Bonaventure would deny the truth. For Bonaventure was set on restoring the order's credibility in Rome: John of Parma had to take the fall.

Since John opposed Gerard's *Eternal Gospel,* the trial had to go afield for Bonaventure and other friars judging with him to find a basis to convict him of heresy. The focus became not Joachim's predictions for history—the issue that prompted the entire crisis—but the late abbot's understanding of the Trinity, which was condemned at the Fourth Lateran Council in 1215. John of Parma believed that Joachim had been misunderstood on a highly technical issue and even on trial could not suppress his honest opinion. Bonaventure seized on this point to convict Brother John of heresy. Acting in consultation with Cardinal Giovanni Gaetano Orsini, the order's protector and the future Pope Nicholas III, he sentenced John of Parma to life in prison. According to Angelo Clareno, the normally wise and tranquil Bonaventure was filled with rage during this trial and sentencing.

The life sentence was so unfair that Cardinal Ottoboni Fieschi, the future Pope Adrian V, intervened. He sent a letter to Bonaventure and the order's cardinal protector that essentially charged that John had been framed. Thereafter an arrangement was made for John to live in a hermitage in Greccio, one of Francis's favorite locales. John lived until he was ninety, dying in 1289; his holiness was officially recognized when he was beatified in 1777.

Having treated the holy John of Parma with extraordinary harshness in his bid to save the order, Bonaventure also went to extremes in a new life of Francis that the order asked him to write in 1260. Although Bonaventure gave the impression in his introduction to *The Major Legend* that he based his account directly on what he had heard from Francis's closest friends, it in fact contains little new. At least eighty percent of it came directly from Celano's prior biographies. Bonaventure took the raw material of previously existing accounts and alloyed it with his great learning, mystic contemplation, theological insight, and desire to solve the order's political problems. While the result is a beautifully wrought meditation on the saint's life, *The Major Legend of Saint Francis* turns the great fool for God into a much more severe and less spontaneous figure. More to the point here, *The Major Legend of Saint Francis* virtually wiped out Francis's activities as a peacemaker who challenged the powers of his day to forsake violence. It did not even hint at the cheeky friar who warned the "rulers of all the people" to shape up or face damnation.

Bonaventure deleted Celano's description of Francis's participation in a war between Assisi and Perugia, as well as the account of his imprisonment and how it shattered him physically and emotionally. He omitted as well the painful conversion experience that Celano recounted.

Similarly, Bonaventure did not use the story of Francis's confrontation with the knights who harassed him while he preached in Perugia, trying to avert a civil war there. He certainly did not use the material from *The Assisi Compilation* that noted that the knights, "supported by the Church," destroyed crops during the civil war. Bonaventure avoided the streak of rebellion that Francis occasionally showed for civil authorities. Celano's story of the warning that Francis had one of his brothers give to Emperor Otto IV, who passed by their hovel at Rivo Torto, did not find space in Bonaventure's work. Nor did he use *The Assisi Compilation*'s story of how Francis made peace late in his life between the mayor of Assisi and the bishop by getting his friars to sing to them.

To be sure, Bonaventure's aim was to focus on Francis's uplifting spiritual journey and not to write a history of his life and times. Even so, the minister general was acutely aware that he needed to silence the outspoken brothers in his order. To do so, he silenced their model, Francis. By eliminating stories that implicitly criticized civil or religious authorities, Bonaventure closed the distance that Francis kept from "the princes of this world." Bonaventure's Francis was all about obedience—an antidote to the likes of Gerard of Borgo San Donnino and his colleagues, who had opposed King Louis's Crusade at Damietta.

Rome's expectations for the proper portrayal of Francis can be heard in a sermon that Cardinal Eudes of Châteauroux delivered to the friars in Paris on the Feast of St. Francis, October 4, 1262. Cardinal Eudes, former chancellor of the University of Paris, had led the papal commission that investigated Gerard of Borgo San Donnino's *Introduction to the Eternal Gospel* and also served as papal legate to the Crusade. In his remarks, the cardinal depicted the encounter between Francis and Sultan al-Kamil as extremely confrontational—even claiming that the sultan's willingness to spare Francis's life was malevolent. The cardinal presented Francis as a man who obeyed Christ's will by confronting the Muslim foe, no matter how implacable.

"He longed so much to die for Christ that he went among infidels to preach the Christian faith and even to the cruel Sultan, in the hope of having to suffer for Christ," the cardinal said. "But when the Sultan realized this, he refused to make him a martyr in order to deprive him of so great a glory."

This story, presented more than four decades after the fact, is very different from the original account given by the Crusade preacher James of

Vitry, who conceded that the sultan softened and listened attentively to Francis. As the Fifth Crusade ended, the Crusaders had praised al-Kamil for his kindness. By the 1260s none of that history mattered any longer. Rome had spoken: the sultan was a cruel tyrant whom Francis approached to achieve martyrdom. And this is the story Bonaventure delivered the following year in *The Major Legend of Saint Francis.*

As already discussed, Bonaventure added the story of Francis's attempt to stage a trial by ordeal, in which he and the sultan's religious advisers would walk through fire. It was the largest block of new material in the entire work. Brother Illuminato is often credited as the source Bonaventure supposedly relied on, although *The Major Legend* does not state this. Illuminato's recollections had been gathered in the 1240s for *The Legend of the Three Companions,* as its prologue notes, and this work informed Celano's second biography. Neither work refers to a trial by fire. If Francis had really made the spectacular proposal to walk through fire to convert the sultan, surely Illuminato would have communicated it sooner than forty years after the fact.

Two other new stories about Francis's encounter with the sultan began to circulate through the Franciscan community in the years Bonaventure was minister general, although they did not appear in *The Major Legend.* One concerned the sultan's test for Francis: whether he would walk across a carpet decorated with crosses. In the other, Sultan al-Kamil challenged Francis on whether the Crusaders had violated their own gospel by attacking his country; Francis purportedly responded with Crusade rhetoric that justified eradicating enemies of the faith.

Both anecdotes were attributed to Bonaventure, who was said to have told others that Illuminato passed along these stories; they were collected at the end of the thirteenth century or in the early fourteenth century in Italy as part of *A Book of Exemplary Stories.* The question arises again about why it took so long for these stories to surface. The Crusade preacher James of Vitry and the French Crusader who wrote *The Chroni-*

cle of Ernoul would certainly have included Francis's ringing defense of the Crusade in the face of the sultan, had they known of it. Pope Gregory IX was close enough to Francis and other brothers, including Elias, to have learned about it as well if Francis really had delivered such a harangue to the sultan. As a staunch supporter of the Crusade, Gregory would have been quick to use Francis's endorsement.

These stories took shape within Franciscan circles because they were sorely needed to correct the order's course—an antidote to the heretical Brother Gerard and his associates. As Salimbene wrote, the taunting prediction by Gerard and a second friar that King Louis IX would be defeated and captured in his Crusade at Damietta had stirred anger even within the order. By this point Franciscans were heavily involved in preaching the Crusades; Gerard's predictions infuriated them.

With the stunning defeat of Louis IX in Egypt in 1250, opposition to the Crusades grew. Humbert of Romans, master general of the Dominican order from 1254 to 1263, went on to write a manual for preaching the Crusade that included a detailed rebuttal of the points opponents raised. It was not written until 1274, more than a decade after Bonaventure's life of Francis, but it captured the controversy that existed at the time Bonaventure wrote the biography—and showed some of the arguments that the church hierarchy had to respond to. For example, some believed the Bible taught nonviolence or that Jesus would have opposed shedding the blood of nonbelievers. Others, he noted, had argued that warfare would only further provoke Muslims against the Christian faith and make it impossible to convert them. This argument was advanced by the philosopher and scientist Roger Bacon, a Franciscan from England who wrote that the Muslims who survived the Crusades—and their children—became so embittered that they would do all they could to harm Christians in the future. He proposed abandoning the Crusades in favor of a carefully reasoned plan to convert Muslims through philosophical disputation, with missionaries required to learn Arabic.

Bonaventure used *The Major Legend of Saint Francis* and subsequent sermons about Francis to stamp out such controversial ideas within the order, demonstrating the Franciscans' loyalty and orthodoxy. He wanted to show that the order's founder and model was not soft on Muslims: he was ready to walk through fire to combat their beliefs.

Bonaventure embellished further in a sermon given on the Feast of St. Francis in Paris in 1267, at a time when King Louis IX, a friend of the Franciscans, was making a dubious attempt at still another Crusade. "Our faith is beyond human reason and reason anyway is of no use except to a believer," Francis supposedly told the sultan, according to the words Bonaventure placed in his mouth. "Besides, I cannot argue from Holy Scripture because your wise men do not believe the Scriptures." The mystic minister general clearly revised the story to suit yet another need of his, this time to show that Francis would have rejected Roger Bacon's scientific approach to ending the Crusades. Bacon had recently sent it directly to Pope Clement IV.

Bonaventure's depiction of Francis and the sultan was shaped by his emphasis on the crucifixion of Jesus, which he saw as the dominant theme in Francis's life, leading up to his stigmata. The theology of the cross permeates Bonaventure's work, giving his erudite writings the inner mystical glow of a medieval icon. His version of Francis also is an icon, a glowing golden figure presented for veneration. In this superheated atmosphere, Francis's interest in achieving martyrdom expanded like a glassblower's bubble.

The story of Francis's *mubahala*—his challenge to the sultan's advisers to an ordeal by fire—was made to order for Bonaventure, who needed to cloak the scandalous disregard for the Crusades that some of his Joachim-dazzled brothers had flaunted. But where did the story come from?

Over time Franciscan missionaries in the East probably heard the story of Muhammad's *mubahala,* when they attempted to explain their faith to Muslims. Why had the Christians of Najran been unwilling to accept Muhammad's challenge to defend their faith? One can imagine that the Franciscan missionaries quickly tired of trying to respond to that question. So the story took shape that Francis too had issued a challenge. In the new version, the sultan's religious advisers shrank from defending their beliefs, much like the Christians of Najran.

If *The Major Legend of Saint Francis* were just one more biography on an already growing shelf of books about Francis, its drawbacks would not have mattered so much. Its highly polished presentation of an ethereal, angelic Francis served to complement the earthier, quirkier saint described in the various works written in the 1240s. But at the order's chapter meeting in 1266 the friars reached the fateful decision to make *The Major Legend* the official biography of Francis and to eliminate all previous versions:

> The Chapter-general ordains on obedience that all the legends of the Blessed Francis formerly made shall be destroyed. The Brothers who shall find any without the order must try to make away with them since the legend made by the General [Bonaventure] is compiled from accounts of three who almost always accompanied Blessed Francis; all that they could certainly know and all that is proven is inserted herein.

With this stroke the friars tried to get beyond the disputes of the past. These controversies were destined to become even more bitter early in the next century; by scotching the earlier biographies, the order succeeded only in obscuring its own story. The Franciscans were efficient about destroying the manuscripts in their own libraries, although a very few lingered in the monasteries of other orders, waiting to be rediscovered centuries later. Just two copies of Celano's second life of Francis, which provided many important details about the saint's conversion, survived.

B onaventure's biography should not carry all the blame for the fact that Francis's novel views about reaching out to Muslims were widely disregarded. These views were overlooked long before Bonaventure ever took up a pen, even in Francis's lifetime.

The disconnect between the Francis of his own writings and the Francis of the early biographers shows through in their choice of Scripture passages. Francis's goal from the start of his ministry was simply to live the gospels. He identified a series of foundational New Testament passages and made them his guide. In terms of his emphasis on being a peacemaker, two passages stand out in his brief writings. He quoted Matthew 5:44—"love your enemies"—four times, twice in his *Admonitions,* and in each of the two known versions of the *Rule.* And he quoted the passage "blessed are the peacemakers" from Matthew 5:9 twice in *Admonitions.*

Like Francis, the early biographers also relied heavily on Scripture to make their points, which was customary in the Middle Ages. Bonaventure's *Major Legend of Saint Francis* contains more than six hundred allusions to Scripture, according to an index by the Franciscan Institute. All told, the known thirteenth- and fourteenth-century documents about Francis add up to more than two thousand pages in today's anthologies, containing thousands of allusions to Scripture. But not once did any of the early biographers of Francis allude to these two lines of Scripture that meant so much to him.

The great cycle of twenty-eight frescoes attributed to Giotto di Bondone in the upper church of the Basilica of St. Francis in Assisi, based on scenes in *The Major Legend,* helped to cement Bonaventure's vision of Francis for future generations. *The Ordeal by Fire,* which depicted Francis preparing to walk through fire as the sultan's scared religious adviser made a hasty retreat, inspired many other artists to re-create the same fictitious scene. Another Giotto work, *Saint Francis of Assisi before the Sultan,* which appears in the Basilica of Santa Croce in Florence, a Franciscan church, also was influential. In both paintings, the blazing but fictitious fire is a key element that heightens the emotional impact.

The huge influence of Bonaventure's legend can be seen by comparing the Giotto work with an anonymous master's earlier panel painting, also located in a chapel in the Basilica of Santa Croce. (See image on this book's jacket.) This work was completed before Bonaventure's legend and perhaps even before Thomas of Celano's second life of Francis, around 1245. (It was transferred later to the Basilica of Santa Croce, which was begun in 1294

The Ordeal by Fire by Giotto di Bondone is part of a cycle of twenty-eight frescoes in the upper church of the Basilica of St. Francis in Assisi depicting scenes
from the saint's life. *Copyright © Scala/Art Resource, New York*

and completed in the mid-fifteenth century). Based on the first biography,
it takes a far more benign view of Francis's encounter with Sultan al-Kamil,
depicting him as preaching peacefully to the attentive sultan and his placid
court. There are no fires or imams slinking into the shadows.

Members of the Spiritual faction recast the story of Francis in their
own revisionist biographies, but they did not tamper with the basics of an
account that was by then enshrined in powerful images on the walls of
their churches. They were content to accept Bonaventure's premise that
their order's founder went to Damietta seeking martyrdom and sought to

stage a trial by the ordeal of fire. The idea that Francis was a zealot willing to risk all for Christ appealed to the Spirituals. The story was embellished in the fourteenth century in *The Deeds of Blessed Francis* and in its popular Italian-language version, *The Little Flowers of Saint Francis,* works associated with the Spirituals. A magical tale of Francis bedding down in a blazing fire to convert a wanton woman—"a certain woman who was very beautiful in face and body but very foul in mind and soul"—in Damietta was added. According to this story, the woman "solicited St. Francis to commit a most shameful act with her." Francis responded by undressing and lying down amid the flames in a fireplace as if it were a bed.

Not only did Francis undergo the ordeal by fire in the new accounts, but he also arranged for Sultan al-Kamil to convert on his deathbed. This reflects the Spirituals' zeal for converting Muslims, which was rooted in their belief that the new age of the Spirit would be brought about through their missionary work. Francis's encounter with Sultan al-Kamil was seen as an alternative to the violence of the Crusades. Peter Olivi, a leading Spiritual thinker in the late thirteenth century, wrote that Francis's journey to Egypt was a step in the history of salvation.

The mystic and poet Raymond Lull, a layman who was influenced by Francis's example, traveled across northern Africa seeking to convert Muslims. He favored a philosophical approach, comparing the two religions with what he regarded as carefully reasoned arguments. It apparently led to his death by stoning in Tunis in 1315.

Meanwhile, the battle over the future of Francis's order between the Spirituals and Conventuals turned deadly. In 1318 Pope John XXII declared doctrines of the Spirituals heretical; among the errors he condemned was the friars' opposition to taking sworn oaths. The angry pope called for friars who held the condemned views to be hunted down. Some escaped into hiding; others recanted. Four brothers were burned at the stake in Marseille on May 7, 1318. In 1323 John XXII even denounced as heresy the teaching that Jesus had no belongings. Poverty and chastity were all well and good, the pope indicated, but obedience came first.

Dante, writing between 1315 and 1318, bemoaned the order's fate in *The Divine Comedy*. He had Thomas Aquinas declare from Paradise that most of the sheep—the friars—had strayed from Francis's fold, although some "to the shepherd cleave; but these so few." Dante put Bonaventure in Paradise and had him introduce Illuminato and Joachim as fellow residents as well. In keeping with Bonaventure's *Major Legend,* he included Francis's visit to the sultan in a summary of the saint's life:

> *And when*
> *He had, through thirst of martyrdom, stood up*
> *In the proud Soldan's presence, and there preach'd*
> *Christ and His followers, but found the race*
> *Unripen'd for conversion; back once more*
> *He hasted.*

Like the poet Henri d'Avranches nearly a century earlier, Dante portrayed Francis's encounter with Sultan al-Kamil as a waste of time for a man who should have been winning souls in Italy. Even Dante, it seems, did not sense the poetry of the encounter between the saint and the sultan.

By the next century Francis's peaceful approach to encountering Muslims was so thoroughly forgotten that a future saint in his order, John of Capistrano, led troops into battle against the Turks in 1454 in Hungary. The dynamic was far different than in Francis's time, when the Muslim rulers were inclined toward peace—the Turks had seized Constantinople the previous year, and Europe stood before them.

This surge of Muslim conquest explains the deeper sense of confrontation pervading the early Renaissance artist Benozzo Gozzoli's fresco *The Trial by Fire before the Sultan,* painted in 1452. It combines the stories of Francis before the sultan and his encounter with the wicked woman of Damietta in one scene; Francis is depicted standing atop a blazing fire before the sultan while the blond enchantress beckons seductively from the sidelines. The painting takes liberties with the fanciful stories in the *Little*

Benozzo Gozzoli's *The Trial by Fire before the Sultan* (1452), in the Church of St. Francis, Montefalco, reimagined the encounter between Francis and the sultan to include a blond seductress. *Copyright © Scala/Art Resource, New York*

Flowers of Saint Francis by including an inscription that says the sultan had sent the woman to tempt Francis. Significantly, the Franciscan order commissioned the fresco, which is part of a cycle of paintings on the life of Francis in the Church of St. Francis in Montefalco, in Umbria.

In short, everything Francis hoped to accomplish by going peacefully into the Muslim world was subverted, even within his own order, to serve the politics of the day. He had counseled love of enemies even at the risk of death; John of Capistrano led troops into battle. He and the sultan re-spected each other; his order depicted a sinister sultan in the art that dec-orated its churches.

By the sixteenth century Franciscans closely aligned with the Spanish crown argued that the use of coercion to convert Indians in the New World was acceptable. The three-century-old ideas of Abbot Joachim, re-heated to suit the times, continued to percolate within some Franciscan circles. Christopher Columbus, mesmerized by the apocalyptic notions the Franciscans kept alive, cast himself as a savior who would use gold taken from the New World to finance a new Crusade in Jerusalem. The seed Francis of Assisi had planted—his plan for fearlessly approaching Muslim enemies to live peacefully among them as friends—fell on rocky ground.

19

The Seed Sprouts

E ven the stump of a tree can grow a new shoot.

That shoot was the desert hermit Charles de Foucauld, a Catholic contemplative who, like Francis, believed in living as a quiet example among Muslims. Born in 1858 in Strasbourg, France, Foucauld grew up a privileged youth in a wealthy household, much as Francis had. As a young man, he soldiered for the French in North Africa, where he became impressed with Muslim religious practices. After leaving the military, he returned to the Sahara as an explorer. Then he underwent a conversion experience that drew him into his Catholic faith and led him to the Holy Land, to the Trappist order, to the priesthood, and finally to life as a hermit in Algeria. While living in the Sahara, he sought to live in fraternity with Muslims by learning the Bedouin tribes' language and culture. Like them, and like Francis, he lived in simplicity. But even in the desert his escape from war and violence went only so far; he was fatally shot in 1916 in a skirmish involving some tribesmen opposed to the French. He was beatified in 2005.

Foucauld's dream of brotherhood between Muslims and Christians did not die with him. Today eight spiritual associations and eleven religious orders trace back to him, including the Little Sisters of Jesus. Moreover, his legacy was kept alive by Louis Massignon, often described as the most prominent Western scholar of Islam. Foucauld was a mentor to Massignon, who was born in Nogent-sur-Marne, France, in 1883.

Massignon had returned to the Christian faith through his study of the great tenth-century Sufi mystic Mansur al-Hallaj, who reminded the Frenchman of Jesus because of his teachings about God's immanent love. He noticed that like Jesus, al-Hallaj was executed over his controversial teachings; he was put to death in Baghdad in 922. Rather than view al-Hallaj only through Christian eyes, according to scholar Seyyed Hossein Nasr, Massignon used his extraordinary knowledge of the nuances of the Arabic language to demonstrate through his scholarship that al-Hallaj's Sufism was rooted in meditation on the Qur'an and was therefore authentically Islamic. Through such scholarly work—and his own spiritual vitality and occasional political activism in behalf of Middle East peace—Massignon became a bridge between Islam and Christianity, a man at home in both belief systems.

Massignon's study of al-Hallaj led him to rediscover the roots of his own Christian faith. As he warmed to Christianity, he became deeply attached to Saint Francis—especially to the story of Francis at Damietta. Massignon so loved Francis that in 1931, after years of consideration, he joined the Franciscans' Third Order for lay people, taking the name Ibrahim (Arabic for Abraham), in honor of the father of the three great monotheistic faiths.

As a frequent traveler to Egypt, where he lectured at the University of Cairo, Massignon drew closer to the story of Francis and Sultan Malik al-Kamil as a way of bridging the chasm between Christians and Muslims. On February 9, 1934, he and his friend Mary Kahil, an Egyptian Christian, went to the site of the abandoned Franciscan church in Damietta—which Francis had founded—to pledge their lives to improving relations between Muslims and Christians. They invoked the same Scripture passage Francis had used to guide his followers: "Love your enemies and pray for those who persecute you." The vow Massignon and Kahil took was called a *badaliya*, taken from the Arabic word for "substitute." It refers to Jesus' willingness to offer himself in love for others. Massignon outlined his efforts to Pope Pius XI in a private audience later that year, telling Kahil in a letter that he had obtained the pontiff's approval. What became known as the Badaliya Prayer Movement received official sanction from the Vatican in 1947.

This movement continues today. In the United States, St. Paul's Church, a Catholic parish in Cambridge, Massachusetts, holds a prayer service monthly. Dorothy C. Buck, a member of the board of the Association of Friends of Louis Massignon, says the aim is to better understand the Islamic community's prayer life. "It's quite profound and deepens everybody's prayer life," she says. ". . . It encourages people to reach out to their Muslim neighbors."

Massignon worked tirelessly at reconciling Muslims and Christians; he was especially interested in getting the Franciscan order to rediscover and nurture the seed that Francis had planted through his encounter with Sultan al-Kamil. Father Giulio Basetti-Sani, a Franciscan from Italy, recalled that when he met Massignon in Paris in 1936, the French scholar urged him to learn more about Francis and Muslims, focusing his attention on passages in the *Earlier Rule*. Then ten years later in Cairo he spoke with Massignon again, and "the seeds began to germinate." He gradually escaped his former view that Muhammad was a prophet of Satan by accepting Massignon's advice to read the Qur'an with a sense of love and respect.

Massignon continued to point out the significance of Francis's visit with Sultan al-Kamil, telling Basetti-Sani that his duty was to get other members of his order to recognize they had a special calling to go peaceably among Muslims. Under Massignon's influence, Basetti-Sani gradually saw Islam in a new way and came to see Francis as a prophet whom God had sent to call the church to a new attitude toward Muslims. Father Basetti-Sani went on to write a key book about Francis and Muslims, *Mohammed et Saint François.* He remained close to Massignon until the French scholar's death in 1962.

Massignon did not live long enough to see a new era in Catholic-Muslim relations begin with the Second Vatican Council's 1965 *Declaration on the Relation of the Church to Non-Christian Religions,* or *Nostra Aetate,*

In Our Age. But his stamp is on that document, which declares that the Catholic Church has a high regard for Muslims:

> They adore the one God, living and subsisting in Himself; merciful and all-powerful, the Creator of heaven and earth, who has spoken to men; they take pains to submit wholeheartedly to even His inscrutable decrees, just as Abraham, with whom the faith of Islam takes pleasure in linking itself, submitted to God. Though they do not acknowledge Jesus as God, they revere Him as a prophet. They also honor Mary, His virgin Mother; at times they even call on her with devotion. In addition, they await the day of judgment when God will render their deserts to all those who have been raised up from the dead. Finally, they value the moral life and worship God especially through prayer, almsgiving and fasting.

Massignon was close to Cardinal Giovanni Battista Montini, the archbishop of Milan, who was elected as Pope Paul VI in 1963 and presided over the council when it issued *Nostra Aetate.* While a cardinal, Montini had defended Massignon when the Vatican's Holy Office (now called the Congregation for the Doctrine of the Faith) assailed his use of the term "the three Abrahamic religions."

While Francis could do no more than hint at his scandalous admiration for Muslim religious practices, Pope John Paul II built on the Vatican Council's foundation by declaring his appreciation for non-Christian religions in his first encyclical, writing that "though the routes taken may be different, there is but a single goal to which is directed the deepest aspiration of the human spirit as expressed in its quest for God and also in its quest . . . for the full meaning of human life."

John Paul's great contribution to Christian-Muslim relations stemmed from the fact that, like Francis, he was a bit of a showman. As a poet, actor, and playwright in his youth, the Polish pope had an uncanny sense for powerful symbolic gestures. Like Francis, he created tableaux of peace; he visited Muslim holy places in Jerusalem that the Crusaders had fought over, for example. Such choreographed events often communicated more through visual images than through the formal statements attached to them. Though his pontificate made many gestures for peace and reconciliation, the World Day of Prayer for Peace held in Assisi on October 26, 1986 stands out. Representatives from twelve religions visited Assisi's many sanctuaries to pray for peace, then gathered to pray side by side in the piazza outside the Basilica of St. Francis. A blustery fall wind and chilling drizzle blew through the town, which was warmed with the colors borne by a multitude of religious leaders, from feather-bedecked Native American shamans to African witch doctors to saffron-robed Buddhists.

That the event was held in Assisi rather than in some center of ecclesiastical power—or at least someplace with a large airport—was a symbolic testament to the ongoing rediscovery of Francis's legacy as a peacemaker who tried to build a bridge to Muslims during the Crusade. "I have chosen this town of Assisi as the place for our Day of Prayer for Peace because of the particular significance of the holy man venerated here—Saint Francis—known and revered by so many throughout the world as a symbol of peace, reconciliation and brotherhood," Pope John Paul said at the day's start in the Basilica of St. Mary of the Angels. Later, as the prayers for peace ended outside the Basilica of St. Francis, the pope invoked Francis's legacy again: "Saint Francis was a man of peace. We recall that he abandoned the military career he had followed for a while in his youth, and discovered the value of poverty, the value of a simple and austere life, in imitation of Jesus Christ whom he intended to serve." The direct link between Francis's rejection of warfare and his decision to adopt a life of holy poverty, downplayed in the past, was clear to John Paul.

The pope, who coined the term "the spirit of Assisi" to define the goodwill created that day, faced serious criticism from conservatives within his own church for praying side by side with people from other faiths. Even the church officials he appointed to create the Day of Prayer for Peace had expressed concerns to him that he might be watering down Catholic beliefs. Representatives of other religions had similar worries. While the "spirit of Assisi" still has its critics, John Paul resolved the objections by saying that participants would not "pray together" but "be together to pray."

"Assisi caused the Church [to] make a great leap forward towards non-Christian religions, which until then appeared to us to live on another planet," England's Cardinal Roger Etchegaray, who organized the event, later said. Even so, powerful Cardinal Joseph Ratzinger, then head of the Vatican's Congregation for the Doctrine of the Faith, insisted that what happened at Assisi must not be the model for future interreligious dialogue. But he later acknowledged during a visit to Assisi in 2007 as Pope Benedict XVI that the gathering had been "a prophetic intuition and a moment of grace."

In an article he wrote in 2002, the then-cardinal Ratzinger noted that Francis's conversion to a life of piety transformed him into an opponent of the Crusades. "Only then did he really know that the Crusades were not the appropriate way to protect the rights of Christians in the Holy Land, but that one had to take literally the message of the imitation of the Crucifix," he wrote.

John Paul continued to seek better relations with Muslims throughout his papacy. When he visited the Umayyad Great Mosque in Damascus in 2001, his remarks echoed Francis's hope that Christians could live peacefully among Muslims. "Interreligious dialogue is most effective," the pope said, "when it springs from the experience of 'living with each other' from day to day within the same community and culture."

Pushed along by John Paul, follow-ups to Assisi's 1986 interreligious gathering were held in 1999 and 2002. Kamel al-Sharif, secretary general of the International Islamic Council for Da'wa and Relief and a leading Muslim participant in the Assisi gatherings, spoke warmly of the example Francis and Sultan al-Kamil gave:

Saint Francis was among the first who called for peace and dialogue, and cast off violence and wars. And for our part, as Muslims, we are reminded of his visit to the Middle East during the Crusader wars, and of his condemnation of the European military actions against the Muslim nations, when he called them irrelevant actions, contrary to Christ's message of peace. It was not such an easy move during that period when fundamentalism, grudge and enmity were so high

among the Crusaders . . . [Sultan al-Kamil] welcomed him and
gathered for him a group of Muslim scholars to exchange with them
their views and ideas about religious matters. Just as St. Francis was a
true believer in Christianity, so also was Sultan al-Kamil with regard
to his Islam.

Members of the Franciscan order had laid the groundwork for John
Paul's "spirit of Assisi" meetings by responding to the Second Vatican
Council's call for religious orders to examine their roots more closely. As
far back as 1969 Franciscans in Egypt had held a prayer service with
Muslims in Damietta to celebrate the seven hundred fiftieth anniversary
of Francis's visit there, praying in a Catholic church and then at the site of
the city's ancient mosque. Franciscan scholars also began to study Francis's
own writings, which had been neglected for centuries.

Franciscans began to look for ways to apply Francis's dramatic gesture
of going to the sultan in their own time. Father GianMaria Polidoro, who
runs the Assisi-based organization Assisi Pax, tried with fellow Franciscans in 1984 to seek peace between the United States and Soviet Union.
They succeeded in arranging meetings with both nations' leaders, meeting Ronald Reagan in the White House and Mikhail Gorbachev during
his visit to Italy. In both cases the Franciscan friars wanted to meet directly with the leader. "This is the same as Saint Francis has done with the
sultan," Father Polidoro said in an interview at his office in the Chiesa
Nuova, a seventeenth-century church built above the house where Francis may have been born.

Father Polidoro, who wore large glasses, had a shock of white hair
across his forehead, and wore blue jeans beneath his brown tunic, said he
thought Francis had been trying to forge a friendly relationship with Sultan al-Kamil: "Francis, when he went to the sultan, he jumped the walls
of culture, of language, of religion, of economy." The priest and his fellow
Franciscans hoped that Reagan and Gorbachev could do the same when
they met. "Try to speak frankly with Gorbachev . . . try to speak to him
as a man who has a family," Father Polidoro said he and fellow friars ad-

vised Reagan. ". . . We told them, 'First of all, speak as a friend. Afterward, speak as leaders.' "

Taking Francis as their example, contemporary Franciscans have launched a host of initiatives aimed at furthering nonviolence and reconciliation. A program called the Damietta Initiative has sent out more than twenty teams of mediators trained in alternatives to violence in eastern and southern Africa. Pointing to "the spirit of mutual respect" between Francis and Sultan al-Kamil, the organization aims to stop violence based on religious differences, which is seen as a major threat to stability and progress in Africa. Conciliation teams try to avert violence over water and grazing rights, elections, and tribal conflicts. "The Muslims are on the whole very positive towards the initiative," says Father Donal O'Mahony, a Capuchin friar from Ireland who has worked more than forty years in Africa. "In a strange way, they relate to Franciscans more closely than to the Catholic Church" through diocesan clergy. Father O'Mahony said that Jan Hoeberichts's 1997 book *Francis and Islam,* which analyzed Francis's instruction to "be subject" to Muslims, inspired him as the Damietta Initiative was created. "Our experience is that the model of Francis and his relation to Islam is very relevant for today," he says.

Another group, the Pace e Bene Nonviolence Service, has offered some five hundred training sessions in how to resolve conflicts peacefully, reaching more than twenty-three thousand people since the program was founded by some Franciscans in California in 1989.

Franciscans also helped to organize interreligious events that Pope John Paul wanted to include in his 2000 pilgrimage to the Holy Land. One of the most intriguing moments occurred on March 22, 2000, when the pope celebrated mass outdoors in Bethlehem's Manger Square. Just after the pope completed his homily, the muezzin's call to noon prayer rang out, a bit late, from speakers that ringed a minaret at the Mosque of Omar along the square. John Paul sat quietly and waited as a sign of respect to Muslims. Afterward Palestinian Christians in the crowded square broke into cheers when the patriarch of Jerusalem, Michel Sabbah, told them that the Muslim prayer had been timed to coordinate with the papal mass. "We witness once again the unity of Muslims and Christians," he said. That sense of unity with Muslims was uncommon enough for the Palestinian Christians, however, that it brought joyful tears when they found out what had occurred.

The Franciscan order held its first conference on Islam in 1982, meeting in Assisi to discuss its mission among Muslims. Since then periodic congresses have been held, including a gathering in Rome on September 17–21, 2007, in which the implications of the encounter between Francis and Sultan al-Kamil for current mission work were discussed extensively. The order's minister general, Brother José Rodríguez Carballo, O.F.M., set the tone for how that encounter is understood today within the order:

> The Sultan discovered a man of faith in Francis. Francis, in turn, discovered a "believer" in the Sultan, a man who prayed five times a day, and was not a "son of the devil." The miracle of the encounter came about. The guns fell silent and dialogue began between these men, separated by religion and culture but united in faith. It is very significant that they both understood and respected each other, even though they spoke different languages. It was faith in the "clement and merciful God" that united them, though their religion was separating them.

Francis may have been frustrated in trying to get his missionary friars to value living quietly among Muslims without arguing about religion, but his forward-thinking approach nowadays inspires his successors. Speakers at the conference, attended by fifty friars who live among Muslims in many nations, stressed the importance of dialogue and working together over conversion. The minister general traced this idea back to a passage in Francis's *Rule* of 1223: "I counsel, warn and exhort my Friars in the Lord Jesus Christ, that when they go about through the world, they are not to quarrel nor contend in words, nor are they to judge others, but they are to be meek, peaceable and modest, meek and humble, speaking uprightly to all, as is fitting."

Nor would Vatican officials of Francis's lifetime have defined the missionary role as one did at the Rome conference. "The important thing is to reflect together in order to continually recover the common, shared values with our Muslim brothers and sisters, while always remaining on the mountain with Jesus and descending regularly for the mission entrusted to you by Him," Father Miguel Ángel Ayuso Guixot, head of the Rome-based Pontifical Institute for Arabic and Islamic Studies, said in remarks he delivered. "This is our mission." The missionary was to be a "promoter of dialogue" who worked "with believers of other religions in a spirit of religious pluralism and sharing the common duty of building a better world with them."

Francis, though he would have phrased this differently, would have been astonished to hear a Vatican official speak of such close cooperation with non-Christian religions. But the fruit being harvested is recognizably Francis's, seeded by his powerful sense of shared humanity with people society designated as his enemy.

Francis's entwined rejection of war and embrace of poverty also came to life in the Catholic Worker Movement, which Dorothy Day founded with Peter Maurin in 1933. Like Francis, its members identify with the poor and avoid catering to powerful religious or civic leaders.

In another sign of Francis's new influence as a peacemaker, the U.S. Catholic bishops cited his example in their much-discussed 1983 pastoral letter, *The Challenge of Peace: God's Promise and Our Response*:

> In the centuries between the fourth century and our own day, the theme of Christian non-violence and Christian pacifism has echoed and re-echoed, sometimes more strongly, sometimes more faintly. One of the great non-violent figures in those centuries was St. Francis of Assisi. Besides making personal efforts on behalf of reconciliation and peace, Francis stipulated that laypersons who became members of his Third Order were not "to take up lethal weapons, or bear them about, against anybody."

These words demonstrate the importance of recovering the true story of Francis, the sultan, and their efforts toward peace. Religion is built on tradition—but the stories comprising that tradition can often be forgotten or skewed. That is what happened to the story of Francis and the sultan: from the start, its meaning was obscured to protect the popes' Crusade dreams. Then it was buried ever deeper in successive biographies of Francis and the artwork they inspired. The church Francis served is now cultivating the political implications in the long-buried story of his nonviolence and radical love. Francis continues to return Christians to their roots, nudging them to reject violence and to approach enemies with love. Though he is dead for close to eight centuries, the story of his encounter with the sultan is blossoming.

Epilogue

W hat can the story of Francis of Assisi and Sultan Malik
al-Kamil mean to us today?

In the fall of 2007 I went to Cairo, Damietta, and
Assisi, looking for an answer to that question as I did
research for this book. I sat for tea with Father Emmanuel Maken, the
wizened Franciscan pastor of red-bricked St. Anthony Church in Cairo,
and asked him about the significance of Francis's trip to Egypt. "It's important because he started Christian-Islamic dialogue," the priest said.
Father Maken has studied the Franciscan presence in Damietta and documented it back all the way to Francis's visit. The Franciscans underwent
some hard times in Damietta, with two martyrdoms and several expul-
sions, he explained. It was, even so, a story of hope. He noted that the encounter between Francis and the sultan provided the foundation for the
World Day of Prayer for Peace in Assisi in 1986.

I also visited the papal nunciature in Cairo, a beautiful palace with a
view over the Nile. When I rang the doorbell at the front gate, Archbishop Michael Fitzgerald, the nuncio, responded on the speaker and
buzzed me in. I walked through a green courtyard, taking in a view of the
Nile through palm trees and vines shaped into leafy arches.

Archbishop Fitzgerald had been the president of the Pontifical Council for Interreligious Dialogue before the new pope, Benedict XVI, sent him to Cairo in 2006 to be the Vatican's representative to Egypt and the Arab League. Some have noted that it was a mistake to reassign Fitzgerald, the Vatican's top expert on Islam, given how Pope Benedict later fumbled relations with Muslims by citing an inflammatory remark about Muhammad in public.

We talked a bit about Fitzgerald's former boss, Pope John Paul II, in the context of Francis's journey to the sultan. "John Paul was convinced that you can't respond to violence with violence," he said, adding that the pope had seen how nonviolence succeeded in ending communist rule in Poland.

Francis's encounter with the sultan "can be an antidote, a reminder that responding to violence through violence cannot succeed, that goodness and respect can change hearts really," he said. "But you have to be realistic in the sense that the meeting of Francis and the sultan didn't have any effect by ending the war. It was of more symbolic importance than political importance."

Many Egyptians I spoke to while researching this book brought up the subject of the war in Iraq. Bishop Yohanna Golta, the Coptic Catholic bishop of Cairo, raised it after he spoke of how the Crusades had poisoned the atmosphere in Egypt for Christians. "It's not finished," he said, referring to the difficulties contemporary Christians face in the Middle East. We spoke in an office behind the large, modern Cathedral of the Blessed Virgin in Nasr City, a brightly lit section of Cairo that is filled with high-rise condominiums. Bishop Yohanna, a sturdy-looking, authoritative-sounding man in a black cassock with white hair combed back from the forehead and a white mustache and goatee, continued with some heat in his voice: "I don't understand your President Bush. He begins a war against Iraq: 'This is a crusade.' You can understand why the Muslims now are against America—because Bush announced a new Crusade."

While I wrote this book, the war in Iraq unfolded, month after month. I found myself drawing parallels to the Fifth Crusade. The comparison can't be precise, but I could not help noticing that both conflicts were sold to the public as preemptive wars; Pope Innocent III claimed that the Crusader state based in Acre faced imminent attack. Nor could I ignore that, much as valid United Nations inspection reports on Iraq were ignored, Pope Innocent also disregarded what we would today call intelligence data: the patriarch of Jerusalem had informed the pope in a letter that the Muslim leaders "are quite willing to return the Holy Land which they [now] hold into the hands of the lord pope for the use of the Christians." Sultan al-Adil and his sons, the patriarch wrote, "wish above all to make peace with the Roman Church." This turned out to be a very accurate intelligence analysis, and Pope Innocent concealed it in his rush to war. It does not take too much imagination to draw parallels to the start of the war in Iraq in 2003. Innocent was a man of action who, in his zeal, did not heed the consequences of the wars he started, including the backlash he would stimulate against Christians in the Middle East. The same can be said for the Iraq war's architects, whose ideological fervor gave them a misguided faith that an undersize army could swiftly accomplish the mission of bringing democracy to a divided people with many scores to settle.

The dynamic of stirring a populace to war has not changed over time; it still begins with demonizing the enemy. Francis saw through it. Going against the grain, he insisted on treating the enemy with love, refusing to denigrate Islam or its followers. Francis's refusal to demonize the enemy remains an important lesson today. Another lesson to glean from Francis's example is that the road to peace is for all of us, not just the government officials who lead in our name. Francis took matters into his own hands by bravely seeking out a personal relationship with the sultan. War is more likely to result when one people is distanced from another and demonized. Peace gets a chance when the divide between peoples is bridged through personal relationships.

In recent times Pope John Paul II stands out as a leader who knew the importance of using personal relationships in trying to make peace. With a U.S. invasion of Iraq imminent in March 2003, John Paul sent envoys to press both countries' leaders for peace. Cardinal Roger Etchegaray met with Saddam Hussein, and Cardinal Pio Laghi with George W. Bush. The aim was to create a dialogue to avert war; the effort went unheeded. Bush's legacy as a president could have been much different had he been open to Cardinal Laghi's criticism.

By dispatching Cardinal Laghi to the White House, the pope was in effect heeding Francis's Scriptural advice to be "shrewd as serpents and simple as doves"—the cardinal, a former papal nuncio to the United States, was a family friend of the Bushes, a tennis partner of the president's father, former President George H. W. Bush. There already was a relationship. In a speech he gave seven months later during a conference at a monastery in Italy, Laghi said he questioned the president on his insistence that Iraq had weapons of mass destruction. Bush told him that Saddam Hussein, Iraq's president, had been training members of al-Qaeda. Laghi responded: "Are you sure? Where is the evidence?" The cardinal said he warned Bush about the chaos that could be unleashed between Sunni and Shiite Muslims if Iraq were attacked.

A church official accompanying Laghi debated with a high-ranking aide to Bush about whether God approved of going to war in Iraq, a source with knowledge of the meeting has told me. Thus the talk at this high-level meeting in the Oval Office eerily echoed the debate over the Fifth Crusade, which started after Pope Innocent announced that the war had divine favor.

According to an account by the Catholic News Service, Laghi said that Bush acted almost as if he felt divinely inspired and "seemed to truly believe in a war of good against evil." This isn't the place for a drawn-out look at whether Bush's religious views affected U.S. foreign policy during his presidency. Nor do I oppose putting religious values into play in the public debate. But the fact that it has been an issue at all says a great deal. We have not come quite so far as we think from the Middle Ages: religious beliefs are still an important part of the public debate over going to war. The religious criteria for a just war are still a source of heated discussion. Beyond that, religion permeates the political process in the nation with the world's most powerful army.

The story of Francis and the sultan even figured in the war of words that preceded the fighting in Iraq. In February 2003 the Iraqi deputy prime minister, Tariq Aziz, visited Assisi and prayed for peace at Francis's tomb. The Franciscan in charge of the Basilica of St. Francis showed Aziz, a Chaldean Catholic, the ivory horn that the sultan gave to Francis, presenting it as a symbol of peace. This action led to some scathing criticism of the Franciscans, who were accused of taking sides.

Religious leaders *should* take a stand on such an important moral issue, though, and of course prominent figures weighed in both for and against starting the Iraq war. The problem, then, is to determine which religious values are authentic. This was the same issue Francis faced as he tried to reform the church. The simplicity valued in the first century had been replaced in the medieval church by a lust for war and wealth. With religion subverted to justify those ends, Francis sought to return his church to the authentic values found in the gospels, including love for the enemy. Today, just as in Francis's time, religion is twisted to justify destructive agendas.

Hence the value of uncovering the true story of Francis as peacemaker; from the depths of his deep piety and his personal experience as a soldier and POW, he gave an authentic religious response to war. As we have seen, he offered that example throughout his life, starting with his decision to follow what he believed to be God's will by turning back from the road to war. Francis believed that God instructed him to befriend and love his enemies and to see war as the devil's work. As he wrote in his *Testament,* the turning point in his life came when he overcame his revulsion and kissed a leper. Francis looked beneath the frightening appearance of those his society considered repulsive and embraced what he found. He was called to radical compassion—to displays of kindness that shocked others into loving what they had considered hateful. He approached the sultan in that spirit, hoping not only to win over an enemy but to show fellow Christians that warfare was the wrong way to approach Islam.

For Francis, this was authentic Christianity, rooted in the gospel. Christians and others who see Francis as a model should value his skepticism for warfare and his courageous willingness to reach out to enemies. As Pope Pius XI wrote in 1926, "There has never been anyone in whom the image of Jesus Christ . . . shone forth more lifelike and strikingly than in St. Francis."

The major religions are all vulnerable to the accusation that they have been used to advance violence rather than to prevent it. Francis's response was to go deeper into his own religious tradition than Pope Innocent and his corps of Crusade preachers did, retrieving Jesus' injunction to love enemies as the basis for his approach to Muslims. And while medieval Christian accounts maintained that Sultan al-Kamil violated Muslim religious law through his willingness to listen to Francis, he in fact went deeper into his own religious tradition, retrieving the theme of respect for holy Christians, even though he was under attack by the pope's forces. Mahmoud Ayoub, professor of Islam at Temple University, says that the sultan's actions should remind Muslims of their tradition of reverence for Christian holiness. "I think one of the greatest lessons [of the encounter between Francis and the sultan] is that we need . . . to appreciate holiness and also show the respect that we have lost for holy people, men and women. The second thing for me is, I think it should remind us both, Muslims and Christians, but from my point of view, Muslims, of the Qur'anic and traditional Islamic reverence for Christian holiness."

Ironically, the war in Iraq drew some of its strongest support from Christian leaders who profess to take the Bible literally. Francis was a biblical literalist; he sought to imitate Jesus as closely as possible. He tried to discover his mission in life by choosing passages in the Bible at random. But his biblical literalism led him to love his enemies even at his own peril, not to attack them. Anyone seeking an answer to the question "What would Jesus do?" would be better advised to look to Francis than to those Christian leaders in the United States who supported the decision to go to war.

Francis's response to the warmongers of his day was to try to return the church to its roots in the time of the apostles, when nonviolence was still the rule and not something to be rationalized away. The task of returning the major religions to their authentic selves remains—and it remains important, given the role that religion plays in shaping public debate in the United States and many other countries.

While the encounter between Francis and Sultan al-Kamil offers valuable lessons for us today, it has to be viewed in the context of its own time, not ours. We should not see Francis as some placard-carrying political demonstrator, the hippie saint. Father GianMaria Polidoro, who leads the peace organization Assisi Pax, stressed that point when I interviewed him in the Chiesa Nuova in Assisi. Scholars differ on whether that church—which boasts a cramped cell where Francis's angry father supposedly imprisoned him—is really built on the site of the Bernardone family home. But Francis's spirit pervades, and Father Polidoro has spent a good deal of time considering and writing about what it means for war and peace. "The peace of Francis is to go back to Eden," he told me. "Because Jesus redeemed us from sin, he redeemed us from war. When we are redeemed we go back to Eden." In other words, the peace Francis spoke of was not the peace of the antiwar movement but something transcendent. It was about creating a new era of reconciliation—in gospel terminology, about creating God's kingdom on earth. Father Polidoro said that members of his order today focus too much on stopping war rather than on the broader peace that Francis preached, which he said is about changing relationships.

The sultan's example—his openness to Francis—is also important. Father Mamdouh Shehab, a round-faced, fifty-three-year-old Egyptian friar at the Franciscan Center of Christian Oriental Studies, located on a side street just off a thoroughfare in a traffic-choked district of Cairo, made that point when we spoke. On entering the center, I was surprised to find a small car in the foyer—parking is difficult in Cairo. We walked through spacious but simple rooms, decorated with a few rugs, and went out to a veranda where we brushed off flies and temperatures were in the mid-nineties under a late October sun. He described Sultan al-Kamil as "a wise voice," adding, "Malik al-Kamil is giving to Christianity a lesson in dialogue, in tolerance." Father Shehab spoke with great passion about the encounter between Francis and al-Kamil, noting that the sultan could have taken a much more severe approach to the two Christian vagabonds who dared to insist that they speak to him. Nowadays it's necessary to hire a lobbyist to talk to a city councilman, much less a monarch. Al-Kamil listened to Francis—and was open to a dialogue—even though he had much else to worry about.

Father Shehab had until recently been the pastor of St. Joseph's Church, an imposing presence in downtown Cairo's banking district, with its rotunda and castlelike bell tower. Outside the church is a statue of a steadfast-looking Saint Francis, stepping forth, jaw jutting forward, eyes

Arnoldo Zocchi depicted *Francis and the Sultan* as part of a 1909 sculpture outside St. Joseph's Church in Cairo. *Copyright © 2007 by Paul Moses*

fixed. Beneath it is a relief sculpture that shows Francis in the same position, approaching the sultan, hand raised. The sultan, meanwhile, leans forward so far that he is nearly coming off his throne. He returns Francis's steady gaze with one of his own. This is the wise sultan Father Shehab saw, crafted by the Italian sculptor Arnoldo Zocchi in the first decade of the twentieth century. This version is more accurate than the one depicted in medieval and Renaissance art; there is no fire blazing between Francis and the sultan.

I think that one reason the sultan leans forward so is that the artist wanted to show how surprised he was to find a Western Christian who was so holy. Sultan al-Kamil had met some pious Coptic monks before but never a Western Christian like Francis, who was irresistible because of the spirituality that emanated from him. Clashing religious views have often provoked discord, but the story of Francis and the sultan demonstrates that religious figures can play a role in building a bridge between Christians and Muslims. Like Francis, they must come with unsoiled hands. But the path Francis offers is not easy to follow; it is based on sacrifice. His peacemaking began when he summoned the courage to kiss a leper.

The story of the sultan and the friar, like any good story, resonates with various levels of meaning rather than with a single precise moral. It doesn't so much prescribe a course of conduct as suggest hope that the right path still can be found. If Francis and Sultan al-Kamil were able to share a common word during the vicious battles of 1219, we should be able to do the same. A lot of history has happened since then; the power relationships between Western Christians and Muslims in the Middle East have changed, still affected by the colonial era in the nineteenth and twentieth centuries. Both sides have played the aggressor in the long history of conflict between Christians and Muslims, and both have resorted to "holy" wars. The destructive power of weaponry has changed, making it difficult to apply what happened in the Middle Ages to our day.

But as the Muslim scholar Seyyed Hossein Nasr said to me, "Usually violence brings violence. And the West during the last two centuries, the colonial period, has always shown its sharp teeth, not the sense of gentleness and love." He said he believes that if more people follow the path of Saint Francis, "the reciprocity will be there." Nasr, a widely recognized expert on Islam and a leader in Muslim-Christian dialogue, has taken his own steps on the path. He recalled that he had sought out the place where Francis is said to have received the stigmata. "We were allowed to pray there," he said.

On a brisk but sunny November morning I took a bus from hilltop Assisi to the lowlands Francis loved, searching for the battlefield where he fought. It's not the usual stop for pilgrims or tourists, and it took some doing to convince the bus driver to let me off in the center of the tiny town of Collestrada rather than at the Collestrada shopping center, then celebrating its tenth anniversary as Umbria's largest mall. I quickly found that the street was called "Hospital of St. Francis." The leper hospital, which was standing in the midst of the Battle of Collestrada, is now a four-story school built of large stones at the bottom and bricks higher up. It had the Perugian insignia, a griffin, and above the door an inscription recalling that the building had once been a leprosarium. I walked a tree-lined road up the hill, which flattened at the top, and found a thick-walled medieval compound with the griffin insignia on the huge wooden gates and again in the wall above them. The site is now a church, with a sculpture outside of two people hugging. Reminders of Francis are noted proudly all over Italy, especially in Umbria, but the reference to his experience at Collestrada was noted only in passing. A sign above the entrance to the compound listed the names of local men who had died in combat. It invoked Francis, in Italian:

> Here where Saint Francis of Assisi
> Made a pledge of peace
> And saw a vision in heaven
> of solemn, holy forgiveness,
> the names of our proud fallen for the defense of Italy . . .

After that I walked along the road, following the signs to the Ponte San Giovanni. The old bridge had washed out during a flood in 2000, but a new one had been built over the spot where Francis was dragged to the dungeon in Perugia. I caught a bus up to the walled city, high up on a hill, and found Il Palazzo del Capitano del Popolo, an austere court building made of gray stone blocks, with two wooden griffins on the dark brown wooden doors, facing each other. Francis was imprisoned someplace on that site, before the palace was built. It is located on the edge of a cliff, and I was struck at how far down below grade it plunged. Next to it was a market that went down four floors beneath street level. Francis's life began to change somewhere in those depths; I could find no plaque pointing out that he had been a resident there.

In the Basilica of St. Francis in Assisi I saw that John of Brienne had found his way back to Francis. Late in his life the Crusader king donated his wealth to building a basilica that Francis would not have wanted, and he was rewarded with a burial in that same edifice. At the end of his colorful life, it is said, he took the habit by joining the laypersons' Third Order. His monument, which features sculptures of angels parting a curtain around his royal-robed likeness, is some forty paces from the stairway leading down to Francis's tomb. Few pilgrims stop at John's monument as they line up to visit the saint who urged a stop to the battle that the king of Jerusalem fought at Damietta.

After leaving Assisi, I also visited the tomb of Pope Innocent III, finding it about two dozen paces from the main altar in the great Basilica of St. John Lateran in Rome. Although he masterminded a series of disastrous wars, some with long-term repercussions, he was entombed in that privileged place with a monument built near the end of the nineteenth century. A statue of a fresh-faced Crusader stood watch by the tomb.

In Cairo I visited a quiet section on the southern fringe of the teeming city, searching for the legacy of Sultan Malik al-Kamil. The taxi driver approached the Mausoleum of Imam al-Shafi'i through narrow, dusty streets, the car bouncing along as it passed through a vast cemetery. The mausoleum was closed when we arrived, and so we waited in an *ahwa*, a café, drinking hot tea and flicking away flies. Sheep and goats fed in the street, parting only slowly for the occasional compact car or donkey-drawn carts carrying onions or other produce.

The Mausoleum of Imam al-Shafi'i has a beautiful ribbed dome that Sultan al-Kamil built. There is a distinctive copper boat on top. The great imam's tomb is beneath the dome, surrounded by intricately decorated wooden slats. Money, donated by visitors, was piled inside the slats. Along the walls, going up about twelve feet, were inlaid marble rectangles in gray, beige, white, and black. There were three prayer niches with more intricate marble designs; people prostrated themselves in prayer, facing the niches. A tall alabaster column next to the imam's tomb told his story. Malik al-Kamil was buried in a place of honor in Damascus after his three daughters purchased property for his mausoleum, which had a window looking out on the Umayyad Great Mosque. His tomb was close by those of his father and his uncle, Saladin. But he is memorialized in the Mausoleum of Imam al-Shafi'i, close to his own mother's tomb. With its towering dome, dim lighting, carpeted floor, and prayerful visitors, it is a quiet place with a feeling of sanctity.

My search for Francis and the sultan took me to Damietta. The city is about three hours' drive north of Cairo, and I visited on a warm, sunny late October day. The air in Damietta was filled with the sounds of hammers and saws, the clip-clopping of horses and ponies, and the shouts of fish vendors. The city has sprawled far beyond where it was in Sultan al-Kamil's day; it was moved south to avoid further invasions after the Crusade of King Louis IX was repelled in 1250. The Nile, in turn, has changed course and moved to the west. The city has expanded to meet it, and a lovely brick promenade runs along the river. Damietta is known for furniture manufacturing, sweets, salted fish. There are stacks of lumber everywhere and workshops where men hone wood into sofas, chairs, beds, and other furniture.

Shaimaa Fouad, an archaeologist from Egypt's Supreme Council for Antiquities who grew up in Damietta, brought me to her native city's ancient mosque, which was being restored. There I met the agency's chief official on the site, Bahaa El-Din Wahba Ramadan, a tall, slim, reserved man in a white shirt. They gave me a tour of the grounds. Egypt's second-oldest mosque dates to early Islamic times, about 643 C.E., just twenty-one years after Muhammad made his hegira, or migration from Mecca. It fell into disrepair when the groundwater rose in the 1960s, swamping the mosque and turning it into a fishing hole. Marble columns sank into the muck, and inlaid marble pathways were obscured.

As I walked around, workers built thick new brick walls based on the originals. Wooden frames were erected to shape and support pointed arches. Vaulted ceilings were constructed over passageways that bordered a central courtyard. New marble columns were being installed, designed to look just like the ancient ones that had been recovered. There were to be 170 columns in all, part of an ambitious, long-term project to create the ancient mosque anew.

As I asked about how the mosque looked at the time of the Crusade, my gracious hosts' eyes darkened; the thought that the site had been in Christian hands seemed to pain them, nearly eight hundred years after the fact. But as I spoke more about Francis, they became curious and asked questions about him.

Restoration expert Mohamed Bahget Elgahary, friendly and bright-eyed, brought me over to see a long wooden beam from the original that had been embedded in a wall of the mosque, Qur'anic verses still visible on it. Workers had restored this piece of wood, inserting parts of the missing letters in the beam, which was about twenty feet long. In a shaded area, workers were restoring and remaking the marble pathways. Copying from the original, skilled stonecutters crafted white and gray marble pieces, angled at the end and interwoven against a black background. Everything left from the original was being reused, even fragments.

Back in the central courtyard under the hot sun in the midst of the 43,000-square-foot complex, I tried to imagine the imam in his *minbar*, exhorting his dying people to have strength during the siege of Damietta. I thought about Francis, who would have visited the mosque during the period it had been converted into a church while the city was under Crusader occupation. Francis went on to leave the city, outraged at the Crusaders' conduct. The voice of Cardinal Pelagius had rung out in that space when he presided at mass. John of Brienne, who had tried to temper

Cardinal Pelagius's fanatical impulse to conquer all Egypt and to get him to give back Damietta in return for Jerusalem, had been there too; perhaps he knelt and prayed on it there. And then I imagined the Crusaders hunkered down in Damietta; they had gone to the same place to debate ferociously whether to turn the city over to the sultan without a fight after the Crusader troops were defeated to the south. And finally I imagined Sultan al-Kamil entering the mosque after winning back the city, triumphant but saddened at the deaths of tens of thousands of his people.

All this occurred in the ancient mosque in Damietta, close to a cemetery where slain soldiers were buried. Not long ago it was a waterlogged grave. Now it is a sparkling house of worship that is 1,350 years old and yet shining new. To see it resurrected so splendidly is a reminder that our history is never so far away as we think and that maybe, just maybe, we can repair the damage left from the mistakes of the past.

The saint and the sultan would have shared that hope.

Main Characters

Francis and the Franciscans

FRANCIS OF ASSISI, 1181/2–1226—Founder of Order of Friars Minor. Canonized in 1228.

BERNARD OF QUINTAVALLE, ?–1241—Wealthy Assisian. One of Francis's first two followers.

BONAVENTURE, 1221–1274—Theologian and minister general of Franciscan order. Doctor of the church. Cardinal. Canonized in 1482.

ELIAS OF CORTONA, 1180?–1253—Began order's mission in Palestine in 1217. Minister general, 1232–1239.

GILES, ?–1262—One of Francis's first companions, from Assisi.

ILLUMINATO, ?–1266?—Friar who accompanied Francis on his visit to the sultan. From Arce, located in valley below Assisi.

JOHN OF PARMA, 1209?–1289—Minister general, 1247–1257. Beatified in 1777.

JORDAN OF GIANO, 1195–1262—Franciscan who went to Germany as missionary. Chronicled the order's early history.

LEO, ?–1272—Close friend of Francis who received a parchment from him at La Verna in 1224.

PETER OF CATANIA, ?–1221—One of Francis's first two followers and his first vicar.

SYLVESTER, ?–1240—Assisi priest who joined Francis and prayed for peace in warring Arezzo.

THOMAS OF CELANO, ?–1255—Franciscan hagiographer. Wrote major works on the life of Saint Francis.

The Sultan and His Circle

MALIK AL-KAMIL NASIR AD-DIN MUHAMMAD, 1180–1238—Sultan of Egypt, 1218–1238. Son of Malik al-Adil.

SALAH AD-DIN YUSUF IBN AYYUB, or Saladin, 1137/8–1193—Sultan who conquered Jerusalem in 1187. Uncle of Sultan al-Kamil.

MALIK AL-ADIL SAYF AD-DIN, 1145–1218—Father of Sultan al-Kamil; brother of Saladin. Sultan of Egypt, 1200–1218. Sultan of Syria, 1196–1218.

MALIK AL-MU'AZZAM SHARAF AD-DIN ISA, 1181?–1227—Younger brother of Sultan al-Kamil. Sultan of Syria, 1218–1227.

MALIK AL-ASHRAF MUSA, 1182/3–1237—Younger brother of Sultan al-Kamil. Sultan of Jezireh, 1210–1220, 1229–1237. Sultan of Syria, 1229–1237.

IMAD AD-DIN IBN AL-MASHTUB, 1179–1222—Emir who attempted an unsuccessful coup against Sultan al-Kamil.

FAKHR AL-FARISI, 1133–1225—Religious adviser to Sultan al-Kamil.

Emperors, Kings, and Counts

EMPEROR FREDERICK I, 1123–1190—His control of Assisi during Francis's youth angered merchants.

EMPEROR HENRY VI, 1165–1197—Son of Frederick I. His death set the stage for battles between the papacy and the imperial forces.

EMPEROR FREDERICK II, 1194–1250—Son of Henry VI. Crowned Holy Roman emperor in 1220.

CONRAD OF URLINGSEN, ?–1202—Count of Assisi, Duke of Spoleto, and lord of the Rocca, the Assisi castle that local merchants destroyed.

JOHN OF BRIENNE, ?–1237—French nobleman who led Christian force in Fifth Crusade. King of Jerusalem.

MARKWARD OF ANWEILER, ?–1202—Led imperial army against Pope Innocent III in southern Italy.

RICHARD THE LION-HEARTED, 1157–1199—King of England, 1189–1199. Led Third Crusade.

WALTER OF BRIENNE, ?–1205—Count from Champagne. Older brother of John of Brienne. Led army that Francis aspired to join in southern Italy.

Church Leaders

POPE CELESTINE III, 1106–1198—Elected pope in 1191.

POPE INNOCENT III, 1160/1–1216—Elected pope in 1198. One of the most powerful popes.

POPE HONORIUS III, ?–1227—Elected pope in 1216. Approved Franciscan *Rule* in 1223.

POPE GREGORY IX, ?–1241—As Cardinal Ugolino, served as protector of Friars Minor. Elected pope in 1227. Nephew of Innocent III.

JOACHIM OF FIORE, 1132–1202—Cistercian abbot from Calabria. Mystic whose biblical prophecies were influential long after his death.

CARDINAL JOHN OF ST. PAUL, ?–1216?—Influential Benedictine cardinal from the Basilica of St. Paul outside the Wall, in Rome. Championed the Friars Minor in the order's early years.

CARDINAL PELAGIUS GALVANI, 1165–1230?—Papal legate who took charge of the Christian army in the Fifth Crusade. Buried in abbey at Montecassino.

JAMES OF VITRY, 1160?–1240—Bishop of Acre. Cardinal. Crusade preacher. Prolific writer.

OLIVER OF PADERBORN, 1170–1227—Cologne scholastic. Cardinal. Wrote chronicle of Fifth Crusade, *The Capture of Damietta.*

Time Line

1095: Pope Urban II calls for Crusade.

1099: Crusaders conquer Jerusalem.

1180: Malik al-Kamil, future sultan of Egypt, is born.

1181/2: Giovanni di Bernardone is born in Assisi and nicknamed Francesco, or Francis.

1187: Crusaders surrender Jerusalem to Muslim forces led by Salah ad-Din Yusuf ibn Ayyub, or Saladin.

1189: Third Crusade is launched.

1190: Death of Emperor Frederick I.

1192: During the Third Crusade, Richard the Lion-Hearted knights Malik al-Kamil in Acre. Crusade concludes with Jerusalem remaining under Muslim control.

1193: Death of Saladin.

1198: After death of Celestine III, Pope Innocent III begins reign.

1200: Malik al-Adil consolidates control over the Ayyubid empire that his brother, Saladin, had led. Appoints his sons as viceroys, with the eldest, Malik al-Kamil, to govern Egypt.

1202: Death of Joachim of Fiore.

1202: Francis fights in Battle of Collestrada and is imprisoned in Perugia.

1203: Francis is ransomed from prison in Perugia.

1204: Fourth Crusade ends with Crusaders sacking Constantinople.

1204: After a dream, Francis turns back from his plan to seek knighthood, beginning his gradual conversion.

1206: Francis, estranged from his father, begins to repair churches and care for lepers.

1208: With a small group of followers, Francis begins to preach.

1208: Murder of papal inquisitor in southern France leads Pope Innocent III to order the Albigensian Crusade against the Cathars.

1209/10: Francis gets verbal approval from Pope Innocent III for the earliest *Rule* of his new order.

1212: Christian forces win key victory over Moors in Battle of Las Navas de Tolosa.

1212: Francis sets out to preach in the Holy Land but returns home after his ship is blown off course.

1213: Pope Innocent III calls for the Fifth Crusade.

1213/14: Francis travels to the shrine of St. James in Spain.

1215: The Fourth Lateran Council approves a new Crusade.

1216: Death of Pope Innocent III. Pope Honorius III is elected.

1217: Francis sends missionaries to Germany, Hungary, North Africa, and Palestine but obeys Cardinal Ugolino's order not to go.

1218: Christian troops lay siege to Damietta. Cardinal Pelagius arrives to take charge. Malik al-Kamil becomes sultan of Egypt.

1219: Francis of Assisi arrives in Crusader camp outside Damietta. Meets Sultan Malik al-Kamil. Crusaders capture Damietta.

1220: Five Franciscan friars are beheaded in Morocco.

1220: Francis returns to Italy and is disturbed at changes in his order.

1220: Frederick II is crowned Holy Roman emperor.

1221: Francis writes *Earlier Rule,* but it does not get approval.

1221: Crusaders are defeated in Egypt. Sultan al-Kamil allows them to return home without further slaughter.

1223: Pope Honorius III approves a much-altered *Rule.*

1224: Francis's mystical experience at La Verna.

1226: Francis dies on October 3.

1227: Cardinal Ugolino becomes Pope Gregory IX.

1228: Gregory IX canonizes Francis on July 16.

1228: The Sixth Crusade is launched.

1229 (or late 1228): Thomas of Celano completes *The Life of Saint Francis.*

1229: Sultan al-Kamil and Emperor Frederick II reach a treaty that gives Christians temporary control of Jerusalem.

1230: Pope Gregory IX redefines meaning of poverty in Franciscan order.

1238: Death of Sultan Malik al-Kamil.

1241: Death of Pope Gregory IX.

1247: Thomas of Celano completes his second official life of Francis, *The Remembrance of the Desire of a Soul.*

1247: John of Parma is appointed to head the order.

1250: After King Louis IX is captured in the Battle of Fariskur, the Seventh Crusade ends with a Christian defeat.

1254: Scandal breaks out in the order over Gerard of Borgo San Donnino's *The Introduction to the Eternal Gospel.*

1266: Bonaventure's *The Major Legend of Saint Francis* is declared the official life of Francis. The order begins destroying earlier versions.

1270: Louix IX dies in Tunisia while leading the Eighth Crusade.

1291: Acre falls to Muslim forces, ending the Christians' military presence in the region.

1318: Pope John XXII declares the doctrines of Franciscan Spiritual faction to be heretical. Four brothers are burned at the stake. Dante bemoans the order's fate in *The Divine Comedy.*

1454: John of Capistrano, a Franciscan friar, leads troops into battle against the Turks in Hungary.

Abbreviations

Writings of Francis

ER: *The Earlier Rule*
LR: *The Later Rule*
LRP: *A Letter to the Rulers of the People*
Test: *Testament*

Early Sources

1 Cel : *The Life of Saint Francis* by Thomas of Celano
2 Cel: *The Remembrance of the Desire of a Soul* by Thomas of Celano
3 Cel: *The Treatise on the Miracles* by Thomas of Celano
AC: *The Assisi Compilation*
AP: *The Anonymous of Perugia*
DBF: *The Deeds of Blessed Francis*
JG: *The Chronicle of Jordan of Giano,* in *XIIIth Century Chronicles,* translated by Placid Hermann, O.F.M.
JS: *The Life of Saint Francis* by Julian of Speyer
L3C: *The Legend of the Three Companions*
LF: *The Little Flowers of Saint Francis*
ML: *The Major Legend of Saint Francis* by Saint Bonaventure
MP: *A Mirror of the Perfection*
Trib: *The Book of Chronicles or of the Tribulations of the Lesser Ones,* by Angelo Clareno
VL: *The Versified Life of Saint Francis* by Henri d'Avranches

Other Works

FA:ED: *Francis of Assisi: Early Documents.* Edited by Regis J. Armstrong, O.F.M. Cap; J. A. Wayne Hellman, O.F.M. Conv.; and William J. Short, O.F.M. 4 vols. New York, London, and Manila: New City Press, 1999–2002.

FH: Roger of Wendover, *Flowers of History.*

HPE: Sawirus Ib al-Muraffa. *History of the Patriarchs of the Egyptian Church, Known as the History of the Holy Church.* Translated by Antoine Khater and O.H.E. KHS Burmeisler. Cairo: Publications of the Coptic Archaelogical Society, 1970.

JV: James of Vitry

Omnibus: Saint Francis of Assisi, Writings and Early Biographies: English Omnibus of the Sources for the Life of Saint Francis. Edited by Marion A. Habig. Translated by Raphael Brown. 2 vols. Quincy, Ill.: Franciscan Press, 1991.

OP: Oliver of Paderborn, *The Capture of Damietta.* In Edward Peters, ed., *Christian Society and the Crusades, 1198–1229.* Translated by John J. Gavigan. Philadelphia: University of Pennsylvania Press, 1971.

RHC: *Recueil des Historiens des Croisades. Oc: Historiens Occidentaux. Or: Historiens Orientaux.* 14 vols. Paris, 1841–1906.

Notes

Introduction

2   "Sultan! Sultan!": JG 10, in *XIIIth Century Chronicles,* 26. The sources for this open-
     ing scene will be explained more fully in Chapter 13.
2   "We are ambassadors . . . Christ": *Chronicle of Bernard the Treasurer,* in FA:ED, 1:608.
2   "If you . . . to God": *Chronicle of Ernoul,* in FA:ED, 1:606.
5   "was deeply moved . . . willingly ": 1 Cel 57, in *Omnibus,* 277.
5   "The saint leapt . . . threatening disaster": 2 Cel 30, in FA:ED, 2:265.
6   *Major Legend:* Meaning "major life."
6   "theologically interpreted 'Francis of faith": Joseph Ratzinger, *The Theology of His-
     tory in St. Bonaventure,* trans. Zachary Hayes, O.F.M. (Chicago: Franciscan Herald
     Press, 1989), 39.
6   treated . . . of heresy: Walter W. Wakefield, *Heresy, Crusade and Inquisition in Southern
     France, 1100–1250* (Berkeley and Los Angeles: University of California Press, 1974),
     245–46.
7   "be subject": ER, in FA:ED, 1:74.
8   "cruel beast": JV, *Historia Occidentalis,* in FA:ED, 1:584.
10   "I knew . . . an idol": Lisa Myers, *NBC Nightly News,* October 15, 2003.
10   Cardinal Stanislaw Dziwisz . . . "holy war": Cardinal Stanislaw Dziwisz, *A Life with
     Karol* (New York: Doubleday, 2008), cited in "John Paul II on War in the Name of
     God," www.zenit.org.
10   "Shame on you . . . the pope": Robert F. Keeler and Paul Moses, *Days of Intense
     Emotion* (Totowa, N.J.: Catholic Book Publishing, 2001), 168.
10   "Show me . . . he preached": www.vatican.va/holy_father/benedict_xvi/speeches/
     2006/september/documents/hf_ben-xvi_spe_20060912_university-regensburg
     _en.html.

Chapter 1: Outfitted to Kill

16   Shops were closed: For details of parade, see Arnaldo Fortini, *Francis of Assisi,* trans. Helen Moak (New York: Crossroad, 1981), 152.

16   One story . . . gave up: Michael Robson, "Assisi, Guido II and Saint Francis," *Greyfriars Review* 12, no. 3 (1998), 225–87.

17   "Frenchy": G. K. Chesterton, *St. Francis of Assisi* (New York: Doubleday Image, 1957), 38.

17   well acquainted with the *Chanson de Roland:* Francis's knowledge of this saga was documented in two early collections of anecdotes about his life that quoted him as saying: "The Emperor Charles, Roland, and Oliver, and all the paladins and valiant knights who were mighty in battle, pursuing unbelievers with great toil and fatigue even to death, had a memorable victory for themselves, and, finally, died in battle as holy martyrs for the faith in Christ." AC 103, in FA:ED, 2:209; MP, 1:4. Some historians have taken this as evidence that Francis supported the Crusades. But respect for soldiers' bravery does not necessarily mean support for a war.

17   "my knights of the round table": AC 103, in FA:ED, 2:208.

18   As former Assisi mayor . . . saddle up: Fortini, *Francis,* 152.

18   "Too often . . . self-identity": Lauro Martines, "Political Violence in the Thirteenth Century," in *Violence and Civil Disorder in Italian Cities, 1200–1500* (Berkeley and Los Angeles: University of California, 1972), 352.

19   Celestine III died: William J. La Due, *The Chair of Saint Peter: A History of the Papacy* (Maryknoll, N.Y.: Orbis, 1999), 117–18.

19   That's when the seething merchants: For details of the conflict between merchants and imperial authorities, see Fortini, *Francis,* 119–20.

19   spurning papal representatives: Paul Sabatier, *Life of St. Francis of Assisi,* trans. Louise Seymour Houghton (New York: Scribner's, 1902), 12.

20   Perugia was becoming the regional powerhouse: Sara Rubin Blanshei, "Perugia, 1260–1340: The Conflict and Change in a Medieval Italian Urban Society," *Transactions of the American Philosophical Society,* new ser., vol. 66, no. 2 (1976), 8–14.

21   Collestrada: On the Battle of Collestrada, events leading to it, and the *Eulistea* account, see Fortini, *Francis,* 147–54.

22   "There was a great massacre . . . Assisi": 2 Cel 4, in FA:ED, 2:243.

22   The Perugians . . . Bonifazio wrote: Fortini, *Francis,* 155.

22   *The American Soldier* . . . the survey: Lt. Col. David Grossman with Loren W. Christensen, *On Combat: The Psychology and Physiology of Deadly Conflict in War and Peace* (PPCT Research Publications, 2004), 9–10.

22   "Any way . . . city defeated," and other information on how the battle would have affected Francis: Lt. Col. David Grossman, interview, August 3, 2007.

22   Penitential manuals: John T. McNeil and Helena M. Gamer, *Medieval Handbooks of Penance* (New York: Columbia, 1938), 187, 192, 225, 317; Bernard J. Verkamp, "Moral Treatment of Returning Warriors in the Early Middle Ages," *Journal of Religious Ethics* 16, no. 2 (Fall 88,) 225.

23   *Four Sons of Aymon:* Omer Englebert, *St. Francis of Assisi: A Biography,* trans. Eve Marie Cooper, 2nd ed. (Cincinnati: Servant, 1979), 33–34; Thomas Bullfinch, *Bull-*

finch's Mythology: Legends of Charlemagne or Romance of the Middle Ages, University of
Adelaide Electronic Texts Collection, chap. 20.

23 Thomas of Chobham: Frederick H. Russell, *The Just War in the Middle Ages* (Cambridge: Cambridge University Press, 1975), 227.

23 mayor, who had been excommunicated: Raffaele Pazzelli, *St. Francis and the Third Order* (Chicago: Franciscan Herald, 1982), 78. The interdict was lifted in 1205 after negotiations with Cardinal Leo Brancaleoni. It was agreed that Assisi would never again "knowingly" elect an excommunicate.

24 "to embark upon a life of penance": Test, in *Omnibus,* 67.

24 he had killed: Ken Butigan, Mary Litell, O.S.F., and Louis Vitale, O.F.M., *Franciscan Nonviolence: Stories, Reflections, Principles, Practices and Resources* (Pace e Bene Nonviolence Services, 2003), 19.

Chapter 2: Shattered

25 Il Palazzo del Capitano del Popolo: Luigi Bonazzi, *Storia di Perugia* (Perugia, 1875), 261.

25 Prisons as we know them . . . improvisations: Jean Dunbabin, e-mail interview, June 6, 2007.

25 tortured and humiliated: Fortini, *Francis,* 54–55.

26 Many were chained . . . disease: Jean Dunbabin, *Captivity and Imprisonment in Medieval Europe, 1000–1300* (New York: Palgrave Macmillan, 2003), 119–21.

26 One of the knights . . . make peace with him: 2 Cel 4, in *Omnibus,* 364.

26 fever, chills: Donald Spoto, *Reluctant Saint: The Life of Francis of Assisi* (New York: Viking, 2002), 37–42.

26 sensory deprivation . . . survivor guilt: Lt. Col. David Grossman, interview, August 3, 2007.

27 "despise himself . . . loved before": 1 Cel 3–4, in *Omnibus,* 232.

28 Saint Martin of Tours: Sulpicius Severus, *Life of St. Martin,* trans. Alexander Roberts, in *A Select Library of Nicene and Post-Nicene Fathers of the Christian Church,* 2nd ser., vol. 11 (New York, 1894), accessed at www.users.csbsju.edu/~eknuth/npnf2-11/sulpitiu/lifemart.html.

28 "A certain . . . and fame": 1 Cel 4, in *Omnibus,* 232.

28 The battle being fought . . . papal force: Most historians who have written on the subject believe Francis planned to join the papal army. His love of French chivalry and his later relationship with Walter's brother, John of Brienne, are evidence that he planned to fight for the pope. Furthermore, if God had told Francis not to fight *against* the pope, Celano would likely have mentioned it. But some scholars have written that Francis had planned to join the imperial force. See Helene Nolthenius, *Een man uit het dal van Spoleto. Franciscus tussen zijn tijdgenoten* [*A Man from the Valley of Spoleto: Francis Among His Contemporaries*] (Amsterdam: Querido, 1988), 55–56. Nolthenius writes that a German bishop who tried to patch up the emperor's relations with Assisi and other communities in the region received a warm welcome in Assisi and that an agreement was reached in 1205 that the Rocca Maggiore would not be rebuilt. My thanks to Dr. J. Hoeberichts for pointing this out.

29   Marwkard: John C. Moore, *Pope Innocent III, 1160/61–1216: To Root Up and to Plant* (Boston: Brill, 2003), 68.

29   "another Saladin": Ibid., 67.

29   threatened to divert: Joseph R. Strayer, "The Political Crusades of the Thirteenth Century," in *A History of the Crusades,* vol. 2, *The Later Crusades, 1189–1311,* eds. Robert Lee Wolff and Harry W. Hazard (Madison: University of Wisconsin Press, 1969), 346–47.

29   "ignoring God's plan": 1 Cel 4, in FA:ED, 1:185.

29   "He led ... crosses": AP 5, in FA:ED, 2:35. AP is believed to be the work of Brother John of Perugia, based on stories he learned from two of Francis's earliest followers, Brother Giles and Brother Bernard of Quintavalle.

30   "I know ... a great prince": L3C 5, in *Omnibus,* 894. Details differ among the various accounts.

30   "lukewarm": JS 3, in FA:ED, 1:371.

30   "Who do you think ... what to do": L3C 6, in *Omnibus,* 895.

30   Dreams ... psychological cinema: Grossman interview, August 3, 2007.

31   stopped off in Foligno: AP 7, in FA:ED, 2:36. The sequence of events varies in other accounts.

32   PTSD: Statement of Matthew J. Friedman, M.D., Ph.D., Executive Director, National Center for PTSD, Committee on House Veterans' Affairs, July 27, 2005, accessed at www.va.gov/OCA/testimony/hvac/050727MF.asp.

32   "prevalence of PTSD": Charles W. Hoge et al., "Association of Posttraumatic Stress Disorder With Somatic Symptoms, Health Care Visits, and Absenteeism Among Iraq War Veterans," *American Journal of Psychiatry* 164, no. 1 (January 2007), 150–53.

32   Pentagon study ... health problems: Deborah Sontag and Lizette Alvarez, "Across America, Deadly Echoes of Foreign Battles," *New York Times,* January 13, 2008.

32   In one story ... forgiveness of his sins: 1 Cel 6, in *Omnibus,* 234.

33   Francis kissed the leper: 2 Cel 4, in *Omnibus,* 364.

33   "What had seemed ... and soul": Test, in FA:ED, 1:124.

33   "repair my house": 2 Cel 10, in *Omnibus,* 370.

34   accusations were shouted at him in the streets: On details on Francis's life at this point, see 1 Cel 10–15.

Chapter 3: His New Way

35   wealth and honor: Francis rejected the values of honor and patronage that predominated in the Mediterranean world. To compare with the life of Jesus, see John Dominick Crossan, *The Historical Jesus: The Life of a Mediterranean Jewish Peasant* (New York: HarperCollins, 1991), 59–71.

35   "like a wolf on a lamb": L3C 17–18, in *Omnibus,* 907–08.

36   "the herald of the great king": 1 Cel 16, in *Omnibus,* 242.

36   "In a word ... counseled them": AP 23; FA: ED, 2:45.

36   "Amid ... with all": 1 Cel 41, in *Omnibus,* 262–63.

36   "revealed": GianMaria Polidoro, *The Greeting of Peace Revealed to Saint Francis,* trans.

Joseph O'Boyle and Paul Reczec (S. Maria degli Angeli: Portiuncula, n.d.), 27–32. See also Lothar Hardick, O.F.M., *The Admonitions of St. Francis of Assisi*, trans. David Smithy, with an appendix by Sr. M. Ethelburga Häcker, O.S.F. (Chicago: Franciscan Herald Press, 1982), 129.

36 greeting of peace: In Scripture, greetings of peace are attributed to David in 1 Samuel 25:6 and Psalm 122:8; the birth of Jesus is in Luke 2:14; the resurrected Christ is in John 20:19, 21, 26; Jesus' instruction, "Peace to this household," is in Luke 10:6 and Isaiah 6–9, 60:17. See Ronald G. Musto, *The Catholic Peace Tradition* (Maryknoll, N.Y.: Orbis, 1986), 7–25. See also "Peace" in Joseph P. Healy and William Klassen, *The Anchor Bible Dictionary*, ed. David Noel Freedman (New York: Doubleday, 1992), 5:206–12.

37 "this greeting of yours . . . this greeting": MP 26, in *Omnibus*, 1152. Also AC 101.

37 "peace and repentance": 1 Cel 29, in *Omnibus*, 252.

37 "Love our neighbors . . . any harm": *Letter to All the Faithful*, in *Omnibus*, 94.

38 "It seems to me . . . in the world": L3C 35, in *Omnibus*, 923. Also AP 17.

38 "The wild beasts . . . lower creatures": *Legend for the Use in a Choir* 7, in FA:ED, 1:322. See also 2 Cel 170, 111, 47.

38 "greedy one . . . end": 2 Cel 47, in FA:ED, 2:279.

39 Emperor Otto IV: 1 Cel 42–43, in FA:ED, 1:221.

39 Otto later betrayed the pope: Almost immediately after Innocent crowned Otto as emperor, Otto reneged on his pledges to the pope and seized lands in Italy. Later Celano did not have to repeat the details; his readers would have known this incident well, since residents of Rome were outraged that Innocent had permitted Otto into their city for the coronation. See Ferdinand Gregorovius, *History of the City of Rome in the Middle Ages*, trans. Annie Hamilton (London: Bell, 1906), 5:85.

39 reading the political climate: For a discussion of how skeptically Francis viewed power, see Jacques Dalarun, *Francis of Assisi and Power*, trans. Anne Baratol, O.S.C. (St. Bonaventure, N.Y.: Franciscan Institute, 2007), 19.

39 Innocent III: La Due, *Chair of Peter*, 118. Also James M. Powell, *Innocent III: Vicar of Christ or Lord of the World?* (Washington: Catholic University, 1994); *The Deeds of Pope Innocent III*, trans. James M. Powell (Washington: Catholic University, 2004), 55.

40 where he found the pope meditating: See FA:ED, 2:548. Jerome of Ascoli, minister general of the Franciscan order from 1274 to 1279 and later Pope Nicholas IV, added this scene to Bonaventure's *The Major Legend of Saint Francis*. The source is identified as Cardinal Riccardo degli Annibaldi.

40 "Go . . . to the pigs . . . preach": FH 494.

41 The Cathars . . . war against them: For details on the Cathars, see Steven Runciman, *The Medieval Manichee: A Study of the Christian Dualist Heresy* (Cambridge: Cambridge University Press, 1969), 179.

41 Innocent then had a famous dream: ML 9; AP 36; John H. R. Moorman, *A History of the Franciscan Order from Its Origins to the Year 1517* (London: Oxford, 1968), 272.

41 "A friar is not bound . . . sin": ER 5, in *Omnibus*, 35.

42 "I strictly forbid the friars": Test, in *Omnibus*, 68.

42 love for enemies: Matthew 5:44.

Chapter 4: The Peacemaker

44   "Listen and understand . . . many of them": AC 75, in FA:ED, 2:178.

44   "The knights . . . as they could": AC 75, in FA:ED, 2:179. See also MP 105.

45   "He saw devils . . . destruction": 2 Cel 108, in *Omnibus,* 451. See also AC 108, in FA:ED, 2:215; ML 6:9–10.

46   "I speak . . . chains": AC 108, in FA:ED, 2:216.

46   the story of Francis and Sylvester: 2 Cel 109, in *Omnibus,* 452–53.

46   the robbers gradually were converted: AC 115, in FA:ED, 2:21–22.

46   "are to be . . . against anybody": www.franciscanfriarstor.com/resources/stf _spirituality_as_reflected_in_the_various_rules.htm.

47   Military leaders . . . make war: Pope Honorius III wrote to the bishop of Rimini in 1221 in support of Third Order penitents who refused to go to war in Faenza. See Ronald G. Musto, *Catholic Peacemakers: A Documentary History* (New York: Garland, 1993), 533.

47   Miracle stories: 3 Cel 89–94.

47   the residents of Gubbio: LF 21, in *Omnibus,* 1348–51.

Chapter 5: Journeys

50   then known as Slavonia: 1 Cel 55, 3 Cel 33, in *Omnibus,* 275; FA:ED, 2:415.

50   "Commander of the Believers": See FA:ED, 1:230. *Almohads* is a Westernized name for the al-Muwahhidun, which translates roughly as "the Unitarians," for their emphasis on the oneness of God.

51   "burning desire for martyrdom": 1 Cel 56, in FA:ED, 1:230.

52   Francis eagerly followed: Ibid.

53   "God revealed . . . various lands": LF 4, in *Omnibus,* 1308–09.

54   opening houses in Spain: Moorman, *Franciscan Order:* 27–28.

55   "while returning . . . had wished": 3 Cel 34, in FA:ED, 2:416; italics added.

55   "Nonviolence . . . die": R. K. Prabhu and U. R. Rao, eds.. *The Mind of Mahatma Gandhi* (Ahemadabad, India, 1945), accessed at www.mkgandhi.org/nonviolence/ phil8.htm, July 23, 2007.

Chapter 6: A New Crusade

57   "At this time . . . great need": Translations from Innocent's encyclical and related letters are from Louise Riley-Smith and Jonathan Riley-Smith, *The Crusades: Idea and Reality, 1095–1274* (London: Edward Arnold, 1981), 119–33.

57   "They are . . . described above": Richard of San Germano, *The Chronicle of Richard of San Germano,* trans. Graham A. Loud (unpublished manuscript), 31–32. The author thanks Loud, of Leeds University, for providing his translation of this important medieval chronicle.

58   Ezekiel's vision: Ezekiel 9:1–11.

58   this speech ... to letters: Omer Englebert, *St. Francis of Assisi: A Biography,* trans. Eve Marie Cooper, 2nd ed. (Cincinnati: Servant, 1979), 139–42.

58   "He favored the sign ... cells everywhere": 3 Cel 3, in FA:ED, 2:402.

59   "will have to answer ... severe Judgment": Riley-Smith, *Crusades,* 126.

59   pressure put ... was enormous: J. Hoeberichts, *Francis and Islam* (Quincy, Ill.: Franciscan Press, 1997), 4–5.

59   he would never preach the Crusade: None of the early biographies record that Francis preached the Crusade. Writers such as Thomas of Celano, Henri d'Avranches, and Bonaventure, all eager for papal approval, would certainly have included it if he had.

59   Innocent never got: JV, Letter I, in FA:ED, 1:579.

60   "They live ... primitive Church": Ibid., in FA:ED, 1:579–80.

60   chapter meeting ... 1217: L3C 62.

61   "They ... put down for heretics": JG 4, in *XIIIth Century Chronicles,* 21.

61   "Some of them ... breeches": JG 5, in *XIIIth Century Chronicles,* 22–23.

62   "Why have you ... many souls": MP 65, in *Omnibus,* 1192. See also AC 108.

62   In a dream ... could provide: L3C 61.

62   Henri d'Avranches: Josiah Cox Russell, "Master Henry of Avranches as an International Poet," *Speculum* 3, no. 1. (January, 1928), 35.

63   "With a martyr's death ... the Syrians": VL 7, 149–54, 171–75, in FA:ED, 1:479–80.

Chapter 7: The Sultan

64   dressed in sackcloth: Raffaele Pazzelli, *St. Francis and the Third Order* (Chicago: Franciscan Herald Press, 1982), 73.

64   Muslims streamed: Thomas Idinopulos, *Jerusalem: A History of the Holiest City as Seen through the Struggles of Jews, Christians and Muslims* (Chicago: Ivan R. Dee, 1994), 250–51.

66   His relations with Arab Christians: HPE, 3:2, preface.

66   "commanded his men ... brotherly love": Beha ed-Din Abu el-Mehasan Yusuf, *The Life of Saladin,* trans. Claude Reignier Conder (London: Hanover Square, 1897), 194.

67   "consented to ... on his part": Ibid., 311.

67   Joan refused: Sidney Painter, "The Third Crusade: Richard the Lionhearted and Philip Augustus," in *A History of the Crusades,* vol. 2 *The Later Crusades, 1189–1311,* eds. R. L. Wolff and Harry W. Hazard (Madison: University of Wisconsin Press, 1969), 77.

67   divide Saladin from his brother: M. R. Morgan, *The Chronicle of Ernoul and the Continuations of William of Tyre* (London: Oxford, 1973), 104.

68   "King Richard ... this purpose": Thomas Andrew Archer, *The Crusade of Richard I, 1189–92: Extracts from the Itinerarium Ricardi Bohâdin* (New York: Putnam's, 1888), 214.

68   That son ... al-Kamil: H. L. Gottschalk, *Al-Malik al-Kamil von Egypten und seine Zeit* (Wiesbaden, 1958), 24.

68   "eighth sacrament": Robert W. Ackerman, "The Knighting Ceremonies in the Middle English Romances," *Speculum* 19, no. 3 (July 1944), 290, quoting Leon Gautier.

68   Lull: Ibid.

68   Ayyubid dynasty: Taqi ad-Din al-Maqrizi, *A History of the Ayubbid Sultans of Egypt,* trans. R.J.C. Broadhurst (Boston: Twayne, 1980), 35. Al-Maqrizi (1364–1442) compiled his account from the works of a variety of thirteenth- and fourteenth-century Arab historians.

69   Ayyub lectured his son: Ibid., 42–43.

70   al-Adil . . . the rest of the empire: Ibid., 117–135.

71   Monastery of Abba Macarius . . . Christianity: HPE, 3:2:198.

72   procession through the streets: Ibid., 3:2:202.

72   felt better immediately: Ibid., 3:2:206.

72   the Qur'an . . . Arabian desert: Mahmoud Ayoub, "Christian-Muslim Dialogue: Goals and Obstacles," *Muslim World* 94 (July 2004), 313. Qur'an 5:82–83.

72   "The Prophet . . . the warriors": Seyyed Hossein Nasr, interview, December 26, 2007.

72   choosing a Coptic patriarch: Al-Maqrizi, *History,* 162, and HPE, 4:1:138.

73   Gottschalk . . . where he lived: Gottschalk, *Al-Malik al-Kamil,* 26.

74   When the Nile failed to flood . . . out of control: Stanley Lane-Poole, *A History of Egypt in the Middle Ages* (New York: Scribner's, 1901), 216, 230.

74   He fortified the walls . . . with robes: HPE, 3:2:7.

74   three thousand European merchants: Steven Runciman, *History of the Crusades* (Cambridge: Cambridge University Press, 1951–54), 3:151.

Chapter 8: The Siege

79   saw clouds form: OP, 60–61; see also 51–55 and 65.

79   by conquering Egypt: Runciman, *Crusades,* 3:150, and Gottschalk, *Al-Malik al-Kamil,* 22.

80   procession . . . barefoot: Joseph Patrick Donovan, *Pelagius and the Fifth Crusade* (Philadelphia: University of Pennsylvania Press, 1950), 33.

80   The campaign began . . . his life: OP, 53. For details of the fighting, see Thomas C. Van Cleve, "The Fifth Crusade," in *A History of the Crusades,* vol. 2, *The Later Crusades, 1189–1311,* eds. Robert Lee Wolff and Harry W. Hazard (Madison: University of Wisconsin Press, 1969), 390–428. See also Runciman, *History,* 3:145–159: HPE, 3:2:217; al-Maqrizi, *History,* 164; and OP, 61–62.

81   "They attribute . . . the stars": FH, 406.

81   Ibn al-Athir: Joseph Michaud, *Bibliothèque des Croisades,* vol. 4, *Extraits des Historiens Arabes,* trans. Joseph Toussaint Reinaud (Paris, 1829), 387.

82   news by carrier pigeon: Gottschalk, *Al-Malik al-Kamil,* 65.

82   unseasoned troops: Christopher Marshall, *Warfare and the Latin East, 1192–1291* (Cambridge: Cambridge University Press, 1992), 36.

83   mangonel . . . into Damietta: Ibid., 212.

84   "fell on . . . matter": FH, 409.

85 The sultan died: al-Maqrizi, *History*, 167.

85 Al-Kamil, grieving and frightened: Ibid., 171.

85 John of Brienne: Étienne Georges, *Jean de Brienne, Empereur de Constantinople et Roi de Jérusalem* (Troyes, 1858), 18–19; Runciman, *History*, 3:132–34.

86 "was a huge man . . . better than he": Salimbene de Adam, *The Chronicles of Salimbene de Adam*, ed. Joseph L. Baird, Giuseppe Baglivi, and John Robert Kane (Binghamton, N.Y.: Center for Medieval and Early Renaissance Studies, University Center at Binghamton, 1986), 17.

88 Grieving the loss of some three thousand soldiers: HPE, 3:2:220–21, 4:1:50–51.

89 "so that we . . . resurrection": Benjamin Z. Kedar, *Crusade and Mission: European Approaches toward the Muslims* (Princeton: Princeton University Press, 1984), 72.

89 "piled into . . . be without": OP, 71.

89 Both men were hung: HPE, 4:1:53.

Chapter 9: Conspiracy Against the Sultan

91 A turncoat Frank . . . their side of the river: FH, 415. For further details, see HPE, 4:1:54–55, and, James M. Powell, *Anatomy of a Crusade, 1213–1221* (Philadelphia: University of Pennsylvania, 1986), 150.

93 "noble . . . awe of him": Ibn Khallikan, *Biographical Dictionary*, trans. William MacGuckin Slane (Paris: Oriental Translation Fund of Great Britain and Ireland, 1843), 1:162.

93 It was a desperate time for al-Kamil: Ibn al-Athir, *Kamel*, in RHC-Or, 2:1:116–17; Abu Shama, *Livre des Deux Jardins*, in RHC-Or 5:175–76; Ibn Khallikan, *Biographical*, 1:162–64; al-Maqrizi, *History*, 174–75.

93 "stirred up . . . was governor": Abu al-Fida, in RHC-Or, 1:90. English spellings for the historian's name vary.

95 "Jerusalem is the city . . . faithful": JV, *The History of Jerusalem*, trans. Aubrey Stewart (1896; reprinted New York: AMS, 1971), 32.

96 "then held . . . in letters": FH, 411.

96 "There was . . . last judgment": trans. from Abu-Shama, *Livre des Deux Jardins*, in RHC-Or, 5:174.

96 "A great number . . . struck Islam": Ibid.

96 On March 31: OP, 78.

Chapter 10: Francis Looks East

98 Chapter of the Mats: The early accounts conflict on which chapter was known as the Chapter of the Mats.

98 Cardinal Ugolino . . . from Perugia: AC 18, in FA:ED, 2:132. See also LP 114 and Arnold of Sarrant, *Kinship of Saint Francis* 24, in FA:ED, 3:709–10.

99 "The cardinal . . . afraid: AC 18, in FA:ED, 2:132.

100 Brother Electus: 2 Cel 108. It is not clear how long Electus was in Tunis before being beheaded.

100 "We are young . . . listen to us": Johannes Jörgensen, *St. Francis of Assisi: A Biography*, trans. T. O'Conor Sloan (New York: Longmans, 1912), 198. See also Arnold of Sarrant, *Chronicle of the Twenty-four Generals of the Order of Friars Minor*, trans. Noel Muscat, O.F.M. (Malta: Tau/Franciscan, 2007), 1:10–12.

101 "To our way . . . period of time": JV, Letter VI, in *Omnibus*, 1609.

101 "The Blessed Father . . . uncertain dangers": JG 10, in *XIIIth Century Chronicles*, 25–26.

101 Peter of Catania: Ibid., 28.

102 He suggested that the youngster . . . decide: *A New Fioretti*, trans. John R. H. Moorman (London, 1946), 27–28.

102 Brother Leonard: Fortini, *Francis*, 124, 395–96.

102 Brother Illuminato: 3 Cel 123; see notes in FA:ED, 2:67.

102 Brother Barbaro: 2 Cel 155.

102 June 24, 1219: Englebert, *Biography*, 174.

102 Fifteen anchors: JV, *Lettres de Jacques de Vitry*, ed. R.B.C. Huygens, trans. Iris Rau, I.S. Moxon, and G.A. Loud (Leiden 1960), 79–97.

103 The route: FA:ED, 1:232. 2 Cel 155 notes Brother Barbaro's presence in Cyprus but does not say whether he was there while accompanying Francis to or from the East. If Francis traveled to Egypt by route of Cyprus, he likely would have stopped at Acre before going on to Egypt. Martiniano Roncaglia, *St. Francis of Assisi and the Middle East*, trans. Stephen A. Janto (Cairo: Franciscan Center of Oriental Studies, 1957), 26–28, speculates that Francis went first to Acre, and that Brother Illuminato met him there. Further, he speculates that Illuminato had learned enough Arabic by being stationed in Acre to serve as Francis's translator before the sultan. He acknowledges, though, that there is no evidence that Illuminato spoke Arabic.

103 a theological controversy . . . the West: 133. *The Cambridge History of Egypt*, vol. 1, *Islamic Egypt, 640–1571*, ed. Carl F. Petry (Cambridge: Cambridge University Press, 1998), 177–79.

103 mainly Melkite: Atiya Aziz, "Ayyubid Dynasty and the Copts," in *The Coptic Encyclopedia* (New York: Macmillan, 1991), 1:314–15.

103 Yohanna Golta: Bishop Yohanna Golta, interview, October 27, 2007.

104 The backlash: HPE, 4:1:62.

Chapter 11: "Forbidding War"

105 a more aggressive attack: Van Cleve, "Fifth Crusade," 412–13.

106 swim across the Nile: al-Maqrizi, *History*, 176.

106 "The insulting . . . increased": FH, 417.

106 handbooks specifying a protocol: Marshall, *Warfare*, 62.

107 the July 31 battle: OP, 79–81; FH, 417–18.

109 Pelagius was quietly planning . . . spies: JV, Letter VI, in *Omnibus*, 1609.

110 "Their swollen . . . fellow citizens": FH, 418.

110 Francis had been born . . . feast days: 2 Cel 3, in *Omnibus*, 364.

110 Deep in prayer: The ensuing account of Francis's objection to the fighting comes from 2 Cel 30, in FA:ED, 2:265–66. Celano did not identify the traveling compan-

ion Francis spoke to. It is sometimes assumed to be Illuminato, but the intimacy of the conversation suggests someone who had been close to Francis from the earliest days of his ministry.

111   fed by a pride and arrogance: See, for example, AC 75, in FA:ED, 2:178, when Francis berated the knights of Perugia by telling them, "Your heart is puffed up by arrogance in your pride and might."

111   heed his own conscience: *Admonitions* 3:7–8, in FA:ED, 1:130.

112   A decade earlier: For background on Pelagius, see Donovan, *Pelagius,* 14–15.

112   "When people falsely . . . it utterly": Riley-Smith, *Crusades,* 68.

112   "a despicable and unknown friar": Fortini, *Francis,* 653, citing *Chronicle of Elemosina,* which dates to 1335.

113   a deeper meaning to the phrase "this day": James Powell, "Francesco d'Assisi e la Quinta Crociata: Una Missione di Pace," *Schede Medievali* 4 (1983), 68–77. Powell revisited the topic in "St. Francis of Assisi's Way of Peace," *Medieval Encounters* 13, no. 2 (June 2007), 275.

113   Proponents: For an argument contrary to Powell's, see John V. Tolan, *Le saint chez le sultan: La rencontre de François d'Assise et de l'islam. Huit siècles d'interprétation* (Paris: Éditions du Seuil, 2007), 453–97.

113   "Thus says the Lord . . . the land": Isaiah 49:8.

113   "acceptable time": 2 Cor. 6:2.

113   "For it was . . . his will": Riley-Smith, *Crusades,* 119.

113   "The end . . . 666 years": Ibid., 120.

114   Joachim of Fiore: Marjorie Reeves, *The Influence of Prophecy in the Later Middle Ages* (Oxford: Clarendon, 1969), 6–10, 17. See Ronald G. Musto, ed., *Catholic Peacemakers: A Documentary History* (New York: Garland, 1993), 605, for a concise summary of Joachim's teachings.

115   "He's saying . . . will of God": Rev. Michael Cusato, interview, May 30, 2007.

115   *bellum,* or war, and not just *pugnam,* or battle: Hoeberichts, *Francis and Islam,* 97.

115   "if the prelate . . . abandon him": *Admonitions* 3: 7–8, in FA:ED, 1:130.

116   "disagreeing amongst themselves": FH, 418.

116   "scarcely any . . . the camp." OP, 81.

116   When the Christian army advanced: For the August 29 battle, see 2 Cel 30; HPE 4:1:63; Marshall, *Warfare,* 168–69; Van Cleve, "Fifth Crusade," 414; OP, 82–83; *A Thirteenth-Century Minstrel's Chronicle,* trans. Robert Levine (Lewiston, Me.: Mellen Press, 1990), accessed at www.bu.edu/english/levine/reims.htm.

118   club-wielding "pagan": *Chronicle of Tolosana Faventino,* cited by Fortini, *Francis,* 408.

119   "Let the princes . . . the Lord": 2 Cel 30, in FA:ED, 2:266.

Chapter 12: The Saint and the Cardinal

120   Sultan al-Kamil decided to try: For the peace negotiations, see Van Cleve, "Fifth Crusade," 414–15.

122   "Trust in . . . brother": ML 9:8, in FA:ED, 2:602. While I have questioned Bonaventure's account of Francis's encounter with the sultan, I have accepted the details used in this chapter because they echo the language in Francis's *Earlier Rule,* which

describes friars sent to preach among Muslims and other nonbelievers as sheep sent before wolves. It's certainly feasible that Francis and Illuminato prayed Psalm 23 at this point, as Bonaventure writes.

123 "The Cardinal . . . come back" and subsequent quotes on encounter between Francis and Pelagius: *Ernoul,* in FA:ED, 1:605–07. *Early Documents* is the source for all quotations from *Ernoul.*

123 Twenty-third Psalm: ML 9:7, in *Omnibus,* 703.

124 "shield of faith": JV, *Historia Occidentalis,* in FA:ED, 1:584.

124 "The thought . . . attracted him": ML 9:7, *Omnibus,* 703.

124 "make themselves . . . enemies": ER 16, in FA:ED, 1:74.

124 "He had a vision . . . of it": Rev. Michael Cusato, interview, May 30, 2007.

124 "Because of . . . ordinate manner": Hugh of Digne's *Rule Commentary, Spicilegium Bonaventurianum,* cited by Kedar, *Crusade and Mission,* 125.

125 "I shall . . . with me": ML 9:7, in FA:ED, 2:602.

Chapter 13: The Saint and the Sultan

126 "What manly courage . . . mortal perils!":VL 110, in FA:ED, 1:486.

126 by the time . . . in late September: Most scholars place Francis's visit with the sultan in the month of September 1219, during a lull in the fighting. See Girolamo Golubovich, *Biblioteca bio-bibliografica della Terra Santa e dell 'Oriente Franciscans* (Quaracchi: Collegio di S. Bonaventura, 1906–27), 1:94. Fortini, *Francis,* 427, argues that it took place after November 5, 1219.

127 "fell upon . . . fiercely": ML 9:8, in *Omnibus,* 703.

127 "flesh . . . his wounds":VL 121–122, in FA:ED, 1:486.

127 Earlier accounts . . . restrained: JV, *Historia Occidentalis,* in *Omnibus,* 1612.

128 "When the . . . the Sultan": *Ernoul,* in FA:ED, 1:606.

128 "Sultan! Sultan!": JG 10, in *XIIIth Century Chronicles,* 26.

128 "He was a most eloquent . . . of all": 1 Cel 83, in *Omnibus,* 298–99.

129 "He had . . . the small": JS 58, in FA:ED, 1:409.

129 "May the Lord . . . preaching that way": 1 Cel 23, in *Ominbus,* 248.

129 "asked if . . . some message": *Ernoul,* in FA:ED, 1:606.

130 "Say not . . . a believer' ": Qur'an 4:94, cited by Mohammad Hashim Kamali, *Freedom of Expression in Islam* (Cambridge: Islamic Texts Society, 1997), 187.

130 "using no . . . flattery": 1 Cel 36, in *Omnibus,* 258.

130 imprisoned Western priests: The priests were taken prisoner at sea during the botched Children's Crusade of 1212.

130 "they never would . . . to God": *Ernoul, in* FA:ED, 1:606.

130 "We are ambassadors": *Chronicle of Bernard the Treasurer,* in FA:ED, 1:608.

131 "If you wish . . . is false": *Ernoul,* in FA:ED, 1:606.

131 "became sweetness itself": JV, *Historia Occidentalis,* in *Omnibus,* 1612.

132 "It is . . . law demands": *Ernoul,* in FA:ED, 1:606.

132 "I will go . . . kind of torture": ML 9:8, in *Omnibus,* 704.

133 "We have seen . . . pleasing to him": JV, *Historia Occidentalis,* in *Omnibus,* 1612.

133 trial by ordeal: Muslims considered trials by ordeal to be repulsive. See *An Arab-*

Syrian Gentleman and Warrior in the Period of the Crusades: Memoirs of Usamah Ibn-Munqidh, trans. Philip K. Hitti (London: I. B. Tauris, 1987), 167–68.

134 "But I say . . . persecute you": Matthew 5:44.

134 "Remember the words . . . eternal life": ER 22, in *Omnibus,* 47. Based on Matthew 5:44, 1 Peter 2:21; Matthew 26:50; John 10:18.

134 a parting testament: David Flood and Thadée Matura, *The Birth of a Movement* (Chicago: Franciscan Herald Press, 1975), 46.

135 a new Elijah: 1 Kings 18:1–40.

135 *mubahala:* Mahmoud Mustafa Ayoub, *The Qur'an and Its Interpreters,* in vol. 2, *The House of 'Imran* (Albany: SUNY Press, 1992), 1–10, 189–198.

136 Francis's actions paralleled: Father Giulio Basetti-Sani, O.F.M., discussed Francis and the *mubahala* in *Mohammed et Saint François* (Ottawa: Commissariat de Terre-Sainte, 1959), 177–83, and in *Muhammad, St. Francis of Assisi and Alvernia* (Florence, 1975), 23–33.

137 that a monarch . . . advisers were evil": Seyyed Hossein Nasr, interview, December 26, 2007.

137 a great deal of provocation: Kedar, *Crusade and Mission,* 15, 125–26.

137 "caught a glimpse . . . proposal": ML 9:8, in *Omnibus,* 704.

137 Mansur al-Hallaj: Louis Massignon, *The Passion of al-Hallaj,* trans. Herbert Mason (Princeton: Princeton University Press, 1982), 1:642.

137 The Sufi influence in the sultan's court: In addition to having a well-known Persian Sufi as his religious adviser, Sultan al-Kamil had close friends who were steeped in a Sufism rooted in Persia, which has a tradition of fusing beliefs from Zoroastrianism and other sources. His confidant and emissary, Fakhr ad-Din, was the grandson of a famous Sufi scholar from Persia who had served the sultan of Damascus during the twelfth century. The family later migrated to Cairo, and the grandson's tradition became a sort of mother's milk for Sultan al-Kamil. It is said that his mother breast-fed the future sultan in his infancy, making her children and al-Kamil the equivalent of siblings. See Hossein Karimi, "L'origine iranienne de Fakhr al-Din Yusof, émir ayyoubide, instigateur de la paix avec Frédéric II pendant la VIe Croisade," in *La signification du bas Moyen Age dans l'histoire et la culture du monde musulman,* Actes du 8ème Congrès de l'Union européenne des Arabisants et Islamisants (Aix-en-Provence, 1976), 115; and Michael Chamberlain, "The Crusader Era and the Ayyubid Dynasty," in *The Cambridge History of Egypt, vol. 1 Islamic Egypt, 640–1517* (Cambridge: Cambridge University Press, 1998), 239.

138 the sultan was so taken . . . al-Farid refused: *Umar Ibn al-Farid: Saintly Life, Saintly Verse,* trans. Th. Emil Homerin, Classics of Western Spirituality (Mahwah, N.J.: Paulist, 2001), 11.

138 "Al-Farid is . . . just a show": Seyyed Hossein Nasr, interview, December 26, 2007. Al-Kamil loved poetry so much that he once released a man from prison upon finding out he had written some verses that moved him. See Ibn Khallikan, *Biographical,* 1:167.

138 Sufis were intrigued by Jesus: David Pinault, "Images of Christ in Arabic Literature," *Die Welt des Islams* 27, nos. 1–3 (1987), 103–25, 109.

138 "I am . . . for God": *Ernoul,* in FA:ED, 1: 607.

138 "He didn't see . . . for Saint Francis": Fareed Z. Munir, interview, January 30, 2008.

139   The Qu'ran doesn not prescribe: Kamali, *Freedom*, 244–45. The accompanying quotations from the Qur'an, 3:186 and 2:109, appear in this work.

139   With a prominent Sufi as his religious adviser: An inscription said to be on the tomb of Fakhr al-Farisi in Cairo raises the possibility that al-Farisi and Francis had long discussions. It declares that al-Farisi's "adventure with al-Malik al-Kamil, and that which befalls him because of the monk are well known." See Roncaglia, *Fancis and Middle East,* 26. Louis Massignon theorized that "the work" referred to Francis, see Massignon, *Passion,* 2:299–301. If so, the epitaph would be the only reference in any Arab source to Francis's visit to the sultan, and an extremely vague one at that. It may well not refer to him. As religious adviser to the sultan, al-Farisi would have dealt routinely with matters concerning Egypt's Christian monks.

139   would even have looked like Sufis: Roncaglia, 26–28.

140   "Although the evangelist . . . ahead of time": 2 Cel 104, in *Omnibus,* 450.

140   Francis spoke to crowds: 1 Cel 72–73, 2 Cel 102, in _____.

140   at least a two-way conversation: al-Maqrizi, *History,* 229–31.

140   "With great steadiness . . . faith": JS 36, in FA:ED, 1:395.

141   the discussions went on . . . for several days: JV, *Historia Occidentalis,* in *Omnibus,* 1612.

141   no detailed record: For a consideration of aspects of Islam that Francis and al-Kamil might have spoken about, see Kathleen A. Warren, *Daring to Cross the Threshold: Francis of Assisi Encounters Sultan Malek al-Kamil* (Rochester, Minn.: Sisters, of St. Francis, 2003), 51–68.

141   a key to his private prayer room: Seyyed Hossein Nasr, interview, December 26, 2007. Dr. Nasr added that the question remains of what the first written source is. This tradition reminds one of the story of the Christians of Najran, who prayed in the Prophet Muhammad's mosque at his invitation.

141   James of Vitry wrote . . . their lives: JV, in *Omnibus,* 1612–13.

142   "you blaspheme . . . themselves": *Omnibus,* 1614; anonymous manuscript, Golubovich, *Biblioteca,* 1:36–37.

142   soon to be . . . disregarded: Kedar, *Crusade and Mission,* 158.

142   "Thieves were . . . symbols of brigands": *Omnibus,* 1614.

142   the chunk of the True Cross: Christoph T. Maier, *Preaching the Crusades: Mendicant Friars and the Cross in the Thirteenth Century* (Cambridge: Cambridge University Press, 1994), 13–17, for the argument that these passages show that Francis supported the Crusade.

143   "to bend . . . different from all others": 1 Cel 57, in *Omnibus,* 277.

143   "great quantities . . . garments": *Ernoul,* in FA:ED, 1:607.

143   "He wanted . . . holiness and poverty ": Mahmoud Ayoub, interview, January 24, 2008.

144   ivory horn: The early accounts of Francis do not mention the horn. The idea that it was a gift from the sultan is not mentioned in inventories of the basilica's relics until 1473, so some caution is necessary in judging its significance. J. Hoeberichts, to author, December 11, 2007. Hoebericts referred to G. P. Freeman, *Umbrië in de voetsporen van Franciscus* (Haarlem, 2003), 51.

144   Such horns: Shaimaa Fouad to author December 26, 2007. Notes at an exhibit of a

similar horn at the Metropolitan Museum of Art in New York say that Muslim workers in Sicily crafted such horns from elephants' tusks; they were often used for hunting.

144 "was deeply moved . . . willingly": 1 Cel 57, in *Omnibus*, 277.

144 "honorably received . . . any fruit": JG 10, in *XIIIth Century Chronicles*, 26.

144 "I could not dare . . . his heart": Morning Sermon on St. Francis, 1267, in FA:ED, 2:757.

144 "The Sultan, the ruler . . . pleased God": JV, Letter VI, in FA:ED, 1:581. James of Vitry included a similar remark in *Historia Occidentalis*.

145 The sultan's authentic voice is heard: Hoeberichts, *Francis and Islam*, 100.

145 "They are not all alike . . . ward off [evil]": Qu'ran 3:113–15, quoted in *A Common Word between Us and You*, 14, accessed at www.acommonword.com. In this statement, issued October 13, 2007, 138 Muslim scholars discussed the common ground between Islam and Christianity.

146 visit the Holy Sepulcher: Trib, Prologue, 395, in FA:ED, 3:398.

146 "with many signs of honor": JV, *Historia Occidentalis*, in *Omnibus*, 1612.

146 "The sultan gave . . . eat": Ernoul, in FA:ED, 1:607.

146 castigated . . . eating sociably: FH, 527.

Chapter 14: "Evil and Sin"

148 "with their usual . . . and violence": OP, 84.

149 Scouts sent ahead . . . impossible: Donovan, *Pelaguis*, 64–65.

149 "found the streets . . . died of hunger": FH, 423–24.

149 "Damietta was captured . . . God alone": OP, 86–87.

150 Abu Shama . . . Damietta's fall: Abu Shama, in RHC-Or, 5:177.

150 terrible embarrassment . . . were captured: HPE, 4:1:67.

150 "passed to the Lord": JV, *Lettres de la Cinquième Croisade*, trans. G. Duchet-Suchaux (Belgium: Brepols, 1998), 147.

150 "The greediness . . . many thieves": FH, 424.

150 "Brother Francis . . . detested it": Hoeberichts, *Francis and Islam*, 58–59.

151 "We have . . . God's help": *Eracles* 15, translated from RHC-Oc, 2:348.

151 *Eracles* added: Ibid.

151 The official dedication . . . restored: Van Cleve, "Fifth Crusade," 420.

151 a grand structure: This description of the mosque is from Shaimaa Fouad, archaeologist, and Bahaa El-Din Wahba Ramadan, inspector, Supreme Council for Antiquities, interview and site visit, October 29, 2007.

151 Francis founded a small convent: Roncaglia, *Francis and Middle East*, 30, notes that it was in the section of the city assigned to the Italians. The Franciscan order continues to own this property. As of this writing, it was being leased for a Coptic girls' school. Franciscan officials said they planned to make use of the site when the lease expired.

152 Pope Honorius . . . Holy Land: Trib 1:23; see note in FA:ED, 3:400.

152 "nuns that are . . . shameful deeds": JV, *History of Jerusalem*, 65–66.

153 eye infection: AC 77. Spoto, *Reluctant Saint*, 167, identifies the disease as trachoma.

153   The five martyrs: Jörgensen, *Biography,* 197–200; Moorman, *History,* 229; Arnold of Sarrant, *Twenty-four Generals,* 1:10–12.

154   Stephen, a lay brother . . . for the order: Rosalind Brooke, *Early Franciscan Government, Elias to Bonaventure* (Cambridge: Cambridge University Press, 1959), 64.

155   "My lord . . . before us": JG, in *XIIIth Century Chronicles,* 27–28. Jörgensen, *Biography,* 205–206, explains the context for the conversation.

155   "When the blessed . . . incurable": Thomas of Pavia, *Deeds of the Emperors and Popes,* in FA:ED, 3:795.

Chapter 15: The Outsider

156   "Not even the sick . . . the others": 2 Cel 58, in *Omnibus,* 412–13.

157   One of Dominic's men . . . doctor of law: Trib 1:158–165, in FA:ED, 3:406–09.

157   Ugolino provided a detour: 2 Cel 58, in *Omnibus,* 412–13.

157   house . . . close to the Portiuncula: AC 56, in FA:ED, 2:157–58.

158   "From now on I am dead to you": 2 Cel 143, in *Omnibus,* 477.

158   "Who are these . . . intention clear": MP 41, in *Omnibus,* 1166. Later accounts such as this one may reflect the anger that a faction of the brothers felt rather than anything Francis really said. But overall the evidence is ample that Francis was disturbed by what was happening in his order.

158   Stephen spilled the fact: On Stephen and the river, see Thomas of Pavia, in FA:ED, 3:795.

159   "a most serious . . . sorrows": 2 Cel 115, in *Omnibus,* 458.

159   "If the brothers . . . compassion for me": AC 118, in FA:ED, 2:227. According to Celano, Francis was very concerned about falling into the "disease" of acedia, one of the seven capital sins, often known as sloth. It is a sort of spiritual malaise or depression. See 2 Cel 125, in FA:ED, 2:329–30. Francis worried that acedia "will produce in the heart permanent rust." This explains his insistence that his brothers put on joyful faces in his presence; it also indicates that he suffered a great deal of anguish. The descriptions of Francis in his youth give no hint of such suffering, portraying it as carefree and self-indulgent. So his anguish may well have been the lingering result of his traumatic wartime experience in Perugia, the destruction he witnessed in the Crusade, his loss of control in his order, and his worsening health. His solution once again was to pray and meditate, the approach that had lifted him from the trauma of his experience as a soldier.

159   "But because . . . not return": Richer of Sens, "Gesta Senonensis Ecclesiae," in FA: ED, 2:810.

159   "to all magistrates . . . this letter": LRP, in *Omnibus,* 115–16.

161   "At the sound . . . reverance": *Letter to a General Chapter,* in *Omnibus,* 103–04.

161   "May you announce . . . bells are rung": *First Letter to the Custodians,* in FA:ED, 1:57.

161   Francis's order buried: FA:ED, 1:56, 58.

162   strong pressure: AC 17.

162   Ferdinand, a Portuguese academic: Carol Ann Morrow, "St. Anthony: Portugal's

Favorite Son," in *St. Anthony Messenger,* June 2001. Accessed at www.american catholic.org/messenger/jun2001/Feature1.asp.

162 "Behold . . . simple as doves": Matthew 10:16.Various translations use "prudent" or "wise" in place of "shrewd."

163 "The minister . . . any other matter": ER 16, in *Omnibus,* 43–44.

164 The idea . . . was revolutionary: See Hoeberichts, *Francis and Islam,* 83–86, for a review of how Francis's wish to "be subject" to Muslims clashed with papal decrees and 61–134 for an illuminating exegesis of the ER.

165 "Everyone should glory . . . another": JG 8, in *XIIIth Century Chronicles,* 24.

165 "offering themselves to death": Ibid., 34–36.

Chapter 16: "Kamil"

166 "Never . . . such a test": RHC-Or, 1:91, 95.

166 "All the provinces . . . to ruins": Translated from RHC-Or, 2:120.

167 "He is believed . . . Asia": OP, 113.

167 sent bribes: Ibid., 112.

167 Al-Kamil . . . Egypt: On al-Kamil and his brothers, see R. S. Humphreys, *From Saladin to the Mongols: The Ayyubids of Damascus* (Albany: SUNY Press, 1977), 167–69.

167 When the brothers arrived: Abu al-Fida, in RHC-Or 1:96.

167 Pelagius was eager to attack: OP, 103–05.

167 "Certain . . . excommunicated": Ibid., 104.

168 "No one can describe . . . wicked gains": Ibid., 106.

168 "waiting with such . . . danger": FH, 433.

168 Similarly, James . . . outnumbered: James M. Powell, *Anatomy of a Crusade, 1213–1221* (Philadelphia: University of Pennsylvania Press, 1986), 178.

169 "It was said . . . this book": *Chronicle of Tours,* quoted in Joseph Michaud, *Histoire des Croisades* (Paris : A. J. Ducollet, 1838), 3:645. See also JV, Letter VII, *Lettres de la Cinquième Croisade,* 200–01; and OP, 113.

169 The pope had lectured . . . for him: Georges, *Jean de Brienne,* 45.

170 "Sane counsel . . . leaders": OP, 124; and, HPE, 4:1:80.

171 ignored a canal: Powell, *Anatomy of a Crusade,* 188.

171 reassembled in secret: Van Cleve, "Fifth Crusade," 426.

171 "wandered . . . like sheep astray": OP, 126. *Chronicle of Tours* noted that the soldiers who burned their tents were Germans.

171 killing those on board: *Chronicle of Tours,* in Michaud, *Histoire,* 3:645.

172 "Our people . . . suffering": FH, 436.

172 "for God": *Eracles,* in RHC-Oc, 2:351; and Van Cleve, "Fifth Crusade," 426.

172 Christian emissaries: The Christian emissaries were preceded by Imbert, a Crusader who took part in strategy meetings with Cardinal Pelagius, who told the sultan of the Christians' dire straits. Oliver of Paderborn portrayed him as a traitor, but Imbert may have been trying to shorten the Crusaders' suffering. In any event, the sultan knew how desperate the Christians were. See OP, 129.

172 Al-Kamil pleaded with his allies: For the Muslims' debate over the peace terms, see

Ibn al-Athir, in RHC-Or, 2:1:124; Abu al-Fida, in RHC-Or, 1:97–98; Gottschalk, *Al-Malik al-Kamil,* 112.

173   "that we might be filled with bread": OP, 130.

173   The sultan bided his time: For details of surrender, see Donovan, *Pelagius,* 93; FH, 438; al-Maqrizi, *History,* 185–186; HPE, 4:1:77; Gwenolé Jeusset, *God Is Courtesy,* trans. Sr. Carolyn Frederick (S.I.: s.n., 1985), 36–37; Gottschalk, *Al-Malik al-Kamil,* 114.

175   The departing Christians: Father Basetti-Sani wrote that Oliver undoubtedly believed Francis had moved the sultan and that al-Kamil might consider conversion. During the contentious debates within the Crusader camp, Oliver had steadfastly supported Pelagius, who wanted to use warfare to coerce Muslims into converting. After thousands died in unnecessary battles, Oliver was essentially taking the tack Francis had urged all along.

175   "The Sultan was moved ... disgrace": Ibid., 138. The translator notes that this concluding appendix to Oliver's history of the battle was probably written by someone else.

175   "Truly ... all princes": Translation based on Basetti-Sani, *Mohammed et Saint François.*

Chapter 17: Weeping

177   Thomas of Split: FA:ED, 2:808.

177   "The whole tenor ... negotiate peace": Augustine Thompson, O.P., *Cities of God: The Religion of the Italian Communes, 1125–1325* (University Park: Pennsylvania State University Press, 2005), cited in Powell, "St. Francis of Assisi's Way of Peace," 274, 276.

178   "go among the Saracens ... be sent": Rule 12, in *Omnibus,* 64.

178   "As the saint ... their deeds": Hugh of Digne, fragments inserted into the *Exposition of the Rule of the Friars Minor,* in FA:ED, 1:95. See Brooke, *Government,* 84–95 for an excellent explanation of the 1223 *Rule* controversies.

179   "to observe the Holy Gospel": Rule 1, in *Omnibus,* 57.

179   John of Brienne's daughter: Runciman, *History,* 3:176.

180   "reserving ... grace": 1 Cel 57, in *Omnibus,* 277.

180   "The memory ... fire of love": ML 9:2, in *Omnibus,* 699.

180   "Given this news ... tent in Damietta": Michael F. Cusato, "Of Snakes and Angels: The Mystical Experience behind the Stigmatization Narrative of 1 Celano," in *The Stigmata of Francis of Assisi: New Studies New Perspectives* (St. Bonaventure, N.Y.: Franciscan Institute, 2006), 60–61. See also Francis de Beer, *"We Saw Brother Francis,"* trans. Maggi Despot and Paul Lachance, O.F.M. (Chicago: Franciscan Herald Press, 1983), 109, and Warren, *Daring,* 96–97.

181   "Oh Lord ... Your praise": LF, in *Omnibus,* 1441.

181   on September 14: Cusato, "Snakes," 38.

182   "The marks ... by a lance": 1 Cel 94–95, in *Omnibus,* 309.

182   he asked Brother Leo ... Ninety-Nine Beautiful Names: Cusato, "Snakes," 61.

182   "You are holy ... Merciful Savior": *Praises of God,* in *Omnibus,* 125–126.

183   "God bless ... you peace": Ibid., 126.

184　"I am weeping for you": Cusato, "Snakes," 67. His analysis on 65–68 offers variations on this translation. Cusato cites John V. Fleming, "The Iconographic Unity of the Blessing for Brother Leo," *Franziskanische Studien* 63 (1981), 203–20. See also Warren, *Daring*, 90–97.

184　"talking head": Cusato, "Snakes," 64.

185　would not reveal the full story: Thomas of Eccleston, in *XIIIth Century Chronicles*, 162.

185　The small portrait on it: This was the experience of the author. Francis's tiny sketch does not reproduce well in a photo but is quite clear when seen in person.

186　"Praised be . . . be crowned": AC 84, in FA:ED, 2:187.

186　"I trust . . . each other": Ibid.

186　performance artist for peace: Lawrence S. Cunningham's biography of Francis is aptly named: *Francis of Assisi: Performing the Gospel Life*. "Performing" was an important part of his mission; his acts of radical compassion and peace helped him change hearts and minds.

187　"seemed bitter . . . you peace": Test 2, 24, 23, in FA:ED, 1:125–26.

187　Tensions rose . . . each other: al-Maqrizi, *History*, 197.

187　planning a new Crusade: The peace agreement reached between the Crusaders and Sultan al-Kamil in 1221 contained a loophole that allowed a "European crowned head" to break the peace. The treaty was written so that Emperor Frederick II could initiate a new Crusade. See Lane-Poole, *History of Egypt*, 225.

188　"He is . . . agent": FH, 506–7.

189　Fakhr ad-Din . . . in negotiations: Karimi, "L'origine," 113; and Gottschalk, *Al-Malik al-Kamil*, 154.

190　"That painful . . . all description": RHC-Or, 2:1:176.

191　"What more . . . the sultan": Dana C. Munro, "Letters of the Crusaders," *Translations and Reprints from the Original Sources of European History*, (Philadelphia: University of Pennsylvania, 1896), vol 1:4: 23–31, accessed at www.fordham.edu/halsall/source/fred2cdelets.html#fred.

191　"In his palace . . . with them": FH, 527.

191　permission to visit the Haram al-Sharif: al-Maqrizi, *History*, 207–08.

192　suffered the indignity: Philip de Novare, *Les Gestes des Chiprois*, cited in James A. Brundage, *The Crusades: A Documentary Survey* (Milwaukee: Marquette, 1962), 48–50.

192　"The most powerful sultan . . . of prosperity": *Matthew Paris's English History: From the Year 1235 to 1273*, trans. J. A. Giles (London: George Bell & Sons, 1889), 1:129–30.

193　this fanciful tale: DBF 27 and LF 24.

Chapter 18: The Story Changes

197　"angel of peace": ML 1, in *Omnibus*, 631.

199　Within a year . . . recruiting for the Crusade: Moorman, *Franciscan Order*, 300–01.

199　Pope Gregory . . . Aleppo: Brooke, *Government*, 146.

199　bull in 1238: Kedar, *Crusade and Mission*, 142.

199　accepting money: Moorman, *Franciscan Order*, 300.

199 "The friars . . . any form": ER 8, in *Omnibus,* 38.

201 "He refused . . . within himself": 1 Cel 6, in *Omnibus,* 233–34.

201 "they had . . . the author:" 2 Cel 2, in *Omnibus,* 360.

201 "Stirred by the venom . . . bodily suffering": 1 Cel 3, in *Omnibus,* 231.

201 driven out of Rome: Ferdinand Gregorovius, *History of the City of Rome in the Middle Ages,* trans. Annie Hamilton(London: George Bell & Sons, 1897), 5:1:148.

202 Brother Crescentius: Angelo Clareno, *A Chronicle or History of the Seven Tribulations of the Order of Brothers Minor,* trans. David Burr and E. Randolph Daniel (St. Bonaventure, N.Y.: Franciscan Institute, 2005), 93.

202 John of Parma: Salimbene, *Chronicle of Salimbene,* 297; Moorman, *Sources,* 139.

203 Joachim's prophecies: Reeves, *Influence,* 39.

203 criticized the popes: Daniel, *Concept of Mission,* 21–22.

203 "These two laughed . . . take place": Salimbene, translated in G. G. Coulton, *From Fancis to Dante: A Translation of All That Is of Primary Interest in the Chronicle of the Franciscan Salimbene* (London: Duckworth, 1908), 153–54.

203 Constantinople . . . that occurred: Clareno, *Seven Tribulations,* 102.

204 *The Introduction to the Eternal Gospel:* Reeves, *Influence,* 59–61, 188.

204 the new age of the Spirit: On the Joachite movement among Franciscans, see E. Randolph Daniel, "A Re-Examination of the Origins of Franciscan Joachitism," *Speculum* 43, no. 4. (October 1968), 671–76.

204 Bonaventure . . . Thomas Aquinas: FA:ED, 2:496.

204 trial for heresy: David Burr, *The Spiritual Franciscans: From Protest to Persecution in the Century after Saint Francis* (University Park: Pennsylvania State University Press, 2001), 32.

205 difficult task for Bonaventure: Moorman, *History,* 146.

205 Like John . . . Abbot Joachim: Clareno, *Trib,* 114.

205 highly technical issue: Reeves, *Influence,* 62.

206 life in prison: Moorman, *History,* 146.

206 filled with rage: Clareno, *Trib,* 126. This may reflect Angelo Clareno's feelings toward the superiors in his own time.

206 beatified in 1777: Livarius Oliger, "Blessed John of Parma," *Catholic Encyclopedia,* vol. 8 (New York: Robert Appleton Company, 1910), accessed at www.newadvent .org/cathen/08475c.htm. Blessed John of Parma's feast day is March 20.

206 At least eighty percent: Moorman, *History,* 286.

206 the order's political problems: On Bonaventure's political aims in writing *The Major Legend,* see Ibid., 287. On his theological aims, see Ewert H. Cousins, *Bonaventure and the Coincidence of Opposites* (Chicago: Franciscan Press, 1978), 73–80.

207 "He longed so much . . . a glory": FA:ED, 2:811–12.

208 *A Book of Exemplary Stories:* FA:ED, 3:796.

209 Humbert of Romans: Musto, *Peacemaker,* 655–61.

209 Roger Bacon: Elizabeth Siberry, *Criticism of Crusading, 1095–1274* (Oxford: Clarendon Press, 1985), 207; Daniel, *Concept of Mission,* 55–62. Bacon's work appeared several years after *The Major Legend,* but his ideas would have circulated sooner.

210 "Our faith . . . believe the Scriptures": *The Morning Sermon on St. Francis, 1267, in* FA:ED, 2:757.

210   sent it directly to Pope Clement IV: Daniel, *Concept of Mission,* 60.

210   Francis also is an icon: Noel Muscat, O.F.M., "Francis of Assisi and Bonaventure's Theology of the Cross," 1–4, accessed at www.ofm.org.mt/fsc/F&C_in_Bonaven .pdf.

211   "The Chapter-general . . . inserted herein": Sabatier, *Life of Francis,* 395.

211   two copies: Brooke, *Government,* 212.

212   index by the Franciscan Institute: FA:ED, 4.

212   The great cycle of twenty-eight frescoes: William R. Cook, interview, December 1, 2007. Cook, an expert on Franciscan art at SUNY Geneseo, provided helpful background on the art depicting Francis and the sultan.

214   "a certain woman . . . act with her": LF 24, in *Omnibus,* 1354.

214   Peter Olivi: *Peter Olivi's Rule Commentary: Edition and Presentation,* ed. David Flood (Wiesbaden: F. Steiner, 1972), cited in Musto, *Peacemakers,* 617–18.

214   Raymond Lull: Moorman, *History,* 232.

214   burned at the stake: Burr, *Spiritual,* 199–200.

214   In 1323 . . . obedience came first: Moorman, *History,* 311.

215   "And when . . . he hasted": Dante Alighieri, "Paradiso," *The Divine Comedy,* Harvard Classics, (1909–14), 11:122 and 11:92–97, accessed at www.bartleby.com/20/ 311.html.

215   Gozzoli's fresco: Web Gallery of Art, accessed at www.wga.hu/frames-e.html?/ bio/g/gozzoli/biograph.html.

217   Franciscans closely aligned . . . in Jerusalem: John Leddy Phelan, *The Millennial Kingdom of the Franciscans in the New World* (Berkeley and Los Angeles: University of California, 1970), 10, 22.

Chapter 19: The Seed Sprouts

219   Massignon used . . . belief systems: Seyyed Hossein Nasr, *Traditional Islam in the Modern World* (London: Keegan, 1990), 255–60.

219   *badaliya:* on the founding of *badaliya* movement, see Mary Louise Gude, *Louis Massignon: The Crucible of Compassion* (South Bend, Ind.: University of Notre Dame Press, 1996), 134–35.

220   "It's quite profound . . . neighbors": Dorothy C. Buck, interview, December 11, 2007. See also www.dcbuck.com/Badaliya/index.html.

220   "the seeds began to germinate": Basetti-Sani, *Muhammad, St. Francis of Assisi and Alvernia ,* 5–9.

220   key book: *Mohammed et Saint François* (Ottawa, 1959).

221   "They adore . . . and fasting": *Declaration on the Relation of the Church to Non-Christian Religions,* October 28, 1965. accessed at www.vatican.va/archive/hist _councils/ii_vatican_council/documents/vat-ii_decl_19651028_nostra-aetate _en.html.

221   Montini had defended Massignon: Peter Hebblethwaite, *Paul VI: The Modern Pope* (New York: Paulist Press, 1993), 384. The author thanks John Borelli for pointing this out and for other helpful background on Massignon.

221   "though the . . . meaning of human life": *Redemptor Hominis,* No. 11, March 4,

1979, accessed at www.vatican.va/edocs/ENG0218/_INDEX.HTM. See also Hoeberichts, *Francis and Islam*, 148.

222 the ongoing rediscovery of Francis's legacy as a peacemaker: Many people associate Francis with the popular "Prayer of St. Francis," beginning, "Lord, make me an instrument of your peace." Francis did not write it, however. According to Christian Renoux of the University of Orleans, it dates to 1912, when it was published in French. A translation into English in the 1930s attributed it to Francis, and Cardinal Francis Spellman of New York popularized it. See Christian Renoux, "The Origin of the Peace Prayer of St. Francis," accessed at www.franciscan-archive .org/franciscana/peace.html.

222 "I have . . . and brotherhood . . . intended to serve": "Address of John Paul II to the Christian Churches and Ecclesial Communities Gathered in Assisi for the World Day of Prayer," www.vatican.va/holy_father/john_paul_ii/speeches/1986/ october/documents/hf_jp-ii_spe_19861027_prayer-peace-assisi_en.html.

222 "be together to pray": William F. Murphy, "Remembering Assisi after 20 Years," *America*, October 23, 2006.

223 "Assisi caused . . . another planet": Accessed at www.vatican.va/jubilee_2000/ magazine/documents/ju_mag_june-sept-1996_etchegaray-assisi_en.html.

223 "prophetic intuition . . . grace": Drew Christiansen, "Benedict XVI: Peacemaker," *America*, July 16, 2007, 11.

223 "Only then . . . the Crucifix": Cardinal Joseph Ratzinger, "Lo splendore della pace di Francesco," *30 Giorni* (January 2002), accessed at www.30giorni.it/it/articolo .asp?id=375; translated in "Cardinal Ratzinger Comments on Lessons of Assisi," accessed at www.ewtn.com/vnews/getstory.asp?number=24103.

223 "Interreligious dialogue . . . and culture": "Address of the Holy Father," May 6, 2001. Accessed at www.vatican.va/holy_father/john_paul_ii/speeches/2001/ documents/hf_jp-ii_spe_20010506_omayyadi_en.html.

223 "Saint Francis was among . . . to his Islam": Dr. Kamel al-Sharif, "St. Francis, Friend of Muslims," accessed at http://hiwar-net.usj.edu.lb/chroniques16.htm.

224 prayer service with Muslims in Damietta: The Franciscan Center for Christian Oriental Studies in Cairo has an archive of photographs of the event. Father Mansour, interview, October 23, 2007.

224 "This is the same . . . speak as leaders' ": Rev. GianMaria Polidoro, interview, November 4, 2007.

225 "The Muslims are . . . for today": Donal O'Mahony, O.F.M. Cap., interview, December 9, 2007.

225 Jan Hoeberichts's: As noted earlier, Dr. Hoeberichts's book made a major contribution with its analysis of the *Earlier Rule*. He was not required to read Francis's writings during his formation, he said in his interview, when he entered the Franciscan order in the 1950s. There was little interest in Francis's writings at the time because he was not seen as a thinker. Franciscan experts such as the American scholar David Flood began studying Francis's writings more closely in the 1970s.

226 "We witness . . . and Christians": Keeler, *Days of Intense Emotion*, 68.

226 "The Sultan discovered . . . separating them": see www.ofm.org/ofmnews/?p=1228 and texts of the statements provided by the Franciscan order.

227 Catholic Worker Movement: Lawrence Cunningham, *Francis of Assisi* (San Francisco: Harper & Row, 1981), 108.

227 "In the centuries . . . anybody": *The Challenge of Peace: God's Promise and Our Response,* accessed at www.osjspm.org/the_challenge_of_peace_1.aspx.

Epilogue

229 "It's important . . . dialogue": Rev. Emmanuel Maken, interview, October 23, 2007.

230 "John Paul . . . political importance": Archbishop Michael Fitzgerald, interview, October 30, 2007.

230 "I don't understand . . . Crusade": Bishop Yohanna Golta, interview, October 27, 2007.

231 "are quite willing . . . Roman Church": *Chronicle of Richard of San Germano,* trans. Graham A. Loud (unpublished), 31–32.

232 "seemed . . . against evil": John Thavis, "Papal Envoy to Bush Says Events Proved Vatican Right about Iraqi War," Catholic News Service, October 6, 2003, accessed at www.catholicnews.com/data/stories/cns/20031006.htm. Cardinal Oscar Rodriguez Maradiaga has described how heated this meeting was. See Brian T. Olszewski, "No Secret Formula for Helping Poor: Cardinal Urges Living Matthew 25:31–36," *Milwaukee Catholic Herald,* October 19, 2006, accessed at www.chnonline.org/2006-10-19/newsstory2.html. For a discussion of how religion may have influenced President Bush's policy toward Iraq, see Kevin Phillips, "Crusader: Bush's Religious Passions," *Christian Century,* no. 14, vol. 121 (July, 13, 2004), 8; Al Kamen, "George Bush and the G-Word," *Washington Post* (October 14, 2005), A17.

233 Tariq Aziz: Frank Bruni, "At Assisi, Iraqi Envoy Traces Saint's Footsteps and Publicly Prays for Peace," *New York Times,* February 16, 2003, 16.

234 "There has never . . . St. Francis": *Rite Expiatis, Encyclical of Pope Pius XI on St. Francis,* April 30, 1926.

234 "I think one . . . Christian holiness": Mahmoud Ayoub, interview, January 24, 2008.

235 "The peace . . . Eden": Rev. GianMaria Polidoro, interview, November 4, 2007.

236 "a wise voice . . . tolerance": Father Mamdouh Shehab, interview, October 23, 2007.

237 in the first decade of the twentieth century: Tolan, *Le Saint chez le Sultan,* 439.

237 "Usually violence . . . pray there": Seyyed Hossein Nasr, interview, December 26, 2007. In November 2008 Dr. Nasr addressed Pope Benedict XVI at the first seminar of the Christiam-Muslim Forum in Rome, on behalf of a worldwide group of Muslim authorities. "Whether we are Christians or Muslims, we are beckoned by our religions to seek peace," he said. For full remarks, see www.acommonword. org.

238 leper hospital: Fortini, *Francis,* 153.

239 took the habit: Bernard of Besse, in FA:ED, 3:56–57.

240 three daughters . . . Saladin: R. Stephen Humphreys, "Women as Patrons of Religious Architecture in Ayyubid Damascus," *Muqarnas* 11 (1994), 41. Nasser Rabbat, interview, January 7, 2008.

Bibliography

Ackerman, Robert W. "The Knighting Ceremonies in the Middle English Romances." *Speculum* 19, no. 3 (July 1944), 285–313.

Adamski, Mary. "Healing the Wound." *Honolulu Star-Bulletin,* September 6, 2003.

Al-Makin Ibn al-'Amid. *Chronique des Ayyoubides: 602–658 / 1205-6-1259-60.* Translated into French by Anne-Marie Eddé and Françoise Micheau. Paris: Académie des In-scriptions et Belles-lettres, 1994.

Al-Maqrizi, Taqi al-Din. *A History of the Ayyubid Sultans of Egypt.* Translated by R. J. C. Broadhurst. Boston: Twayne, 1980.

Andrews, Frances. *The Early Humiliati.* Cambridge Studies in Medieval Life and Thought, 4th ser., no. 43. New York: Cambridge University Press, 1999.

Archer, Thomas Andrew. *The Crusade of Richard I, 1189–92: Extracts from the Itinerarium Ricardi Bohâdin.* New York: Putnam's, 1888.

Armstrong, Regis J., O.F.M. Cap.; J. A. Wayne Hellman, O.F.M. Conv.; and William J. Short, O.F.M., eds. *Francis of Assisi: Early Documents.* 4 vols. New York, London, and Manila: New City Press, 1999–2002.

Arnold of Sarrant. *Chronicle of the Twenty-four Generals of the Order of Friars Minor.* Part I: *Saint Francis and His Companions.* Translated by Noel Muscat, O.F.M. Malta: Tau/Franciscan, 2007.

Ayoub, Mahmoud. "Christian-Muslim Dialogue: Goals and Obstacles." *Muslim World* 94 (July 2004), 313–19.

———. *The Qur'an and Its Interpreters.* Vol. 2, *The House of 'Imran.* Albany: SUNY Press, 1992.

Basetti-Sani, Giulio, O.F.M. *Mohammed et Saint François.* Ottawa: Commissariat de Terre-Sainte, 1959.

Beha ed-Din Abu el-Mehasan Yusuf. *The Life of Saladin.* Translated by Claude Reignier Conder. London: Hanover Square, 1897.

Bigaroni, Marino, O.F.M. "The Church of San Giorgio in Assisi and the First Expansion of the Medieval City Walls." Translated by Lori Pieper, S.F.O. *Greyfriars Review* 8, no. 1 (1994).

Bird, Jessalynn Lea. "Crusade and Conversion after the Fourth Lateran Council (1215): Oliver of Paderborn's and James of Vitry's Missions to Muslims Reconsidered." *Essays in Medieval Studies* 21 (2004), 23–47.

Blanshei, Sara Rubin. "Perugia, 1260–1340: The Conflict and Change in a Medieval Italian Urban Society." *Transactions of the American Philosophical Society*, new ser., vol. 66, no. 2 (1976), 1–128.

Boase, T. R. R. *St. Francis of Assisi.* Bloomington: Indiana University Press, 1968.

Brooke, Rosalind. *Early Franciscan Government, Elias to Bonaventure.* Cambridge: Cambridge University Press, 1959.

Brundage, James A. *The Crusades: A Documentary Survey.* Milwaukee: Marquette, 1962.

Burr, David. *The Spiritual Franciscans: From Protest to Persecution in the Century after Saint Francis.* University Park: Pennsylvania State University Press, 2001.

Butigan, Ken, Mary Litell, O.S.F., and Louis Vitale, O.F.M. *Franciscan Nonviolence: Stories, Reflections, Principles, Practices and Resources,* Pace e Bene Nonviolence Services, 2003. Online www.ofm-jpic.org/peace/nonviolence/nonviolence_en.pdf.

Clareno, Angelo. *A Chronicle or History of the Seven Tribulations of the Order of Brothers Minor.* Translated by David Burr and E. Randolph Daniel. St. Bonaventure, N.Y.: Franciscan Institute, 2005.

Cook, William R. *The Art of the Franciscan Order in Italy.* Boston: Brill, 2005.

Coulton, G. G. *From Francis to Dante: A Translation of All That Is of Primary Interest in the Chronicle of the Franciscan Salimbene.* London: Duckworth, 1908.

Cousins, Ewert H. *Bonaventure and the Coincidence of Opposites.* Chicago: Franciscan Press, 1978.

Crossan, John Dominick. *The Historical Jesus: The Life of a Mediterranean Jewish Peasant.* New York: HarperCollins, 1991.

Cunningham, Lawrence. *The Meaning of Saints.* San Francisco: Harper & Row, 1980.

———. *Francis of Assisi: Performing the Gospel Life.* Grand Rapids, Mich.: Eerdmans, 2004.

Cusato, Michael F. "An Unexplored Influence on the *Epistola ad fideles* of St. Francis of Assisi: The *Epistola universis Christi fidelibus* of Joachim of Fiore." *Franciscan Studies* 61 (2003), 253–78.

———. "Of Snakes and Angels: The Mystical Experience behind the Stigmatization Narrative of 1 Celano." In *The Stigmata of Francis of Assisi: New Studies New Perspectives.* St. Bonaventure, N.Y.: Franciscan Institute, 2006.

Dalarun, Jacques. *Francis of Assisi and Power.* Translated by Anne Baratol, O.S.C. St. Bonaventure, N.Y.: Franciscan Institute, 2007.

Daniel, E. Randolph. *The Franciscan Concept of Mission in the High Middle Ages.* Lexington: University of Kentucky Press, 1975.

———. "A Re-Examination of the Origins of Franciscan Joachitism." *Speculum* 43, no. 4 (October 1968), 671–76.

de Beer, Francis. *"We Saw Brother Francis."* Translated by Maggi Despot and Paul Lachance, O.F.M. Chicago: Franciscan Herald Press, 1983.

Donovan, Joseph Patrick. *Pelagius and the Fifth Crusade.* Philadelphia: University of Pennsylvania Press, 1950.

Dunbabin, Jean. *Captivity and Imprisonment in Medieval Europe, 1000–1300.* New York: Palgrave Macmillan, 2002.

Englebert, Omer. *St. Francis of Assisi: A Biography.* Translated by Eve Marie Cooper. 2nd ed. Cincinnati: Servant, 1979.

Fitzgerald, Michael, and John Borelli. *Interfaith Dialogue: A Catholic View.* Maryknoll, N.Y.: Orbis, 2006.

Flood, David, and Thadée Matura. *The Birth of a Movement.* Chicago: Franciscan Herald Press, 1975.

Fortini, Arnaldo. *Francis of Assisi. A Translation of Nova Vita di San Francesco.* Translated by Helen Moak. New York: Crossroad, 1981.

Francke, Linda Bird. *On the Road with Francis of Assisi.* New York: Random House, 2005.

Gabrieli, Francesco, ed. *Arab Historians of the Crusades.* Translated by E. J. Costello. Berkeley and Los Angeles: University of California Press, 1969.

Georges, Étienne. *Jean de Brienne, Empereur de Constantinople et Roi de Jérusalem.* Troyes, 1858.

Golubovich, Girolamo. *Biblioteca bio-bibliografica della Terra Santa e dell'Oriente francescano.* 5 vols. Quaracchi: Collegio di S. Bonaventura, 1906–27.

Gordon, Lina Duff. *The Story of Assisi.* London: Dent, 1900.

Gottschalk, H. L. *Al-Malik al-Kamil von Egypten und seine Zeit.* Wiesbaden: O. Harrassowitz, 1958.

Grossman, Lt. Col. David, with Loren W. Christensen. *On Combat: The Psychology and Physiology of Deadly Conflict in War and Peace.* PPCT Research Publications, 2004.

Gude, Mary Louise. *Louis Massignon: The Crucible of Compassion.* South Bend, Ind.: University of Notre Dame Press, 1996.

Habig, Marion A., ed. *St. Francis of Assisi, Writings and Early Biographies: English Omnibus of the Sources for the Life of St. Francis.* Translated by Raphael Brown et al. 2 vols. Quincy, Ill.: Franciscan Press, 1991.

Hallam, Elizabeth, ed. *Chronicles of the Crusades: Eye-Witness Accounts of the Wars between Christianity and Islam.* London: Weidenfield and Nicolson, 1989.

Hardick, Lothar, O.F.M. *The Admonitions of St. Francis of Assisi.* Translated by David Smithy. Chicago: Franciscan Herald Press, 1982.

Healy, Joseph P., and William Klassen. "Peace." In *The Anchor Bible Dictionary.* Edited by David Noel Freedman. New York: Doubleday, 1992.

Heer, Friedrich. *The Medieval World: Europe 1100–1350.* Translated by Janet Sondheimer. New York: Praeger, 1969.

Hermann, Placid, O.F.M., trans. *XIIIth Century Chronicles: Jordan of Giano, Thomas of Eccleston, and Salimbene degli Adam.* Chicago: Franciscan Herald Press, 1961.

Hillenbrand, Carole. *The Crusades: Islamic Perspectives.* Edinburgh: Edinburgh University Press, 1999.

Hoeberichts, J. *Francis and Islam.* Quincy, Ill.: Franciscan Press, 1997.

Hoge, Charles W., et al. "Association of Posttraumatic Stress Disorder With Somatic Symptoms, Health Care Visits, and Absenteeism Among Iraq War Veterans." *American Journal of Psychiatry* 164, no. 1 (2007), 150–53.

House, Adrian. *Francis of Assisi: A Revolutionary Life.* New York: Paulist, 2003.

Huber, Raphael. *A Documented History of the Franciscan Order from the Birth of St. Francis to the Divison of the Order, 1182–1517.* Milwaukee: Nowiny Publishing Apostolate, 1944.

Humphreys, R. S. *From Saladin to the Mongols: The Ayyubids of Damascus.* Albany: SUNY Press, 1977.

Ibn-Khallikan. *Biographical Dictionary.* Translated by William MacGuckin Slane. Paris: Oriental Translation Fund of Great Britain and Ireland, 1843.

Idinopulos, Thomas. *Jerusalem: A History of the Holiest City as Seen Through the Struggles of Jews, Christians and Muslims.* Chicago: Ivan R. Dee, 1994.

Iriarte, Lazaro, O.F.M. Cap. "Francis of Assisi and the Evangelical Movements of His Time." *Greyfriars Review* 12, no. 2 (1998).

Jacques de Vitry. *The History of Jerusalem.* Translated by Aubrey Stewart. 1896; Reprinted New York: AMS, 1971.

———. *Lettres de la Cinquième Croisade.* Translated by G. Duchet-Suchaux. Brépols: Turnhout, 1998.

Jeusset, Gwenolé. *God Is Courtesy: Francis of Assisi, His Order, and Islam.* Translated by Sr. Carolyn Frederick. S.I.: s.n., 1985.

Jörgensen, Johannes. *St. Francis of Assisi: A Biography.* Translated by T. O'Conor Sloan. New York: Longmans, 1912.

Kamali, Mohammad Hashim. *Freedom of Expression in Islam.* Cambridge: Islamic Texts Society, 1997.

Karimi, Hossein. "L'origine iranienne de Fakhr al-Din Yusof, émir ayyoubide, instigateur de la paix avec Frédéric II pendant la VIe Croisade." In *La signification du bas Moyen Age dans l'histoire et la culture du monde musulman.* Actes du 8ème Congrès de l'Union européenne des Arabisants et Islamisants. Aix-en-Provence, 1976.

Kastner, L. E. "Gavaudan's Crusade Song." *Modern Language Review* 26, no. 2 (April 1931).

Kedar, Benjamin Z. *Crusade and Mission: European Approaches Toward the Muslims.* Princeton: Princeton University Press, 1984.

Küng, Hans. *The Catholic Church: A Short History.* Translated by John Bowden. New York: Random/Modern Library, 2001.

La Due, William J. *The Chair of Saint Peter: A History of the Papacy.* Maryknoll, N.Y.: Orbis, 1999.

Lane-Poole, Stanley. *A History of Egypt in the Middle Ages.* New York: Scribner's, 1901.

Macgregor, James B. "Negotiating Knightly Piety: The Cult of the Warrior-Saints in the West, ca. 1070–ca. 1200." *Church History* 73, no. 2 (June, 2004).

Maier, Christoph T. *Preaching the Crusades: Mendicant Friars and the Cross in the Thirteenth Century.* New York: Cambridge University Press, 1994.

Mallon, Elias D. *Islam: What Catholics Need to Know.* Washington: NCEA, 2006.

Marshall, Christopher. *Warfare and the Latin East, 1192–1291.* New York: Cambridge University Press, 1992.

Martines, Lauro. "Political Violence in the Thirteenth Century." In *Violence and Civil Disorder in Italian Cities, 1200–1500.* Berkeley and Los Angeles: University of California Press, 1972.

Massignon, Louis. *The Passion of al-Hallaj.* Translated by Herbert Mason. 4 vols. Princeton: Princeton University Press, 1982.

Mastnak, Tomaz. *Crusading Peace: Christendom, the Muslim World, and Western Political Order.* Berkeley and Los Angeles: University of California Press, 2002.

Matthew Paris's English History. From the Year 1235 to 1273. Translated by J. A. Giles. London: George Bell & Sons, 1889.

McNeill, John T. "Asceticism versus Militarism in the Middle Ages." *Church History* 5 (1936).

McNeil, John T., and Helena M. Gamer. *Medieval Handbooks of Penance.* New York: Columbia University Press, 1938.

Michaud, Joseph. *Histoire des Croisades.* 6 vols. Paris: A. J. Ducollet, 1838.

Moore, John C. *Pope Innocent III (1160/62–1216): To Root Up and to Plant.* Boston: Brill, 2003.

Moorman, John H. R. *The Sources of the Life of Saint Francis.* Manchester: Manchester University Press, 1940.

———, trans. *A New Fioretti: A Collection of Early Stories About St. Francis Assisi.* London: S.P.C.K., 1946.

———. *A History of the Franciscan Order from Its Origins to the Year 1517.* Oxford: Clarendon Press, 1968.

Morgan, M. R. *The Chronicle of Ernoul and the Continuations of William of Tyre.* London: Oxford University Press, 1973.

Musto, Ronald G. *The Catholic Peace Tradition.* Maryknoll, N.Y.: Orbis, 1986.

———, ed. *Catholic Peacemakers: A Documentary History.* New York: Garland, 1993.

Nasr, Seyyed Hossein. *Traditional Islam in the Modern World.* London: Keegan, 1990.

———. "Islamic-Christian Dialogue—Problems and Obstacles to Be Pondered and Overcome." *Muslim World* 88, no. 3–4 (July–October 1998), 218–37.

Navone, John. "Spiritual Acedia, Torpor and Depression." *Homiletic and Pastoral Review.* (August 1999). Online at www.catholic.net/rcc/Periodicals/Homiletic/Aug-Sept99/depression.html.

Owen, D. D. R. *The Legend of Roland: A Pageant of the Middle Ages.* New York: Phaedon/Praeger, 1973.

Pazzelli, Raffaele. *St. Francis and the Third Order.* Chicago: Franciscan Herald Press, 1982.

Peters, Edward, ed. *Christian Society and the Crusades, 1198–1229; Sources in Translation, including The Capture of Damietta by Oliver of Paderborn.* Translated by John J. Gavigan. Philadelphia: University of Pennsylvania Press, 1971.

Petry, Carl F., ed. *The Cambridge History of Egypt.* Vol. 1, *Islamic Egypt, 640–1571.* Cambridge: Cambridge University Press, 1998.

Phelan, John Leddy. *The Millennial Kingdom of the Franciscans in the New World.* 2nd ed., rev. Berkeley and Los Angeles: University of California Press, 1970.

Pinault, David. "Images of Christ in Arabic Literature." *Die Welt des Islams* 27, no. 1–3 (1987), 103–25.

Polidoro, GianMaria. *The Greeting of Peace Revealed to Saint Francis.* Translated by Joseph O'Boyle and Paul Reczec. S. Maria degli Angeli: Portiuncula, n.d.

Powell, James M. "Francesco d'Assisi e la Quinta Crociata: Una Missione di Pace." *Schede Medievali* 4 (1983), 68–77.

———. *Anatomy of a Crusade, 1213–1221.* Philadelphia: University of Pennsylvania Press, 1986.

————. *Innocent III: Vicar of Christ or Lord of the World?* Washington, D.C.: Catholic University of America Press, 1994.

————, trans. *The Deeds of Pope Innocent III.* Washington, D.C.: Catholic University of America Press, 2004.

————. "St. Francis of Assisi's Way of Peace." *Medieval Encounters* 13, no. 2 (June 2007), 271–80.

Ratzinger, Joseph. *The Theology of History in St. Bonaventure.* Translated by Zachary Hayes, O.F.M. Chicago: Franciscan Herald Press, 1989.

Recueil des Historiens des Croisades. 14 vols. Paris, 1841–1906.

Reeves, Marjorie. *The Influence of Prophecy in the Later Middle Ages: A Study of Joachimism.* London: Oxford University Press, 1969.

Renaud, Joseph Toussaint. *Histoire de la Sixième Croisade et de la Prise de Damiette.* Paris, 1826.

Richard of San Germano. *The Chronicle of Richard of San Germano.* Translated by G. A. Loud. Unpublished ms.

Riley-Smith, Louise, and Jonathan Riley-Smith. *The Crusades: Idea and Reality, 1095–1274.* London: Edward Arnold, 1981.

Robson, Michael. "Assisi, Guido II and Saint Francis." *Greystone Review* 12, no. 3 (1998), 225–87.

Roger of Wendover. *Roger of Wendover's Flowers of History.* Translated by J. A. Giles. London: Bohn, 1849.

Roncaglia, Martiniano. *St. Francis of Assisi and the Middle East.* Translated by Stephen A. Janto. Cairo: Franciscan Center of Oriental Studies, 1957.

Runciman, Steven. *History of the Crusades.* 3 vols. Cambridge: Cambridge University Press, 1951–54.

————. *The Medieval Manichee: A Study of the Christian Dualist Heresy.* Cambridge: Cambridge University Press, 1969.

Russell, Frederick H. *The Just War in the Middle Ages.* Cambridge: Cambridge University Press, 1975.

Russell, Josiah Cox. "Master Henry of Avranches as an International Poet." *Speculum* 3, no. 1 (January 1928), 34–63.

Sabatier, Paul. *Life of St. Francis of Assisi.* Translated by Louise Seymour Houghton. New York: Scribner's, 1902.

Salimbene de Adam. *The Chronicles of Salimbene de Adam.* Edited by Joseph L. Baird, Giuseppe Baglivi, and John Robert Kane. Medieval and Renaissance Texts and Studies. Binghamton, N.Y.: Center for Medieval and Early Renaissance Studies, 1986.

Sawirus Ibn al-Mukaffa. *History of the Patriarchs of the Egyptian Church, Known as the History of the Holy Church.* Translated by Antoine Khater and O.H.E. KHS Burmester. Cairo: Publications of the Coptic Archaeological Society, 1970.

Siberry, Elizabeth. *Criticism of Crusading, 1095–1274.* Oxford: Clarendon Press, 1985.

Sibt Ibn al-Farid. *Umar Ibn-al-Farid: Sufi Verse, Saintly Life.* Translated by Th. Emil Homerin. New York: Paulist Press, 2001.

Spoto, Donald. *Reluctant Saint: The Life of Francis of Assisi.* New York: Viking, 2002.

Sulpicius Severus. *Life of St. Martin.* Translated by Alexander Roberts. New York: The Christian Literature Co., 1894.

Throop, P. A. *Criticism of the Crusade: A Study of Public Opinion and Crusade Propaganda.* 1940; reprinted. Philadelphia, 1975.

Tolan, John V. *Saracens: Islam in the Medieval European Imagination.* New York: Columbia University Press, 2002.

———. *Le saint chez le sultan: La rencontre de François d'Assise et de l'islam. Huit siècles d'interprétation.* Paris: Éditions du Seuil, 2007.

Usamah Ibn-Munqidh. *An Arab-Syrian Gentleman and Warrior in the Period of the Crusades: Memoirs of Usamah Ibn-Munqidh.* Translated by Philip K. Hitti. London: I. B. Tauris, 1987.

Van Cleve, Thomas C. "The Fifth Crusade." In *A History of the Crusades,* vol. 2, *The Later Crusades, 1189–1311.* Edited by R. L. Wolff and Harry W. Hazard. Madison: University of Wisconsin Press, 1969– 89.

Vauchez, Andre. *Sainthood in the Later Middle Ages.* Translated by Jean Birrell. New York: Cambridge University Press, 1997.

Verkamp, Bernard J. "Moral Treatment of Returning Warriors in the Early Middle Ages." *Journal of Religious Ethics* 16, no. 2 (Fall 1988), 223–49.

Wakefield, Walter W. *Heresy, Crusade and Inquisition in Southern France.* Berkeley and Los Angeles: University of California Press, 1974.

Waley, D. P. "Papal Armies in the Thirteenth Century." *English Historical Review* 72, no. 282 (January 1957).

Warren, Kathleen A. *Daring to Cross the Threshold: Francis of Assisi Encounters Sultan Malek al-Kamel.* Rochester, Minn.: Sisters of St. Francis, 2003.

Wilkinson, Isambard. "Public Outcry Forces Church to Keep Moor Slayer's Statue." *Daily Telegraph,* July 22, 2004.

Websites

www.crusades-encyclopedia.com/recueil.html
Recueil des Historiens des Croisades is presented online through the Bibliothèque Nationale de France.

www.fordham.edu/halsall/sbook.html
The Internet Medieval Sourcebook, from Fordham University.

www.franciscan-archive.org/patriarcha/opera/fwintro.html
The writings of Saint Francis of Assisi, from the Franciscan Archive.

www.peacedocs.com/Site/Texts.html
Documents from the peace traditions of various religions, compiled by Ronald G. Musto.

Acknowledgments

I'm fortunate to be part of a supportive community at Brooklyn College of the City University of New York, where my colleagues helped me in many ways. The Ethyle R. Wolfe Institute for the Humanities provided a fellowship that gave me the gift of time. I thank Nicola Masciandaro, Ellen Tremper, and Robert Viscusi for their insights and encouragement. I am grateful to Anthony Mancini, director of the Journalism Program in which I teach, for encouraging me throughout and helping with some key translations. I also appreciate the enthusiasm our students expressed.

I've relied heavily on the work of many scholars, especially Franciscan experts. Their translations and other material in the *Omnibus* and the more recent *Francis of Assisi: Early Documents* are a great, great service. My thanks also to Father Michael Cusato of the Franciscan Institute and Sister Kathy Warren for speaking to me about their research concerning Francis and the sultan. I'm grateful to Father Michael Calabria, who followed Francis's footsteps to Egypt, for his help. In Assisi, Father GianMaria Polidoro was perceptive and inspiring. Jan Hoeberichts, a former Franciscan but still one in spirit, was generous in accepting my questions and thoughtful and authoritative in his answers. My thanks also to the friars and staff at the Franciscan Center for Christian Oriental Studies in Cairo.

I'm grateful to the people at Egypt's Supreme Council of Antiquities, under the leadership of Dr. Zahi Hawass, for all their help. My thanks to Bahaa El-Din Wahba Ramadan, Mohamed Bahget Elgahary, and all those who generously showed me the very impressive work being done to restore two ancient mosques in Damietta. The joy they took in their work was catching. Special thanks to Naguib Amin and the archaeologist Shaimaa Fouad.

A number of other experts provided valuable assistance by discussing their work and views with me. These include Mahmoud Ayoub, John Borelli, Dorothy Buck, William Cook, Archbishop Michael Fitzgerald, Bishop Yohanna Golta, David Grossman, Fareed Munir, Ronald Musto, Seyyed Hossein Nasr, John F. Romano, and Neslihan Senocak. I owe a great debt to the published work of many others, particularly James M. Powell and including Frances Andrews, Rosalind Brooke, Thomas Van Cleve, E. Randolph Daniel, Joseph P. Donovan, Arnaldo Fortini, Benjamin Kedar, Helen Moak, John H. R. Moorman, Marjorie Reeves, and Steven Runciman. Recent biographies by Lawrence Cunningham, Adrian House, and Donald Spoto were a valuable help, as was Linda Bird Francke's *On the Road with Francis of Assisi*.

I thank Adel Awny, who guided me in Cairo with grace and humor. He gave me the opportunity to speak about Francis and the sultan to his students at the Carmelite Sisters' school for girls in Cairo; I enjoyed the dialogue with these perceptive young women.

My thanks to the staff at the Brooklyn College Library and affiliated CUNY libraries; to the New York Public Library; and to other libraries that permitted me to use their collections, including American University of Cairo, the Dominican Institute for Oriental Studies in Cairo, St. Francis College, New York Theological Seminary, and Yale University.

My thanks also to Paul Baumann, Mohamad Bazzi, Gary Brandl, Joseph C. Donnelly, Father Jim Gardiner, David Gibson, Patrick Jordan, Omar Khalidi, Amina Khan, Lamberto Laccisaglia, Graham A. Loud, Father Emmanuel Maken, Dan Morrison, James Moses, Nasser Rabat, Father Mamdouh Shehab, and Craig Sparks. I thank the Franciscan Sisters of the Atonement in Assisi for their wonderful hospitality. My former *Newsday* colleague Bob Keeler, an expert on the Catholic peace tradition, offered perceptive comments on the manuscript.

I am especially grateful to literary agent Stephen Hanselman, who grasped this idea immediately when I sent it to him on the Feast of St. Francis in 2006, and to Doubleday's Trace Murphy and Gary Jansen, who made many excellent suggestions on the manuscript. It is a writer's delight to work with an agent and editors who are so knowledgeable about his subject—and perhaps an especially uncommon delight for those who write on religion. My thanks also go to Julia Serebrinsky for her excellent observations on the proposal, to Kathleen Digrado for her beautiful jacket design, and to John Burke and Janet Biehl for their help in turning the manuscript into a book.

My parents, Bernard and Anne Moses, continued to inspire and encourage me as I worked on this book. My father long ago passed up a career as a scholar of European history to manage public housing for the poor, a decision Francis would have appreciated. He was there to help me with this book, translating key scholarly work written in German. Calls and visits from my children, Matthew and Caitlin, always lifted my spirits, thrilling me with all they were doing. Maureen had the hardest job, to be the author's spouse; I was lost in the thirteenth century, which filled my thoughts through my waking hours and sometimes even in my sleep. I'm thankful to her for sustaining me on this journey with her love and compassion.

Grateful acknowledgment is made to the following for permission to quote from published works:

Arizona Center for Medieval and Renaissance Studies: Joseph L. Baird, Giuseppe Baglivi, and John Robert Kane, eds., Excerpt from *The Chronicles of Salimbene de Adam*. METS Volume 40 (Binghamton, NY, 1986). Copyright Arizona Board of Regents for Arizona State University. Reprinted with permission.

Edward Arnold (Publishers) Ltd.: Louise Riley-Smith and Jonathan Riley-Smith, *The Crusades: Idea and Reality, 1095–1274*. Reproduced by permission of Edward Arnold (Publishers) Ltd.

Franciscan Institute: Michael F. Cusato, "Of Snakes and Angels: The Mystical Experience behind the Stigmatization Narrative of 1 Celano," in *The Stigmata of Francis of Assisi: New Studies New Perspectives.*

Franciscan Press: Marion A. Habig, ed., *St. Francis of Assisi, Writings and Early Biographies: English Omnibus of the Sources for the Life of St. Francis;* J. Hoeberichts, *Francis and Islam;* Joseph Ratzinger, *The Theology of History in St. Bonaventure; XIIIth Century Chronicles,* trans. Placid Hermann, O.F.M.

Islamic Texts Society: Mohammad Hashim Kamali, *Freedom of Expression in Islam.*

New City Press: Regis J. Armstrong, O.F.M. Cap., J. A. Wayne Hellman, O.F.M. Conv., and William J. Short, O.F.M., eds., *Francis of Assisi: Early Documents,* 4 vols.

Princeton University Press: Benjamin Z. Kedar, *Crusade and Mission: European Approaches toward the Muslims.*

University of California Press: Lauro Martines, *Violence and Civil Disorder in Italian Cities 1200–1500.*

University of Pennsylvania Press: Edward Peters, ed., *Christian Society and the Crusades, 1198–1229.* Reprinted with permission of the University of Pennsylvania Press.

Index

Note: Page numbers in *italics* refer to illustrations.